CARNEGIE LEARNING MATH SERIES COURSE 2

STUDENT EDITION
VOLUME 1
3RD EDITION

SANDY BARTLE FINOCCHI

WILLIAM S. HADLEY

MARY LOU METZ

MARY LYNN RAITH

JANET SINOPOLI

JACLYN SNYDER

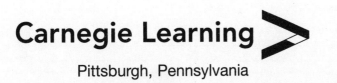

Carnegie Learning

Pittsburgh, Pennsylvania

Carnegie Learning >

437 Grant St., Suite 1906
Pittsburgh, PA 15219
Phone 888.851.7094
Customer Service Phone 888.851.7094, option 3

www.carnegielearning.com

Printing History
First Edition 2011
Second Edition 2014
Third Edition 2015

ISBN: 978-1-60972-590-7
Set ISBN: 978-1-60972-111-4

Printed in the United States of America by Cenveo Corporation
1 2 3 4 5 6 7 8 9 CC 18 17 16 15

Dear Student,

You are about to begin an exciting journey! These mathematical materials were written specifically for *you*, a middle school student. The book you are holding is *your* book. There is lots of space for writing, sketching, drawing, cutting, pasting, and constructing new mathematical ideas. You may want to highlight key terms, take notes in the margins, or even doodle on the cover.

Connections are important in life. The popularity of social networks shows the importance of connections. In much the same way, mathematics connects with so many activities in our lives. Throughout the lessons, you will build new knowledge based upon your prior knowledge. You will apply math to real-world situations so that you can see why it's meaningful. You will encounter models that portray mathematical concepts. Models will be presented in all sorts of ways—from lesson openers, to pictures, to different student methods and approaches to problem solving. You will also use manipulatives, which are objects that you can use to model or reinforce key mathematical concepts.

Of course, if you need additional practice, you can find it in your Assignments and Skills Practice book. Keep in mind, no professional athlete practices by just playing an entire game—ballet dancers repeat some basic steps, moves, and dances; basketball players practice dribbling, shooting, and defending; even writers jot ideas for novels in their spare time—all to improve their skills. Mathematics is no different and these materials enable and encourage you to practice.

> I bet the folks at home would like to know what we're going to do this year!

Don't worry—you will not be working alone. We encourage students to work together in pairs or in groups because it gets you talking about your insights. Everyone will share his or her ideas and thoughts in class. Sometimes you will help your classmates, and other times they will help you.

Today's workplace demands teamwork and self-confidence. At Carnegie Learning, we have designed a Math Series to help you to make the most of your math course. Enjoy the journey and share your thoughts with others. Have fun while Learning by Doing!

The Carnegie Learning® Curriculum Development Team

ACKNOWLEDGMENTS

Carnegie Learning Curriculum Development Team

- David Dengler
  Director, Curriculum Development
- Jen Gansberger
  Editorial Assistant
- Lezlee Ross
  Curriculum Developer
- Joshua Fisher
  Math Editor
- David "Augie" Rivera
  Math Editor

Advisory Board

- Shelly Allen, Richmond County Schools
- Ryan Baker, Worcester Polytechnic Institute
- Bill Bush, University of Louisville
- John McCook, McCook and Associates
- Roxana Moreno, University of New Mexico
- Doug Rohrer, University of South Florida
- Bob Siegler, Carnegie Mellon University
- Mary Ann Stine, Private Consultant

Vendors

- Bookmasters, Inc.
- Mathematical Expressions
- ESI Design
- Cenveo Corporation

Special Thanks

- Content contributors: Janet Falkowski, Ken Labuskes, Marianne O'Connor, Jennifer Panasko, Agnes Pavolovich
- Peter Arkle for the design and rendering of "The Crew"
- Richmond County School District, Georgia, for piloting lessons and providing implementation feedback
- Carnegie Learning Managers of School Partnership for content and design review
- The Children of Carnegie Learning employees for providing a "middle-schooler's" perspective, with special recognition to:
  - Matthew B.
  - Dawson D.
  - Allison M.
  - Adam, Nic, and Shane R.
  - Aaron and Melinda R.

Photograph Credits

Chapter 1 © istockphoto.com/gaffera;
Chapter 2 © istockphoto.com/Amanda Rohde;
Chapter 3 © istockphoto.com/Nathan Maxfield;
Chapter 4 © istockphoto.com/Michael Flippo;
Chapter 5 © istockphoto.com/Pgiam;
Chapter 6 © istockphoto.com/Pavels Sabelnikovs;
Chapter 7 © istockphoto.com/Michael Smith;
Chapter 8 © istockphoto.com/Peter Andersen;
Chapter 9 © istockphoto.com/Richard Hobson;
Chapter 10 © istockphoto.com/Gary Blakeley;
Chapter 11 © istockphoto.com/Daniel Cooper;
Chapter 12 © istockphoto.com/Joze Pojbic;
Chapter 13 © istockphoto.com/sandramo;
Chapter 14 © istockphoto.com/Mark Rose;
Chapter 15 © istockphoto.com/Sam Kittner/Courtesy Newseum;
Chapter 16 © istockphoto.com/Patrick Heagny;
Chapter 17 © istockphoto.com/Suzanne Tucker

Acknowledgments

TABLE OF CONTENTS

DIRECT VARIATION AND CONSTANT OF PROPORTIONALITY_____65

Table of Contents

Table of Contents

MULTIPLICATION AND DIVISION WITH RATIONAL NUMBERS___251

NUMERICAL AND ALGEBRAIC EXPRESSIONS AND EQUATIONS___293

SOLVING EQUATIONS AND INEQUALITIES_____339

SOLVING PROBLEMS WITH EQUATIONS AND INEQUALITIES___385

Table of Contents

THE CREW

The Crew is here to help you on your journey. Sometimes they will remind you about things you already learned. Sometimes they will ask you questions to help you think about different strategies. Sometimes they will share fun facts. They are members of your group—someone you can rely on!

Teacher aides will guide you along your journey. They will help you make connections and remind you to think about the details.

MATHEMATICAL REPRESENTATIONS

Introduction

During this course, you will solve problems and work with many different representations of mathematical concepts, ideas, and processes to better understand the world. Each lesson will provide you with opportunities to discuss your ideas, work within groups, and share your solutions and methods with your class. These process icons are placed throughout the text.

Discuss to Understand

- Read the problem carefully.

- What is the context of the problem? Do we understand it?

- What is the question that we are being asked? Does it make sense?

- Is this problem similar to some other problem we know?

Think for Yourself

- Do I need any additional information to answer the question?

- Is this problem similar to some other problem that I know?

- How can I represent the problem using a picture, a diagram, symbols, or some other representation?

Work with Your Partner

- How did you do the problem?

- Show me your representation.

- This is the way I thought about the problem—how did you think about it?

- What else do we need to solve the problem?

- Does our reasoning and our answer make sense to each other?

- How will we explain our solution to the class?

Share with the Class

- Here is our solution and the methods we used.

- Are we communicating our strategies clearly?

- We could only get this far with our solution. How can we finish?

- Could we have used a different strategy to solve the problem?

ACADEMIC GLOSSARY

Key Terms of the Course

There are important terms you will encounter throughout this book. It is important that you have an understanding of these words as you get started on your journey through the mathematical concepts. Knowing what is meant by these terms and using these terms will help you think, reason, and communicate your ideas. The Graphic Organizers shown display a definition for a key term, related words, sample questions, and examples.

DEFINITION

To study or look closely for patterns. Analyzing can involve examining or breaking a concept down into smaller parts to gain a better understanding of it.

RELATED WORDS

- examine
- evaluate
- determine
- observe
- consider

- investigate
- what do you notice?
- what do you think?
- sort and match

ASK YOURSELF

- Do I see any patterns?
- Have I seen something like this before?
- What happens if the shape, representation, or numbers change?

ANALYZE

EXAMPLE

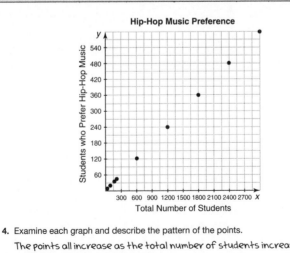

4. Examine each graph and describe the pattern of the points.

The points all increase as the total number of students increase. The points seem to be in a straight line.

DEFINITION

To give details or describe how to determine an answer or solution.
Explaining your reasoning helps justify conclusions.

RELATED WORDS

- show your work
- explain your calculation
- justify
- why or why not?

ASK YOURSELF

- How should I organize my thoughts?
- Is my explanation logical?
- Does my reasoning make sense?
- How can I justify my answer to others?

Don't forget to check your answers!

EXPLAIN YOUR REASONING

EXAMPLE

In order to build a balsa wood model of the Wright brothers' plane, you would need to cut long lengths of wood spindles into shorter lengths for the wing stays, the vertical poles that support and connect the two wings. Each stay for the main wings of the model needs to be cut $3\frac{1}{4}$ inches long.

Show your work and explain your reasoning.

1. If the wood spindles are each 10 inches long, how many stays could you cut from one spindle?

$$10 \div 3\frac{1}{4} = \frac{10}{1} \times \frac{4}{13}$$
$$= \frac{40}{13}$$
$$= 3\frac{1}{13}$$

I could cut three stays because 10 divided by $3\frac{1}{4}$ is $3\frac{1}{13}$, so there are 3 full pieces and $\frac{1}{13}$ of a stay left over.

DEFINITION

To display information in various ways. Representing mathematics can be done using words, tables, graphs, or symbols.

RELATED WORDS

- show
- sketch
- draw
- create
- plot
- graph
- write an equation
- complete the table

ASK YOURSELF

- How should I organize my thoughts?
- How do I use this model to show a concept or idea?
- What does this representation tell me?
- Is my representation accurate?

REPRESENT

EXAMPLE

4. During the summer, Matthew and Devan started their own business mowing lawns for people in the Lake Section. Before starting any work, Matthew spent $15 to fill up the gas tank for the lawnmower. The boys agreed that each person would earn the same amount after Matthew was reimbursed the money he spent for gas. After a week of work, the boys were paid a total of $243. Matthew filled up the gas tank just once. How much did each boy earn?

a. Draw a picture to represent the situation. Label the unknown parts with variables and the known parts with their values.

Matthew's earnings: $\boxed{m}$ $\boxed{15}$ ⎫
                                              ⎬ $243
Devan's earnings: $\boxed{m}$ ⎭

DEFINITION

To make an educated guess based on the analysis of given data.
Estimating first helps inform reasoning.

RELATED WORDS

- predict
- approximate
- expect
- about how much?

ASK YOURSELF

- Does my reasoning make sense?
- Is my solution close to my estimation?

Estimating gets you in the neighborhood, calculating gets you the address.

ESTIMATE

EXAMPLE

Most restaurant patrons add a tip to the final bill to show their appreciation for their wait staff. Usually, a patron will determine 15% or 20% of the bill, and then add that amount to the total. Many times, patrons will just round off the tip to the nearest dollar. For patrons tipping 20%, determining the amount of a tip is easier. Twenty percent is one-fifth, so to determine the tip, patrons only need to divide the rounded bill by 5.

> For example, if the bill is $38.95, you would round to 40, and then divide by 5. The 20% tip should be about $8.

1. Estimate a 20% tip for each of the bills shown.
   a. $89.45
      This is about $90. So, a reasonable tip will be about $90 divided by 5, which is $18.

DEFINITION

To represent or give an account of in words. Describing communicates mathematical ideas to others.

RELATED WORDS

- demonstrate
- label
- display
- compare
- define
- determine
- what are the advantages?
- what are the disadvantages?
- what is similar?
- what is different?

ASK YOURSELF

- How should I organize my thoughts?
- Is my explanation logical?
- Did I consider the context of the situation?
- Does my reasoning make sense?

DESCRIBE

EXAMPLE

1. The amount a contractor gets paid (p) is directly proportional to the number of days worked (d).

   a. Complete the table of values.

d	p (dollars)
0	0
1	250
2	500
3.5	875

   b. Determine the constant of proportionality and describe what it represents in this problem situation.

   The constant of proportionality, or k, is 250. The contractor makes $250 for every day he or she works.

Problem Types You Will See

Worked Example

When you see a Worked Example:
▶ Take your time to read through it,
▶ Question your own understanding, and
▶ Think about the connections between steps.

Ask yourself:
▶ What is the main idea?
▶ How would this work if I changed the numbers?
▶ Have I used these strategies before?

Problem Types

A number line can be used to model integer addition.
When adding a positive integer, move to the right on a number line.
When adding a negative integer, move to the left on a number line.

Example 1: The number line shows how to determine $5 + 8$.

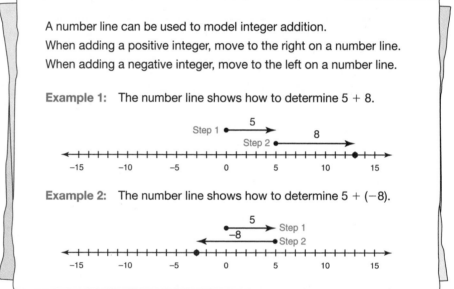

Example 2: The number line shows how to determine $5 + (-8)$.

2. Compare the first steps in each example.

   a. What distance is shown by the first term in each example?

   The distance shown by the first term in each example is the same: 5 units.

   b. Describe the graphical representation of the first term. Where does it start and in which direction does it move? Why?

   The graphical representation for the first term begins at 0 and moves to the right. It moves to the right because the first term is positive.

   c. What is the absolute value of the first term in each example?

   The absolute value of 5 is 5.

Thumbs Down

Katie used Corinne's method to solve this problem:

1. Explain why Katie's answer is incorrect. Then, determine the correct answer.

   The $46 was the discount, not what Katie paid for the flight. Katie must subtract the discount:
   $229.99 - $46 = $183.99.

Katie

My flight was $229.99 but I got 20% off because I booked it online. What did I pay?

$$\frac{\text{Percent part}}{\text{Percent whole}} = \frac{\text{Part of quantity}}{\text{Whole quantity}}$$

$$\frac{20}{100} = \frac{x}{229.99}$$

$$\frac{4599.8}{100} = \frac{100x}{100}$$

$$45.998 = x$$

So, I paid about $46.

Problem Types

Thumbs Up

<table>
<tr>
<td>

When you see a Thumbs Up icon:

▶ Take your time to read through the *correct* solution.

▶ Think about the connections between steps.

</td>
<td>

Ask yourself:

▶ Why is this method correct?

▶ Have I used this method before?

</td>
</tr>
</table>

Vicki also used Corinne's method but, got the answer without having to subtract:

2. Explain why Vicki's method worked.

Twenty percent off is the same as 80% of something.

If I take 40% off $100, that's $100 − $40. That leaves me with $60, which is 100% − 40%, or 60%. Hmmmm . . .

Vicki

My flight was $229.99 but I got 20% off because I booked it online. What did I pay?

$$\frac{\text{Percent part}}{\text{Percent whole}} = \frac{\text{Part of quantity}}{\text{Whole quantity}}$$

$$\frac{80}{100} = \frac{x}{229.99}$$

$$\frac{18399.2}{100} = \frac{100x}{100}$$

$$183.99 = x$$

Who's Correct?

Examine the spinner shown.

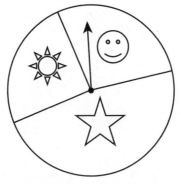

1. Jonah makes the follow predictions for the spinner landing on each symbol. Do you think his predictions are correct?

$$P(\textcircled{\cdot\cdot}) = \frac{1}{4} \qquad P(\text{☀}) = \frac{1}{4} \qquad P(\text{☆}) = \frac{2}{5}$$

Jonah's predictions are incorrect because the sum of the probabilities of the three outcomes is not equal to 1.

Problem Types

1 RATIOS AND RATES

Whether it is to celebrate wedding anniversaries or the center piece for gala dinners, flowers brighten up the event. For florists, ordering the correct amount of flowers is challenging. This is because florists pride themselves in selling fresh flowers.

1.1 SHOW SOMEONE YOU CARE—SEND FLOWERS!

Introduction to Ratios and Rates

Learning Goals

In this lesson, you will:

▶ Identify ratios, rates, and unit rates.
▶ Use ratios, rates, and unit rates to analyze problems.

Key Terms

▶ ratio
▶ rate
▶ proportion
▶ equivalent ratios
▶ unit rate
▶ scaling up
▶ scaling down

You probably don't think about flowers on a daily basis, but there are some people who do! Florists routinely think about different types of flowers, arrangements of those flowers, ordering flowers, plants, balloons, baskets, and vases, and—phew! There's a lot to floristry! But make no mistake, the business of floristry is more than just flowers—it's dollars and cents and mathematics. For example, there are certain days of the years when there is a huge demand for roses, vases, and baby's breath. When this occurs, florists must accurately order roses and baby's breath in comparison to other flowers to make sure they can fulfill the demand, but not have a lot of these flowers left over. What certain days do you think might have a higher demand for roses or vases? How do you think mathematics can help florists order and arrange flowers?

Baby's breath are plants that have tiny white flowers and buds. They are usually with roses in flower arrangements.

Problem 1   Representing Ratios

Pat's Flower Shop specializes in growing and selling large daisies. On a typical summer day, you may hear a florist say one of these statements:

- In the Daisy Smile Bouquet, there are 2 white daisies for every 3 orange daisies.
- In the Daisy Smile Bouquet, 2 out of every 5 daisies are white.
- Five daisies cost $7.50.
- There are 10 daisies in a small vase.

In each statement, the florist is comparing two different quantities. In mathematics, we use *ratios* to make comparisons. A **ratio** is a comparison of two quantities using division.

Let's consider the statement:

"In the Daisy Smile Bouquet, there are 2 white daisies for every 3 orange daisies."

The relationship between the two different types of daisies can be represented in several ways. One way to represent the relationship is to draw picture, or model.

From the model, you can make comparisons about the different quantities.

- White daisies to orange daisies
- Orange daisies to white daisies
- White daisies to total daisies
- Orange daisies to total daisies

Each comparison is ratio. The first two comparisons are part-to-part ratios. The last two comparisons are part-to-whole ratios because you are comparing one of the parts (either white or orange) to the total number of parts.

The table shows three different ways to represent the part-to-part ratios.

Part-to-Part Ratios		
In Words	**With a Colon**	**In Fractional Form**
2 white daisies to every 3 orange daises	2 white daisies : 3 orange daisies	$\dfrac{2 \text{ white daisies}}{3 \text{ orange daises}}$
3 orange daisies to every 2 white daisies	3 orange daisies : 2 white daisies	$\dfrac{3 \text{ orange daisies}}{2 \text{ white daisies}}$

You can also write a part-to-whole ratio to show the number of each daisy compared to the total number of daisies. The table shows two different ways to represent part-to-whole ratios.

Part-to-Whole Ratios		
In Words	**With a Colon**	**In Fractional Form**
2 white daisies to every 5 total daisies	2 white daisies : 5 total daisies	$\dfrac{2 \text{ white daisies}}{5 \text{ total daises}}$
3 orange daisies to every 5 total daisies	3 orange daisies : 5 total daisies	$\dfrac{3 \text{ orange daisies}}{5 \text{ total daisies}}$

Notice that when you write a ratio using the total number of parts, you are also writing a fraction. A fraction is a ratio that shows a part-to-whole relationship.

Ratios

$$\dfrac{\text{part}}{\text{part}} \qquad \underbrace{\dfrac{\text{part}}{\text{whole}}}$$

Fraction

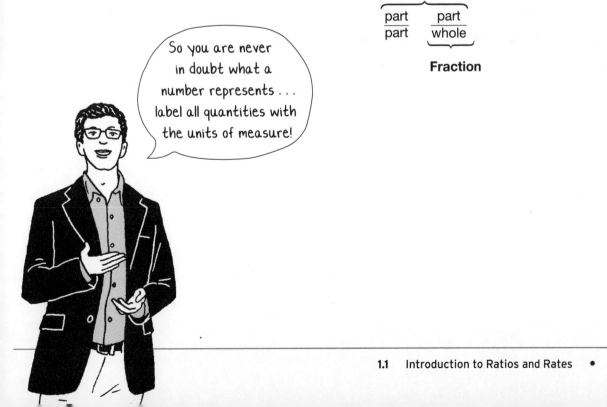

So you are never in doubt what a number represents . . . label all quantities with the units of measure!

So far, you have seen ratios with the same unit of measure—in this case, daisies. However, remember ratios are comparison of two quantities. Sometimes, ratios can be a comparison of two different quantities with two different units of measure. When this occurs, we call this type of ratio a *rate*. A **rate** is a ratio that compares two quantities that are measured in different units. The two shown statements represent rates.

- Five daisies cost $7.50.
- There are 10 daisies in one small vase.

1. Write each statement as a rate using colons and in fractional form.

   a. Five daisies cost $7.50.

   With a colon: ___2 : $3___

   In fractional form: ___$\frac{2}{\$3}$___

   b. There are 10 daisies in one small vase.

   With a colon: ___20 : 2___

   In fractional form: ___$\frac{20}{2}$___

A **unit rate** is a comparison of two measurements in which the denominator has a value of one unit.

2. Which statement from Question 1 represents a unit rate?

   B: There are 10 daisies in
   One small hat.

Problem 2   Selling Daisies

In any size of the Daisy Smile Bouquet, 2 out of every 5 daisies are white.

1. Complete the model for each question using the ratio given. Then, calculate your answer from your model and explain your reasoning.

   a. How many total daisies are there if 8 daisies are white?

$$20 \quad daisies$$

   b. How many daisies are white if there are a total of 25 daisies?

$$10 \quad daisies$$

   c. How many daisies are white if there are a total of 35 daisies?

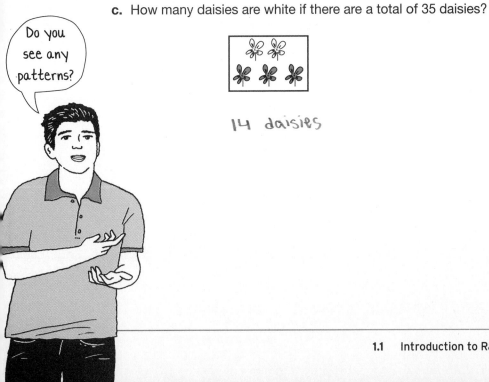

Do you see any patterns?

$$14 \quad daisies$$

Pat's Flower Shop is having a one-day sale. Two daisies cost $1.50.

2. Complete the model for each question using the ratio given. Then, calculate your answer from your model and explain your reasoning.

a. How much would 7 daisies cost?

$1.50

3

$5.25

b. How many daisies could you buy for $8.25?

$1.50

11 daisies

Problem 3 Equivalent Ratios and Rates

Previously, you used models to determine whether ratios and rates were equivalent. To determine when two ratios or rates are equivalent to each other, you can write them as a *proportion* to determine if they are equal. A **proportion** is an equation that states that two ratios are equal. You can write a proportion by placing an equals sign between the two *equivalent ratios*. **Equivalent ratios** are ratios that represent the same part-to-part relationship or the same part-to-whole relationship.

For example, from Pat's Daisy Smile Bouquet problem situation, you know that 2 out of every 5 daisies are white. So, you can determine how many total daisies there are when 8 daisies are white.

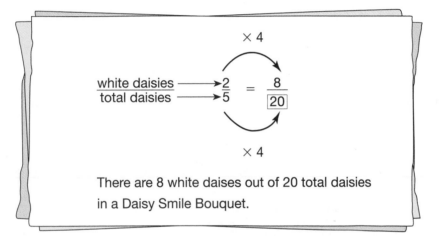

There are 8 white daises out of 20 total daisies in a Daisy Smile Bouquet.

When you rewrite a ratio to an equivalent ratio with greater numbers, you are *scaling up* the ratio. **Scaling up** means to multiply the numerator and the denominator by the same factor.

It is important to remember to write the values representing the same quantity in both numerators and in both denominators. It doesn't matter which quantity is represented in the numerator; it matters that the unit of measure is consistent among the ratios.

Another way you can write equivalent ratios to determine the total number of daisies if 8 are white is shown.

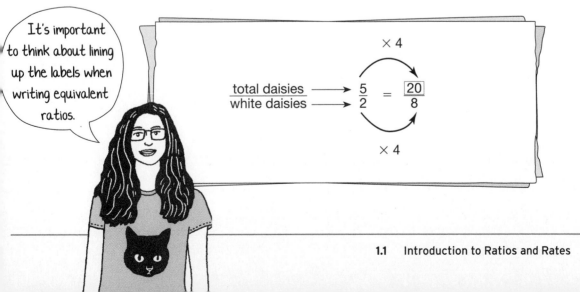

It's important to think about lining up the labels when writing equivalent ratios.

1. The Daisy Smile Bouquets are sold in a ratio of 2 white daisies for every 3 orange daisies. Scale up each ratio to determine the unknown quantity of daisies. Explain how you calculated your answer.

a. $\dfrac{2 \text{ white daisies}}{3 \text{ orange daisies}} = \dfrac{? \text{ white daisies}}{21 \text{ orange daisies}}$

14 white daisies

b. $\dfrac{2 \text{ white daisies}}{3 \text{ orange daisies}} = \dfrac{? \text{ white daisies}}{33 \text{ orange daisies}}$

22 white daisies

c. $\dfrac{2 \text{ white daisies}}{3 \text{ orange daisies}} = \dfrac{12 \text{ white daisies}}{? \text{ orange daisies}}$

18 orange daisies

d. $\dfrac{2 \text{ white daisies}}{3 \text{ orange daisies}} = \dfrac{24 \text{ white daisies}}{? \text{ orange daisies}}$

36 orange daisies

When you rewrite a ratio to an equivalent ratio with lesser numbers, you are *scaling down* the ratio. **Scaling down** means you divide the numerator and the denominator by the same factor.

For example you know that 5 daisies cost $7.50. So, you can determine the cost of 1 daisy.

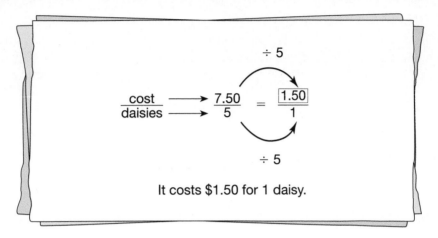

$$\frac{\text{cost}}{\text{daisies}} \longrightarrow \frac{7.50}{5} = \frac{\boxed{1.50}}{1}$$

$\div 5$

$\div 5$

It costs $1.50 for 1 daisy.

The unit rate $1.50 : 1, $\frac{\$1.50}{1}$ daisy is also a rate because the two quantities being compared are different. Recall that any rate can be rewritten as a unit rate with a denominator of 1.

2. Scale down each rate to determine the unit rate.

a. $\dfrac{60 \text{ telephone poles}}{3 \text{ miles}}$ $= \dfrac{20 \text{ telephone poles}}{1 \text{ mi}}$

d. $\dfrac{3000 \text{ sheets of paper}}{5 \text{ reams}}$ $= \dfrac{600 \text{ sheets of paper}}{1 \text{ ream}}$

b. $\dfrac{10,000 \text{ people}}{5 \text{ rallies}}$ $= \dfrac{2,000 \text{ people}}{1 \text{ rally}}$

e. $\dfrac{15 \text{ dollars}}{2 \text{ T-shirts}}$ $= \dfrac{\$7.50}{1 \text{ T-shirt}}$

c. $\dfrac{45 \text{ yard of fabric}}{5 \text{ dresses}}$ $= \dfrac{9 \text{ yards of fabric}}{1 \text{ dress}}$

f. $\dfrac{10 \text{ km}}{60 \text{ min}}$ $= \dfrac{1 \text{ km}}{6 \text{ min}}$

Talk the Talk

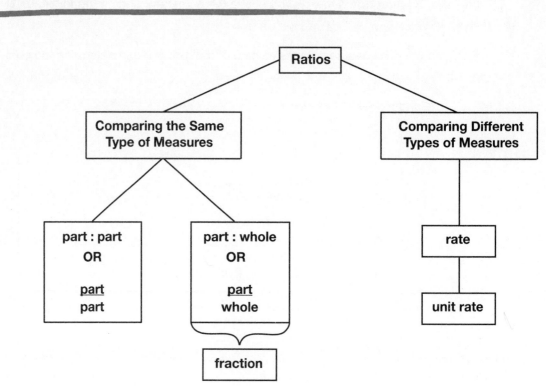

1. Identify each as a ratio that is either part-to-part, part-to-whole, a rate, or a unit rate.

   a. 25 bricks on each pallet   *unit rate*

   b. $\dfrac{5 \text{ inches}}{2 \text{ worms}}$ *part-to-part*

   c. $\dfrac{5 \text{ small dolls}}{1 \text{ large doll}}$ *part-to-part*

   d. $\dfrac{33 \text{ girls}}{100 \text{ total students}}$ *part-to-whole*

   e. $\dfrac{5 \text{ tons}}{1 \text{ railway car}}$ *unit rate*

2. Scale each ratio or rate up or down to determine the unknown term.

a. $\dfrac{3 \text{ people}}{9 \text{ granola bars}} = \dfrac{?}{3 \text{ granola bars}}$ *1 person*

b. $\dfrac{2 \text{ sandwiches}}{6 \text{ people}} = \dfrac{1 \text{ sandwich}}{?}$ *3 people*

c. $\dfrac{4 \text{ pencils}}{1 \text{ person}} = \dfrac{?}{25 \text{ people}}$ *100 pencils*

d. $\dfrac{8 \text{ songs}}{1 \text{ CD}} = \dfrac{?}{5 \text{ CDs}}$ *40 songs*

e. $\dfrac{3 \text{ tickets}}{\$26.25} = \dfrac{1 \text{ ticket}}{?}$ *$8.75*

f. $\dfrac{10 \text{ hours of work}}{\$120} = \dfrac{1 \text{ hour of work}}{?}$ *$12*

g. $\dfrac{2 \text{ hours}}{120 \text{ miles}} = \dfrac{12 \text{ hours}}{?}$ *720 mi*

h. $\dfrac{6 \text{ gallons of red paint}}{4 \text{ gallons of yellow paint}} = \dfrac{?}{1 \text{ gallon of yellow paint}}$ *1.5 gallons of red paint*

Be prepared to share your solutions and methods.

1

1.2 MAKING PUNCH
Ratios, Rates, and Mixture Problems

Learning Goals

In this lesson, you will:

▶ Use ratios to make comparisons.

▶ Use rates and proportions to solve mixture problems.

Do you like smoothies? Perhaps one of the best things about smoothies is that you can make one with just about any ingredients. Just throw them in the blender and turn it on!

Smoothies can be very healthy too. Try this healthy smoothie recipe sometime.

- 1 banana
- 1 cup of vanilla yogurt
- 1 cup of grapes
- $\frac{1}{2}$ of an apple
- 2 cups of spinach leaves

If this recipe serves 3 people, how much of each ingredient would you need to make smoothies your whole class?

Problem 1 May the Best Recipe Win

1

Each year, your class presents its mathematics portfolio to parents and community members. This year, your homeroom is in charge of the refreshments for the reception that follows the presentations. Four students in the class give their recipes for punch. The class wants to analyze the recipes to determine which will make the punch with the strongest grapefruit flavor, and which will make the strongest lemon-lime soda flavor. The recipes are shown.

Adam's Recipe
4 parts lemon-lime soda
8 parts grapefruit juice

Bobbi's Recipe
3 parts lemon-lime soda
5 parts grapefruit juice

Carlos's Recipe
2 parts lemon-lime soda
3 parts grapefruit juice

Zeb's Recipe
1 part lemon-lime soda
4 parts grapefruit juice

1. How many total parts are in each person's recipe?

Adam: 12   zeb: 4
Carlos: 5
Bobbi: 8   Total: 29

2. For each recipe, write a ratio that compares the number of parts of grapefruit juice to the total number of parts in each recipe. If possible, simplify each rate.

Adam's recipe: 2 : 3

Bobbi's recipe: 5 : 8

Carlos's recipe: 3 : 5

Zeb's recipe: 4 : 5

3. Which recipe will make the punch with the strongest grapefruit taste? Explain how you determined your answer.

Adam, because he has the biggest difference of Grapefruit and lemon-lime.

4. For each recipe, write a rate that compares the number of parts of lemon-lime soda to the total number of parts in each recipe. If possible, simplify each rate.

Adam's recipe: 1:3

Bobbi's recipe: 3:8

Carlos's recipe: 2:5

Zeb's recipe: 1:5

5. Which recipe will make the punch with the strongest lemon-lime soda flavor? Explain how you determined your answer.

Carlos, because he has the smallest difference between lemon-lime and grape-fruit.

Problem 2   Making the Refreshments

1. You are borrowing glasses from the cafeteria to serve the punch. Each glass holds 6 fluid ounces of punch. Your class expects that 70 students and 90 parents and community members will attend the reception. You decide to make enough punch so that every person who attends can have one glass of punch. How many fluid ounces of punch will you need for the reception?

960 fl oz

$$\begin{array}{r} \overset{3}{16}00 \\ \times \quad 6 \\ \hline 9600 \end{array}$$

Previously, you wrote rates to compare parts of each ingredient to total parts of all the ingredients. Recall that a rate is a ratio in which the units of the parts or the whole being compared are different.

2. Determine the unit rate for the fluid ounces of punch there would be in one part of the recipe if your class uses Adam's recipe.

0.5 fl oz of punch in one part

3. How many fluid ounces of lemon-lime soda and grapefruit juice are needed to make enough punch if your class uses Adam's recipe? Show all your work.

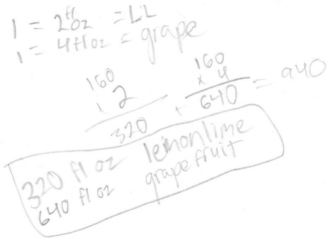

$1 = 2$ fl oz $= L\cdot L$
$1 = 4$ fl oz $=$ grape

$\dfrac{160}{\times 2}$ $\dfrac{160}{\times 4} = 240$
320 $\dfrac{}{640}$

320 fl oz lemonlime
640 fl oz grapefruit

4. How many fluid ounces of lemon-lime soda and grapefruit juice are needed to make enough punch if your class uses Bobbi's recipe? Show all your work.

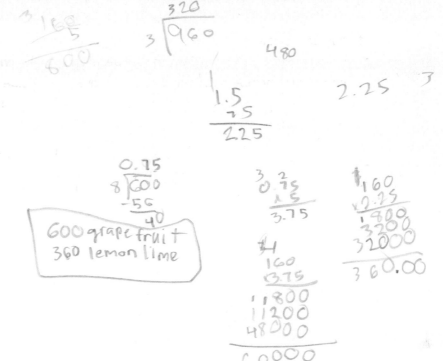

5. How many fluid ounces of lemon-lime soda and grapefruit juice are needed to make enough punch if your class uses Carlos's recipe? Show all your work.

6. How many fluid ounces of lemon-lime soda and grapefruit juice are needed to make enough punch for the reception if your class uses Zeb's recipe? Show all your work.

$$\begin{array}{r} 160 \\ \times 4.8 \\ \hline 768 \end{array}$$

$$\begin{array}{r} 160 \\ \times 1.2 \\ \hline 320 \\ 1600 \\ \hline 192.0 \end{array}$$

$$\dfrac{1.2}{4.8}$$

$$5\overline{\smash{)}6}^{\,1.2}$$

7. Complete the table with the calculations you determined for each person's recipe.

	Amount of Lemon-Lime Soda (fluid ounces)	Amount of Grapefruit Juice (fluid ounces)	Total Amount of Punch (fluid ounces)
Adam's recipe	320	640	960
Bobbi's recipe	360	600	960
Carlos's recipe	384	576	960
Zeb's recipe	192	768	960

8. In Problem 1, Question 3 you determined which recipe would have the strongest grapefruit flavor? How does the table confirm your choice?

It shows the same thing, but in a different way!

9. In Problem 1, Question 5 you determined which recipe would have the strongest lemon-lime soda flavor? How does the table confirm your choice?

It shows the same thing in a different way.

10. If you would use 8-ounce glasses for the reception rather than 6-ounce glasses, how would that affect the amount of punch you would need to make?

I would have more flozs per part.

11. Will the ratio of the parts for any of the recipes change by putting more punch in each glass? Explain your reasoning.

No because only the fl oz per part will change.

Talk the Talk

1. Explain how ratios and rates helped you solve the problems in this lesson.

Be prepared to share your solutions and methods.

1.3 FOR THE BIRDS
Rates and Proportions

Which bird lays the largest egg for its size? That honor goes to the little spotted kiwi—a native of New Zealand with no tail, a long ivory beak, and poor eyesight. The little spotted kiwi lays an egg that is more than one quarter its own body weight.

By contrast, the bird that lays the smallest egg for its size is—you guessed it—the ostrich! (Perhaps you didn't guess that.) Although ostriches lay the largest eggs, a typical ostrich egg weighs less than $\frac{15}{1000}$ of its mother's weight.

Why do you think that the ostrich egg is both the largest egg that any bird lays, but is also the smallest egg in comparison to the mother's weight?

Problem 1   Eggsactly!

The table shows the weights of four different adult birds and the weights of their eggs.

	Mother's Weight (oz)	Egg Weight (oz)
Pigeon	10	0.75
Chicken	80	2
Swan	352	11
Robin	2.5	0.1

1. Compare the weights of the eggs. List the birds in order from the bird with the largest egg to the bird with the smallest egg.

2. Determine the ratio of egg weight to mother's weight for each bird. Use your calculator to help you. Write the ratios as decimals.

Remember to carefully read which quantity should come first in the ratio!

3. Use your decimal representations 2 to answer each question. Explain your reasoning.

   a. Which of the birds listed lays the largest egg for its size?

   b. Which of the birds listed lays the smallest egg for its size?

   c. Compare the ratios of egg weight to mother's weight. List the birds in order from greatest ratio to least ratio.

Problem 2   The Coyote and the . . . Ostrich?

Although the ostrich is the largest living bird, it is also the fastest runner. The table shows distances that four birds ran, and the amount of time it took each bird to run that distance.

Bird	Distance Covered	Time
Ostrich	22 miles	30 minutes
Great Roadrunner	300 yards	30 seconds
Quail	20 yards	2.5 seconds
Pheasant	200 yards	50 seconds

Each row in the table shows a rate. The rate for each bird in this situation is the distance covered per the amount of time.

> The rate, or running speed, for the ostrich is 22 miles per
> 30 minutes, or $\frac{22 \text{ mi}}{30 \text{ min}}$.

1. Write the rates for the other three birds.

  a. Great roadrunner:

  b. Quail:

  c. Pheasant:

Remember, a rate is a ratio that compares two quantities that are measured in different units.

There are many situations in which you need to *convert* measurements to different units. To **convert** a measurement means to change it to an equivalent measurement in different units. Converting measurements can help you compare rates. When the units of measure are the same, you can more easily compare the rates.

The table shows some common measurement conversions.

Length	Weight	Capacity	Time
12 in. = 1 ft	16 oz = 1 lb	8 fl oz = 1 c	60 sec = 1 min
36 in. = 1 yd	2000 lb = 1 t	2 c = 1 pt	60 min = 1 hr
3 ft = 1 yd		4 c = 1 qt	3600 sec = 1 hr
5280 ft = 1 mi		2 pt = 1 qt	24 hrs = 1 day
		4 qt = 1 gal	

You can use the table of common measurements as rates to change one measurement to an equivalent measurement in different units.

2. Write each length in the table as a rate.

   a. 12 in. = 1 ft

   b. 36 in. = 1 yd

   c. 3 ft = 1 yd

   d. 5280 ft = 1 mi

3. Write each amount of time in the table as a rate.

   a. 60 sec = 1 min

   b. 60 min = 1 hr

   c. 3600 sec = 1 hr

   d. 24 hrs = 1 day

You can convert the running speed of the ostrich from being represented in miles per minute to show the units in miles per hour.

You know that the ostrich ran 22 miles in 30 minutes. You can use a proportion to describe the ostrich's speed in miles per hour.

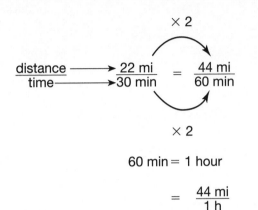

$$\frac{\text{distance}}{\text{time}} \longrightarrow \frac{22\text{ mi}}{30\text{ min}} = \frac{44\text{ mi}}{60\text{ min}}$$

$$60 \text{ min} = 1 \text{ hour}$$

$$= \frac{44\text{ mi}}{1\text{ h}}$$

The ostrich's speed is 44 miles per hour.

You can also use the unit rate, $\frac{60\text{ min}}{1\text{ hr}}$, to convert the ostrich's speed from miles per minute to miles per hour.

$$\frac{22\text{ mi}}{30\text{ min}} \cdot \frac{60\text{ min}}{1\text{ hr}} = \frac{22\text{ mi}}{\cancel{30\text{ min}}^{1}} \cdot \frac{\cancel{60\text{ min}}^{2}}{1\text{ hr}}$$

$$= \frac{22 \cdot 2\text{ mi}}{1\text{ hr}}$$

$$= \frac{44\text{ mi}}{1\text{ hr}}$$

The ostrich's speed is 44 miles per hour.

> You can represent multiplication by using · or by using parenthesis like (22)(2).

You can scale up the rate for the roadrunner to describe its speed in miles per hour.

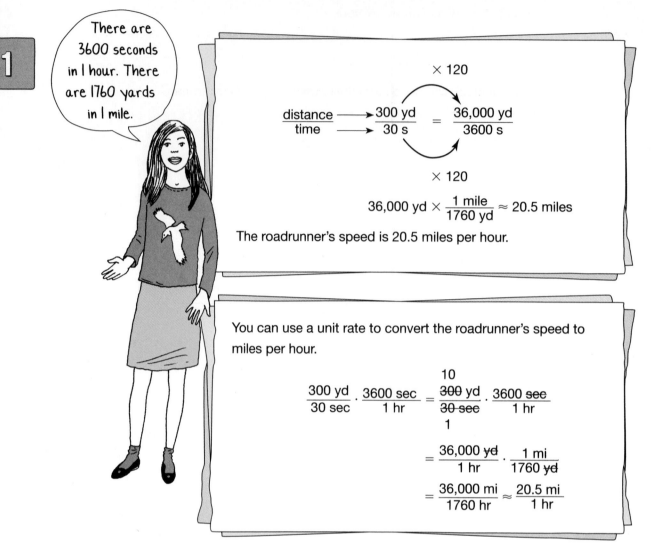

There are 3600 seconds in 1 hour. There are 1760 yards in 1 mile.

$\times\ 120$

$$\frac{\text{distance}}{\text{time}} \longrightarrow \frac{300\ \text{yd}}{30\ \text{s}} = \frac{36{,}000\ \text{yd}}{3600\ \text{s}}$$

$\times\ 120$

$$36{,}000\ \text{yd} \times \frac{1\ \text{mile}}{1760\ \text{yd}} \approx 20.5\ \text{miles}$$

The roadrunner's speed is 20.5 miles per hour.

You can use a unit rate to convert the roadrunner's speed to miles per hour.

$$\frac{300\ \text{yd}}{30\ \text{sec}} \cdot \frac{3600\ \text{sec}}{1\ \text{hr}} = \frac{\overset{10}{\cancel{300}}\ \text{yd}}{\underset{1}{\cancel{30}\ \cancel{\text{sec}}}} \cdot \frac{3600\ \cancel{\text{sec}}}{1\ \text{hr}}$$

$$= \frac{36{,}000\ \cancel{\text{yd}}}{1\ \text{hr}} \cdot \frac{1\ \text{mi}}{1760\ \cancel{\text{yd}}}$$

$$= \frac{36{,}000\ \text{mi}}{1760\ \text{hr}} \approx \frac{20.5\ \text{mi}}{1\ \text{hr}}$$

4. Write a proportion or use rates to determine the quail's and pheasant's speeds in miles per hour. Use your calculator to help you.

   a. Quail's speed:

   b. Pheasant's speed:

5. Write the birds in order from the fastest run to the slowest run.

You can scale down the ratio for the ostrich to describe its speed in miles per minute.

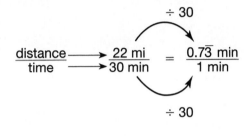

$$\dfrac{\text{distance}}{\text{time}} \longrightarrow \dfrac{22 \text{ mi}}{30 \text{ min}} = \dfrac{0.7\overline{3} \text{ min}}{1 \text{ min}}$$

The ostrich's speed was about 0.73 mile per minute.

Problem 3 Up and Down

1. Scale each common measurement up or down to determine the unknown quantity.

a. $\dfrac{12 \text{ in.}}{1 \text{ ft}} = \dfrac{48 \text{ in.}}{?}$

b. $\dfrac{3 \text{ ft}}{1 \text{ yd}} = \dfrac{?}{4 \text{ yd}}$

c. $\dfrac{360 \text{ min}}{6 \text{ hrs}} = \dfrac{?}{1 \text{ hr}}$

d. $\dfrac{300 \text{ cm}}{3 \text{ m}} = \dfrac{100 \text{ cm}}{?}$

e. $\dfrac{64 \text{ fl oz}}{8 \text{ cups}} = \dfrac{?}{1 \text{ cup}}$

f. $\dfrac{16 \text{ c}}{8 \text{ pt}} = \dfrac{?}{1 \text{ pt}}$

g. $\dfrac{32 \text{ oz}}{2 \text{ lb}} = \dfrac{16 \text{ oz}}{?}$

h. $\dfrac{1 \text{ km}}{0.6 \text{ mi}} = \dfrac{5 \text{ km}}{?}$

i. $\dfrac{5280 \text{ ft}}{1 \text{ mi}} = \dfrac{?}{2 \text{ mi}}$

j. $\dfrac{72 \text{ hours}}{3 \text{ days}} = \dfrac{?}{1 \text{ day}}$

2. Use a rate and multiply to determine each measurement conversion.

    a. How many quarts in 12 cups?

    b. How many gallons in 16 quarts?

    c. How many pounds in 2 tons?

    d. How many ounces in 4 pounds?

    e. How many seconds in 1 day?

 Be prepared to share your solutions and methods.

1.4 TUTOR TIME!
Using Tables to Solve Problems

Learning Goals

In this lesson, you will:

▶ Use tables to represent equivalent ratios.

▶ Solve proportions using unit rates.

It was not too long ago that if you needed help with homework or grasping a concept in one of your classes, you would either stay after school and speak with your teacher, or you may have gotten the help of a tutor. However, technology has made tutoring a snap! For many struggling students, accessing a tutor online is much easier and more convenient that traveling to a physical location.

And tutoring in school studies is not the only help that is in demand. Up and coming chess players used to rely on chess coaches or teachers in their city or town. But you were out of luck if your town did not have a chess teacher. Now, aspiring chess players can access almost any chess teacher available in the entire world. But of course, academic tutoring or chess coaching are not just for free—generally there is a fee. Sometimes, chess coaches charge up to 80 dollars per hour for their services. What do you think academic tutors charge their students? Have you used online tutors before?

Problem 1   Using Tables to Scale Up and Scale Down

1. A Girl Scout troop of 16 members sells 400 boxes of cookies in one week. Assume that this rate of sales continues.

a. Write the relationship between the number of boxes of cookies and the members in this situation as a rate or ratio. Explain your reasoning.

b. Complete the table.

Number of Boxes	400				
Members	16	8	32	24	20

c. Determine the unit rate for this situation.

> Remember, a unit rate is a rate with a 1 in the denominator.

d. Use the unit rate to calculate the number of boxes of cookies 50 Girl Scouts could sell in a week. Explain your reasoning.

e. Use the unit rate to calculate the number of Girl Scouts that it would take to sell 575 boxes of cookies in a week. Explain your reasoning.

f. Does having the unit rate help you to answer these questions? Explain why or why not.

2. About 13 people out of 100 are left-handed.

    a. Write the relationship in this situation as a ratio or rate and explain your reasoning.

    b. Complete the table with the number of people you would expect to be left-handed.

Left-handed People	13		
Total People	100	1000	25

    c. Complete the sentence that states another equivalent ratio or rate that you did not use in the table. Explain your reasoning.

        About _____ people out of _____ are left-handed.

3. Three robot lawn mowers can mow five regulation football fields in a day.

    a. Write the relationship between the mowers and the football fields in this situation as a ratio or rate. Explain your reasoning.

    b. Complete the table.

Mowers	3		12
Fields	5	15	

    c. Complete the sentence that states another equivalent ratio or rate that you did not use in the table. Explain your reasoning.

        _____ robot lawn mowers can mow _____ regulation football

fields in a day.

4. A color printer can print 7 color photos in one minute.

  a. Write the relationship between the photos and the time in this situation as a unit rate and explain your reasoning.

  b. How many color photos can this printer print in one hour? Explain your reasoning.

  c. If you need to print 500 photos, how many minutes will it take?
  Explain your reasoning.

  d. Complete the sentence that states another equivalent ratio. Explain your reasoning.
  A color printer can print _____ color photos in _____ minutes.

5. Tony needs a rate table for his tutoring jobs so that he can look up the charge quickly.

a. Complete the rate table.

Hours	0.5	1	1.5	2	3	3.5	4
Charge		$2.50					

b. Describe how you used the table to determine each tutoring charge. Then, use the table to determine the tutoring charges for:

i. 6 hours.

ii. 7 hours.

iii. 7.5 hours.

c. Tony made $21.25 last weekend. How many hours did he tutor? Explain your reasoning.

d. If Tony made $125 for one week of tutoring over the summer vacation, how many hours did he tutor?

6. Hayley's cat eats 3 large cans of food every 8 days. Determine the answer to each question. Explain your reasoning for the method you chose.

   a. How many cans of food will her cat eat in 24 days?

   b. How many days will 1 large can of cat food last? How did you determine your answer?

   c. How many days will 20 large cans of cat food last?

7. One pound of bananas costs $0.64. Describe the strategy you used to determine the cost of each.

   a. What is the cost of $\frac{1}{2}$ pound?

   b. What is the cost of 2 pounds?

   c. What is the cost for $2\frac{1}{2}$ pounds?

Be prepared to share your solutions and methods.

1.5 LOOKS CAN BE DECEIVING!

Using Proportions to Solve Problems

1

Learning Goals

In this lesson, you will:

▶ Solve proportions using the scaling method.

▶ Solve proportions using the unit rate method.

▶ Solve proportions using the means and extremes method.

Key Terms

▶ variable

▶ means and extremes

▶ solve a proportion

▶ inverse operations

H ave you ever seen a shark up close? Perhaps you have seen sharks at an aquarium or on the Internet. Would you say that sharks generally look scary? Well, looks can be deceiving. If you encountered a basking shark, you might be startled, but there is nothing to fear. These mighty beasts actually swim around with their mouths wide open looking quite intimidating, but actually, they are just feeding on plankton. Unfortunately, these sharks are on the "endangered" list in the North Atlantic Ocean.

Have you ever wondered how scientists keep track of endangered species populations? How would you track endangered species?

Problem 1 Does That Shark Have Its Tag?

Because it is impossible to count each individual animal, marine biologists use a method called the capture-recapture method to estimate the population of certain sea creatures. Biologists are interested in effectively managing populations to ensure the long-term survival of endangered species. In certain areas of the world, biologists randomly catch and tag a given number of sharks. After a period of time, such as a month, they recapture a second sample of sharks and count the total number of sharks as well as the number of recaptured tagged sharks. Then, the biologists use proportions to estimate the population of sharks living in a certain area.

Biologists can set up a proportion to estimate the total number of sharks in an area.

$$\frac{\text{Original number of tagged sharks}}{\text{Total number of sharks in an area}} = \frac{\text{Number of recaptured tagged sharks}}{\text{Number of sharks caught in the second sample}}$$

Although capturing the sharks once is necessary for tagging, it is not necessary to recapture the sharks each time. At times, the tags can be observed through binoculars from a boat or at shore.

Biologists originally caught and tagged 24 sharks off the coast of Cape Cod, Massachusetts, and then released them back into the bay. The next month, they caught 80 sharks with 8 of the sharks already tagged. To estimate the shark population off the Cape Cod coast, biologists set up the following proportion:

$$\frac{24 \text{ tagged sharks}}{p \text{ total sharks}} = \frac{8 \text{ recaptured tagged sharks}}{80 \text{ total sharks}}$$

Notice the p in the proportion. The p is a *variable*. A **variable** is a letter or symbol used to represent a number. In the proportion given, let p represent the total shark population off the coast of Cape Cod.

A proportion can be written several ways. Think about equivalent fractions using the same four numbers. You can rearrange the numbers in equivalent fraction statements to make more equivalent fraction statements.

So you can rearrange the proportion if you maintain equality.

	Example 1	**Example 2**
Equation 1	$\frac{2}{3} = \frac{4}{6}$	$\frac{5}{7} = \frac{15}{21}$
Equation 2	$\frac{6}{3} = \frac{4}{2}$	$\frac{21}{7} = \frac{15}{5}$
Equation 3	$\frac{2}{4} = \frac{3}{6}$	$\frac{5}{15} = \frac{7}{21}$

1. In each example, use arrows to show how the numbers were rearranged from the:

   a. first equation to the second.

   b. first equation to the third.

2. Write three more different proportions you could use to determine the total shark population off the coast of Cape Cod.

Think about how you changed the position of the numbers in the fraction examples to write other proportions to estimate the shark population.

3. Estimate the total shark population using any of the proportions.

4. Did any of the proportions seem more efficient than the other proportions?

5. Wildlife biologists tag deer in wildlife refuges. They originally tagged 240 deer and released them back into the refuge. The next month, they observed 180 deer, of which 30 deer were tagged. Approximately how many deer are in the refuge? Write a proportion and show your work to determine your answer.

A proportion of the form $\frac{a}{b} = \frac{c}{d}$ can be written in many different ways.

Another example is $\frac{d}{b} = \frac{c}{a}$ or $\frac{c}{a} = \frac{d}{b}$.

6. Show how the variables were rearranged from the proportion in the "if" statement to the two proportions in the "then" statement to maintain equality.

If $\frac{a}{b} = \frac{c}{d}$, then $\frac{d}{b} = \frac{c}{a}$ or $\frac{c}{a} = \frac{d}{b}$.

7. Write all the different ways you can rewrite the proportion $\frac{a}{b} = \frac{c}{d}$ and maintain equality.

Problem 2   Quality Control

The Ready Steady battery company tests batteries as they come through the assembly line and then uses a proportion to predict how many of its total production might be defective.

On Friday, the quality controller tested every tenth battery and found that of the 320 batteries tested, 8 were defective. If the company shipped a total of 3200 batteries, how many might be defective?

A quality control department checks the product a company creates to ensure that the product is not defective.

Let's analyze a few methods.

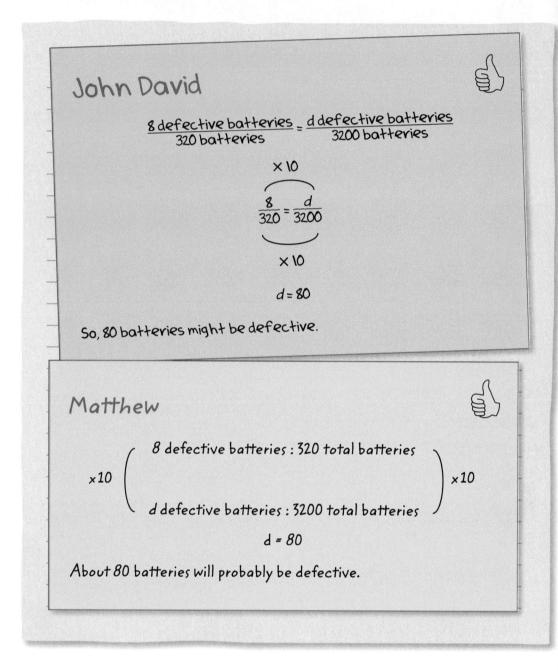

John David

$$\frac{8 \text{ defective batteries}}{320 \text{ batteries}} = \frac{d \text{ defective batteries}}{3200 \text{ batteries}}$$

$\times 10$

$$\frac{8}{320} = \frac{d}{3200}$$

$\times 10$

$d = 80$

So, 80 batteries might be defective.

Matthew

$\times 10$ (8 defective batteries : 320 total batteries

d defective batteries : 3200 total batteries) $\times 10$

$d = 80$

About 80 batteries will probably be defective.

1. How are Matthew's and John David's methods similar?

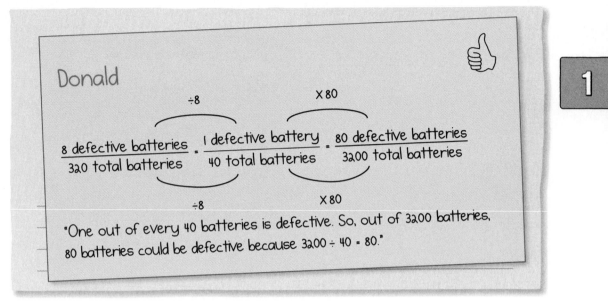

Donald

÷8

$\frac{8 \text{ defective batteries}}{320 \text{ total batteries}}$ = $\frac{1 \text{ defective battery}}{40 \text{ total batteries}}$ = $\frac{80 \text{ defective batteries}}{3200 \text{ total batteries}}$

×80

÷8

×80

"One out of every 40 batteries is defective. So, out of 3200 batteries, 80 batteries could be defective because 3200 ÷ 40 = 80."

2. Describe the strategy Donald used.

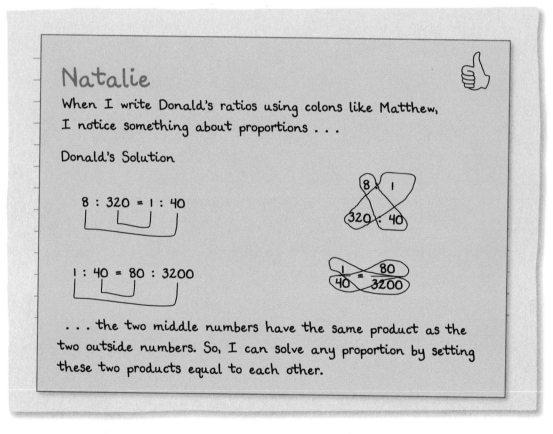

Natalie

When I write Donald's ratios using colons like Matthew, I notice something about proportions . . .

Donald's Solution

8 : 320 = 1 : 40

1 : 40 = 80 : 3200

. . . the two middle numbers have the same product as the two outside numbers. So, I can solve any proportion by setting these two products equal to each other.

3. Verify that Natalie is correct.

4. Try the various proportion-solving methods on these proportions and determine the unknown value. Explain which method you used.

a. $\dfrac{3 \text{ granola bars}}{420 \text{ calories}} = \dfrac{g \text{ granola bars}}{140 \text{ calories}}$

b. 8 correct: 15 questions = 24 correct: q questions

c. $\dfrac{d \text{ dollars}}{5 \text{ miles}} = \dfrac{\$9}{7.5 \text{ miles}}$

Natalie noticed a relationship between the *means* and *extremes* method. In a proportion that is written a: b = c: d, the product of the two values in the middle (the **means**) equals the product of the two values on the outside (**extremes**).

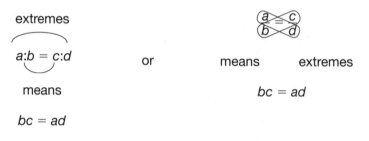

When $b \neq 0$, $d \neq 0$

To solve a proportion using this method, first, identify the means and extremes. Then, set the product of the means equal to the product of the extremes and solve for the unknown quantity. To **solve a proportion** means to determine all the values of the variables that make the proportion true.

> Multiplying the means and extremes is like "cross-multiplying."

In general, a proportion can be written in two ways: using colons or setting two ratios equal to each other.

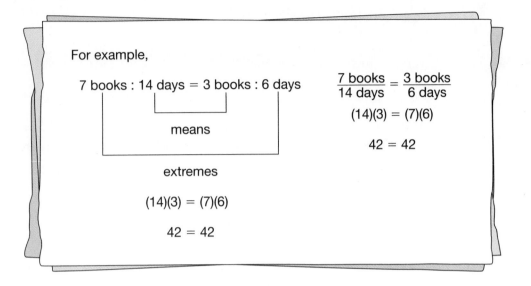

For example,

7 books : 14 days = 3 books : 6 days

$$\frac{7 \text{ books}}{14 \text{ days}} = \frac{3 \text{ books}}{6 \text{ days}}$$

means

extremes

$$(14)(3) = (7)(6)$$

$$42 = 42$$

$$(14)(3) = (7)(6)$$

$$42 = 42$$

5. You can write four different equations using means and extremes. Analyze each equation.

$$3 = \frac{(7)(6)}{14} \qquad 14 = \frac{(7)(6)}{3} \qquad \frac{(3)(14)}{7} = 6 \qquad \frac{(3)(14)}{6} = 7$$

a. Why are these equations all true? Explain your reasoning.

A different number was isolated in each equation.

b. Compare these equations to the equation showing the product of the means equal to the product of the extremes. How was the balance of the equation maintained in each?

6. Why is it important to maintain balance in equations?

In the proportion $\frac{a}{b} = \frac{c}{d}$, you can multiply both sides by b to *isolate the variable a.*

$$b \cdot \frac{a}{b} = \frac{c}{d} \cdot b \longrightarrow a = \frac{cb}{d}$$

When you isolate the variable in an equation, you perform an operation, or operations, to get the variable by itself on one side of the equals sign. Multiplication and division are *inverse operations*. **Inverse operations** are operations that "undo" each other.

Another strategy to isolate the variable a is to multiply the means and extremes, and then isolate the variable by performing inverse operations.

$$\frac{a}{b} = \frac{c}{d}$$

Step 1: $ad = bc$

Step 2: $\frac{ad}{d} = \frac{bc}{d}$

Step 3: $a = \frac{bc}{d}$

7. Describe each step shown.

8. Rewrite the proportion $\frac{a}{b} = \frac{c}{d}$ to isolate each of the other variables: b, c, and d. Explain the strategies you used to isolate each variable.

Problem 3   Using Proportions

1. The school store sells computer games for practicing mathematics skills. The table shows how many of each game were sold last year.

Game	Fast Facts	Fraction Fun	Percent Sense	Measurement Mania
Number of Games Sold	120	80	50	150

a. How many total games were sold last year?

b. The store would like to order a total of 1000 games this year. About how many of each game should the store order?

c. If the store would like to order a total of 240 games this year, about how many of each game should the store order?

2. You are making lemonade to sell at the track meet. According to the recipe, you need 12 ounces of lemon juice for every 240 ounces of sugar water. You have 16 ounces of lemon juice.

a. How many ounces of sugar water do you need?

Make sure you show your work.

b. How many ounces of lemonade can you make?

3. A maintenance company charges a mall owner $45,000 to clean his 180,000 square foot shopping mall.

    a. How much should a store of 4800 square feet pay? Show your work.

    b. How much should a store of 9200 square feet pay?

4. The National Park Service has to keep a certain level of bass stocked in a lake. They tagged 60 bass and released them into the lake. Two days later, they caught 128 fish and found that 32 of them were tagged. What is a good estimate of how many bass are in the lake? Show your work.

5. An astronaut who weighs 85 kilograms on Earth weighs 14.2 kilograms on the moon. How much would a person weigh on the moon if they weigh 95 kilograms on Earth? Round your answer to the nearest tenth.

6. Water goes over Niagara Falls at a rate of 180 million cubic feet every 30 minutes. How much water goes over the Falls in 1 minute?

7. The value of the U.S. dollar in comparison to the value of foreign currency changes daily. Complete the table shown. Round to the nearest hundredth.

Euro	U.S. Dollar
1	1.44
	1.00
	6.00
6	
10	

Do you see how to set up proportions by using two different rows of the table?

8. To make 4.5 cups of fruity granola, the recipe calls for 1.5 cups of raisins, 1 cup of granola, and 2 cups of blueberries. If you want to make 18 cups of fruity granola, how much of each of the ingredients do you need?

Be prepared to share your solutions and methods.

1.6

THE PRICE IS . . . CLOSE

Using Unit Rates in Real World Applications

Learning Goals

In this lesson, you will:

▶ Estimate and calculate values using rates.

▶ Use unit rates to determine the best buy.

Have you ever bought something on sale? Was the item on sale for a percentage off, like 50% or 25%? How did you know that you paid the correct amount for the item? Did you calculate the discount or did you just let the store clerk calculate it?

Problem 1 A Special on Unit Rates in Aisle 9

Marta and Brad go to the store to buy some laundry detergent for a neighbor. They see that the brand he wants comes in two different sizes: 26 fluid ounces for $9.75 and 20.5 fluid ounces for $7.50.

1. Which one should Marta and Brad buy? Explain the reason for your decision.

Shouldn't you just buy the cheaper one?

2. Which is the better buy? How do you know?

One way to compare the values of products is to calculate the unit rate for each item. Remember that a unit rate is a rate with a bottom term of 1.

Marta estimated the unit rates this way:

The first one is about 25 fluid ounces for about $10.

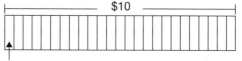

1 fl oz

So, 1 fluid ounce costs about $\frac{\$10}{25}$, which is $\frac{\$2}{5}$, or $\frac{\$0.40}{1}$.

The second one is about 21 fluid ounces for about $7.

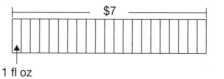

1 fl oz

So, 1 fluid ounce of that detergent costs about $\frac{\$7}{21}$, which is $\frac{\$1}{3}$, or about $\frac{\$0.33}{1}$.

That means that you pay less for each fluid ounce of the second one, so it is the better buy.

Brad estimated the unit rates this way:

For the first one, you spend about $10 for about 25 fluid ounces.

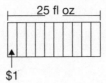

So, for each dollar you spend on the first one, you get about $\frac{25 \text{ fl oz}}{\$10}$, or $\frac{2.5 \text{ fl oz}}{\$1}$.

For the second one, you spend about $7 for about 21 fluid ounces.

So, for each dollar you spend on the second one, you get about $\frac{21 \text{ fl oz}}{\$7}$, or $\frac{3 \text{ fl oz}}{\$1}$.

Because you get more of the second one for each dollar you spend, the second one is the better buy.

3. Marta and Brad both chose the second one as the better buy, but which one of them reasoned correctly? Explain your reasoning.

4. Calculate the unit rates for each of these products.

5. Using the unit rates, is it now possible to decide which is the better deal? Explain your reasoning.

6. Calculate the unit rates for each item.

    a. A bottle of 250 vitamins costs $12.50.

    b. A pack of 40 AAA batteries costs $25.95.

    c. A package of 24 rolls of toilet paper costs $16.25.

    d. A box of 500 business cards costs $19.95.

7. Estimate the unit rates to determine which is the better buy. Explain your reasoning.

   a. 22 vitamins for $1.97 or 40 vitamins for $3.25

   b. 24.3 ounces for $8.76 or 32.6 ounces for $16.95

8. Bottles of water are sold at various prices and in various sizes. Write each as a ratio, and then as a unit rate. Which bottle is the best buy? Explain how you know.

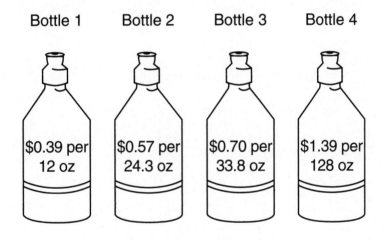

Bottle 1 — $0.39 per 12 oz

Bottle 2 — $0.57 per 24.3 oz

Bottle 3 — $0.70 per 33.8 oz

Bottle 4 — $1.39 per 128 oz

 Be prepared to share your solutions and methods.

Chapter 1   Summary

Key Terms

▶ ratio (1.1)
▶ rate (1.1)
▶ proportion (1.1)
▶ equivalent ratios (1.1)

▶ scaling up (1.1)
▶ scaling down (1.1)
▶ unit rate (1.1)
▶ convert (1.3)

▶ variable (1.5)
▶ means and extremes (1.5)
▶ solve a proportion (1.5)
▶ inverse operations (1.5)

Identifying Ratios, Rates, and Unit Rates

A ratio is a comparison of two quantities using division. A rate is a ratio that compares two quantities that are measured in different units. A unit rate is a comparison of two measurements in which the denominator has a value of 1 unit.

Example

$\dfrac{50 \text{ gallons}}{1 \text{ hour}}$	Unit Rate
$\dfrac{4 \text{ red crayons}}{15 \text{ total crayons}}$	Ratio
$\dfrac{168 \text{ hours}}{7 \text{ days}}$	Rate

1.1 Using Ratios, Rates, and Unit Rates to Analyze Problems

Ratios, rates, and unit rates are commonly used to analyze and solve a variety of real-world problems. Any rate can be rewritten as a unit rate by determining an equivalent rate with a denominator of 1 unit.

Example

Four employees can package 1920 crates per day. The rate $\dfrac{1920 \text{ crates}}{4 \text{ employees}}$ can be rewritten as the following unit rate: $\dfrac{480 \text{ crates}}{1 \text{ employee}}$.

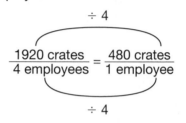

$$\overset{\div\,4}{\overbrace{\dfrac{1920 \text{ crates}}{4 \text{ employees}} = \dfrac{480 \text{ crates}}{1 \text{ employee}}}}$$
$$\div\,4$$

1.1 Scaling a Ratio to Write a Proportion

A proportion is an equation that states two ratios are equal. In a proportion, the first terms of each ratio must have the same units and the second terms of each ratio must have the same units. To rewrite a ratio to an equivalent ratio with larger numbers, you scale up. To scale up means to multiply the numerator and the denominator by the same factor. To rewrite a ratio to an equivalent ratio with smaller numbers, you scale down. To scale down means to divide the numerator and the denominator by the same factor.

Example

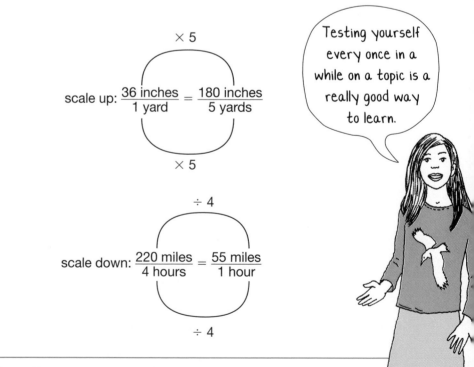

$$\text{scale up: } \overset{\times\,5}{\overbrace{\dfrac{36 \text{ inches}}{1 \text{ yard}} = \dfrac{180 \text{ inches}}{5 \text{ yards}}}}$$
$$\times\,5$$

Testing yourself every once in a while on a topic is a really good way to learn.

$$\text{scale down: } \overset{\div\,4}{\overbrace{\dfrac{220 \text{ miles}}{4 \text{ hours}} = \dfrac{55 \text{ miles}}{1 \text{ hour}}}}$$
$$\div\,4$$

58 • **Chapter 1** Ratios and Rates

1.2 Using Ratios to Make Comparisons

Ratios can be used to compare similar items.

Example

Ted wants to determine which fertilizer has the highest nitrogen content. A-Plus Fertilizer contains 1 part nitrogen for every 10 parts fertilizer. True Grow Fertilizer contains 2 parts nitrogen for every 25 parts fertilizer. Sky High Fertilizer contains 3 parts nitrogen for every 20 parts fertilizer.

A-Plus Fertilizer: $\dfrac{1 \text{ part nitrogen}}{10 \text{ parts fertilizer}} = \dfrac{10 \text{ parts nitrogen}}{100 \text{ parts fertilizer}}$

True Grow Fertilizer: $\dfrac{2 \text{ parts nitrogen}}{25 \text{ parts fertilizer}} = \dfrac{8 \text{ parts nitrogen}}{100 \text{ parts fertilizer}}$

Sky High Fertilizer: $\dfrac{3 \text{ parts nitrogen}}{20 \text{ parts fertilizer}} = \dfrac{15 \text{ parts nitrogen}}{100 \text{ parts fertilizer}}$

Sky High Fertilizer has the highest nitrogen content of the three brands.

1.2 Using Rates and Proportions to Solve Mixture Problems

In order to solve mixture problems, set up and solve a proportion with the given rate to determine the unknown value.

Example

Ted is using Sky High Fertilizer to fertilizer his crops. Each bag of fertilizer contains 15 pounds of nitrogen and 4 pounds of phosphorus. Ted wants to determine how many pounds of phosphorus he will use if he uses 300 pounds of nitrogen.

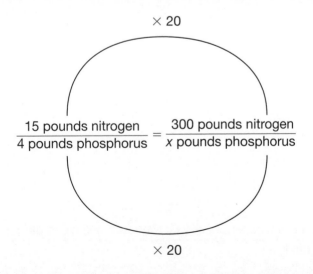

$\times 20$

$$\dfrac{15 \text{ pounds nitrogen}}{4 \text{ pounds phosphorus}} = \dfrac{300 \text{ pounds nitrogen}}{x \text{ pounds phosphorus}}$$

$\times 20$

Ted will use $4(20) = 80$ pounds of phosphorus if he uses 300 pounds of nitrogen.

1.3 Comparing Rates with Different Units of Measure

When comparing rates between two items, the units of measure of each item may be different. When this occurs, converting two different measures to one measure makes comparing the rates easier. To convert the units of measure, it is helpful to know the conversion rate to set up and solve a proportion.

Example

A jet plane travels 250 miles in 30 minutes. A bullet train travels 98 miles in 900 seconds. By converting the units of measure to one measure will help determine that the jet plane travels faster in one hour than the bullet train.

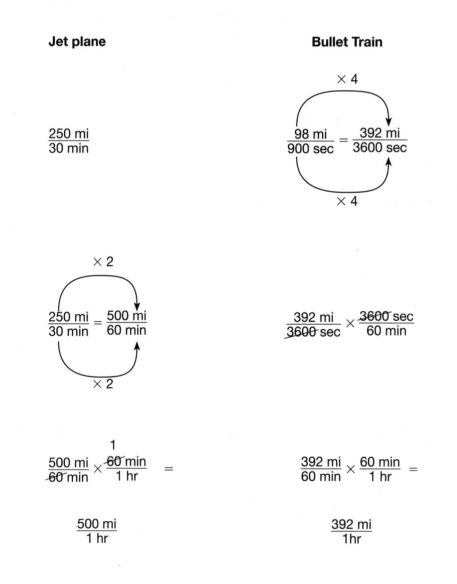

The jet plane travels faster because it travels at 500 miles per hour. The bullet train travels at 392 miles per hour.

1.4 Using Tables to Represent Equivalent Ratios

Using a table can be a convenient and orderly way to represent equivalent ratios.

Example

Six-hundred pounds of grass seed will cover 4 acres. The unit rate is $\dfrac{150 \text{ pounds}}{1 \text{ acre}}$, because $\dfrac{600 \text{ pounds}}{4 \text{ acres}} = \dfrac{150 \text{ pounds}}{1 \text{ acre}}$. The unit rate can be used to complete the table.

Grass Seed (pounds)	150	750	1500	3000
Acres Covered	1	5	10	20

1.5 Solving Proportions Using the Scaling Method

The scaling method should be used when it is easy to determine which number to multiply by when scaling up or which number to divide by when scaling down.

Example

In a survey, 4 out of 5 people preferred peppermint gum to spearmint gum. To estimate how many people out of 100 prefer peppermint gum to spearmint gum, scale up.

$$\overset{\times\, 20}{\overbrace{}}$$
$$\frac{4}{5} = \frac{p}{100}$$
$$\underset{\times\, 20}{\underbrace{}}$$

$$p = 80$$

It is expected that 80 people out of 100 prefer peppermint gum to spearmint gum.

1.5 Solving Proportions Using the Unit Rate Method

Use the unit rate method to rewrite a ratio when it is easy to first calculate the unit rate and then scale up to the rate needed.

Example

If you ran 18 miles in 3 hours, you could except to run 30 miles in 5 hours as shown.

Calculate the unit rate: $\dfrac{18 \text{ miles}}{3 \text{ hours}} = \dfrac{6 \text{ miles}}{1 \text{ hour}}$

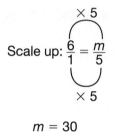

Scale up: $\dfrac{6}{1} = \dfrac{m}{5}$

$m = 30$

1.5 Solving Proportions Using the Means and Extremes Method

Use the means and extremes method when you need to solve a proportion with an unknown quantity by setting the product of the means equal to the product of the extremes. For any numbers a, b, c, and d where b and d are not zero:

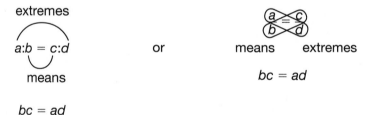

$$bc = ad$$

Example

You need 6.75 cups of sugar to make 3 batches of cookies. To determine how much sugar you will need to make 7 batches of cookies, use the means and extremes method.

$$\frac{6.75}{3} = \frac{s}{7}$$

$$3s = (6.75)(7)$$

$$\frac{3s}{3} = \frac{47.25}{3}$$

$$s = 15.75$$

You will need 15.75 cups of sugar to make 7 batches of cookies.

Estimate and Calculate Values Using Unit Rates

One way to compare the values of products is to calculate the unit rate for each item. Remember that a unit rate is a rate in which the denominator has a value of 1 unit.

Example

A 16-ounce bottle of Dazzle shampoo costs $6.40. A 24-ounce bottle of Dazzle shampoo costs $10.80. The steps to determining which shampoo bottle size is the better buy are shown.

The unit rate for the 16-ounce bottle is $\dfrac{\$0.40}{1 \text{ oz}}$, because $\dfrac{\$6.40}{16 \text{ oz}} = \dfrac{\$0.40}{1 \text{ oz}}$.

The unit rate for the 24-ounce bottle is $\dfrac{\$0.45}{1 \text{ oz}}$, because $\dfrac{\$10.80}{24 \text{ oz}} = \dfrac{\$0.45}{1 \text{ oz}}$.

The 16-ounce bottle of Dazzle shampoo is the best buy, because it costs less per ounce.

2 DIRECT VARIATION AND CONSTANT OF PROPORTIONALITY

Equivalent ratios and direct variation are vital to chemists. Too much of one solution can result in a smoldering reaction, while too little of a solution may not result in a reaction at all. But the correct solution can be used for all sorts of things like medicines to cleaning products.

2.1

WHAT MAKES YOU TAP YOUR FEET?

Introduction to Direct Variation

Learning Goals

In this lesson, you will:

▶ Determine how quantities in different situations vary.

▶ Use multiple representations to explore the types of variation.

Key Terms

▶ direct variation (direct proportion)

▶ origin

Bob is four times as old as his brother. Will he ever be three times as old? Twice as old? Will they ever be the same age? Do you know how old each of them is? How do the ages of two people vary over their lives?

These are math riddles. To solve a math riddle, you need to know some information about the riddle. For example, you know that Bob is four times as old as his brother. That is a bit of information. However, do you think you can answer the rest of the questions with the information you are given?

Problem 1   Do You Rock Out or Are You Feeling Funky?

A recent survey of middle school students found that:

- 1 out of 4 students like country music,
- 1 out of 3 students like rock music,
- 1 out of 5 students like hip-hop music,
- the rest of the students no musical preference.

> How can unit rates help you complete this table?

1. Use this information to interpret the survey results given the total number of students. Then, complete the table.

Total Students	Prefer Country	Prefer Rock	Prefer Hip-Hop	No Preference
60				
120				
180				
240				

2. As the total number of students increases by 60, by how much does each increase?

   a. the number of students who like country

   b. the number of students who like rock

   c. the number of students who like hip-hop

   d. the number of students who have no preference

> Sometimes I listen to classical music when I do homework.

3. How does the increase in total students as a multiple of 60 make the calculations more efficient? Why 60?

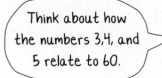

Think about how the numbers 3, 4, and 5 relate to 60.

4. Complete the table.

Total Students	Prefer Country	Prefer Rock	Prefer Hip-Hop	No Preference
600				
	300			
		600		
			480	
				650

5. How do the number of students in this table compare to the previous table?

How can the values from the first table help you complete the table?

Problem 2   Using Graphs to Show Middle School Learners Musical Tastes

1. Complete the graph to show the relationship between the total number of students and those students who prefer country music using the information you completed in Problem 1.

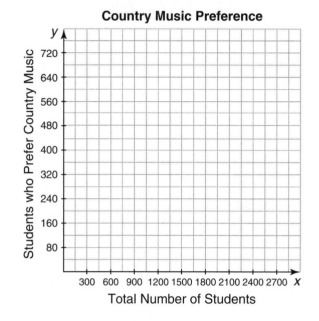

Country Music Preference

2. Complete the graph to show the relationship between the total number of students and the students who prefer rock music using the information you completed in Problem 1.

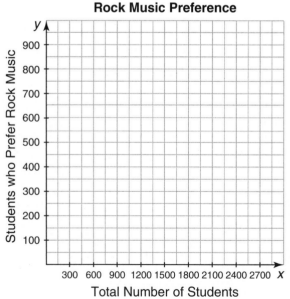

Rock Music Preference

3. Complete the graph to show the relationship between the total number of students and the students who prefer hip-hop music using the information you completed in Problem 1.

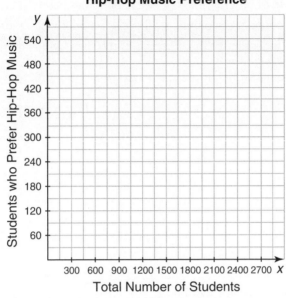

Hip-Hop Music Preference

4. Examine each graph and describe the pattern of the points.

Data sets can either be discrete or continuous data. As quantitative data, discrete data are counts of how many, where the data can only have values that are counting numbers. Continuous data are measurements and can have values that fall between counting numbers.

5. Are the data in your graphs continuous or discrete data? Would it make sense to connect the points in the graph? Why or why not?

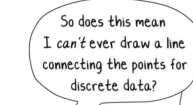 Drawing a line through the data set of a graph is a way to represent relationships. The points on the line represent a set of equivalent ratios. In certain problems, all the points will be on a line. It will sometimes make sense in terms of the situation to connect the points on the line. At other times, not all the points will end up on the line, or it does not make sense to connect the points. It all depends on the situation. It is up to you to consider each situation and interpret the meaning of the data values from a line drawn on a graph.

6. In each graph, if there were zero total students, how many would like each type of music?

So does this mean I *can't* ever draw a line connecting the points for discrete data?

Drawing a line is a way to model connections between equivalent ratios. But it is up to you to determine when it makes sense to connect the points or not using the knowledge you know about discrete and continuous data.

In the tables and graphs in Problems 1 and 2, you saw that the number of students who prefer one type of music varied based on the total number of students. For example, for each increase in four students, one more student liked country music. For every additional student who prefers rock, the total number of students increases by three.

A function represents a **direct variation** if the ratio between the output values and input values is a constant. If two quantities vary directly, the points on a graph form a straight line, and the line runs through the *origin*. The **origin** is a point on a graph with the ordered pair (0, 0). You can also describe the quantities of a direct variation relationship as **direct proportions**.

2

A car driving at a constant rate of 60 miles per hour is an example of direct variation.

A sketch of a graph that could represent this situation is shown.

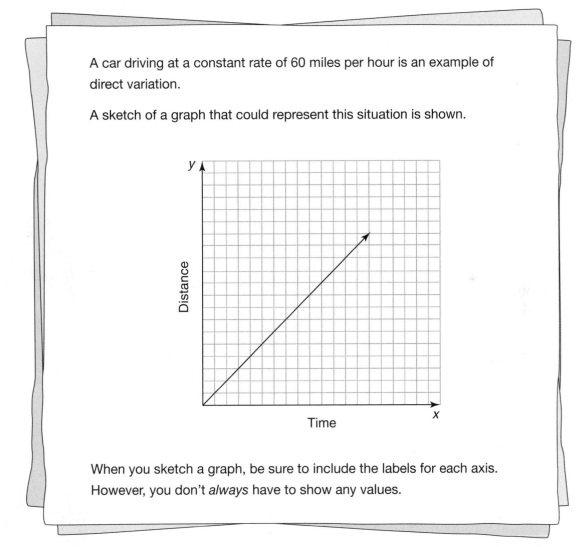

When you sketch a graph, be sure to include the labels for each axis. However, you don't *always* have to show any values.

7. Explain how this situation is an example of direct variation.

Think about the definition of direct variation as you explain your reasoning.

8. List another example of quantities that vary directly. Then, sketch a graph that could represent the relationship between the quantities.

2

Be prepared to share your solutions and methods.

2.2 BUILDING BIRD FEEDERS IS FOR THE BIRDS!

Determining Equivalent Ratios

Learning Goal

In this lesson, you will:

▶ Determine if the points on a graph are equivalent ratios.

Woodworkers create and repair all sorts of items and structures that are made primarily of wood. If the item is made of wood, they probably know how to sand it, glue it, build it, stain it. Woodworkers use tools such as jigsaws, levels, T-squares, and chisels. Woodworkers can create tables and chairs, chess sets, bird houses and feeders, and—well, just about anything that is made of wood. They are the pros of pine, wizards of walnut, champions of chestnut, and maestros of mahogany. How do you think wood workers might use equivalent ratios? Do you think woodworkers work together to complete projects?

Problem 1   Building Feeders

Bob and his little brother Jake want to build bird feeders to sell at a local farmers market. They have enough money to buy materials to build 10 bird feeders.

1. If Bob builds 5 bird feeders, how many will Jake need to build?

2. Complete the table by listing all the possible ways in which they can divide up the work.

Bird Feeders Built by Bob	Bird Feeders Built by Jake
10	
9	
8	
7	
6	
5	
4	
3	
2	
1	
0	

3. Complete the graph by plotting the quantities from the table you completed.

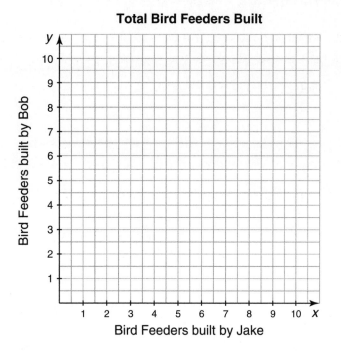

Total Bird Feeders Built

(y-axis: Bird Feeders built by Bob, x-axis: Bird Feeders built by Jake)

4. Draw a line to connect the points on this graph.

5. Describe the line you drew. Do all the points on your line make sense in terms of the problem situation?

6. Describe how the number of bird feeders built by Bob affects the number Jake builds.

7. What is the ratio of bird feeders that Bob builds to the number that Jake builds? Explain your reasoning.

8. Dontrell claims that the number of bird feeders Bob builds directly varies with the number of bird feeders Jake builds. Do you agree with Dontrell's claim? Explain your reasoning.

Problem 2   Varying Areas of Rectangles—But Do They Directly Vary?

Vanessa was given a math problem to determine how many different rectangles can be constructed with an area of 12 square inches.

1. Vanessa thinks that there are only two: one with a width of 2 inches and a length of 6 inches, and another with a width of 3 inches and a length of 4 inches. Is she correct? Explain your reasoning.

2. Complete the table by determining the unknown value.

Width of Rectangle (in.)	Length of Rectangle (in.)
1	
	2
4	
1.5	
$1\frac{1}{3}$	
20	
	$\frac{3}{4}$

Remember, the area of the rectangle is 12 square inches.

3. Complete the graph by plotting the quantities from the table you completed.

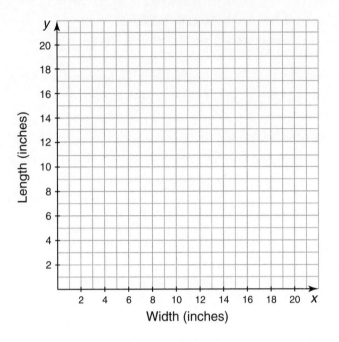

4. Draw a line to connect the points on this graph.

5. Describe the line you drew. Do all the points on your line make sense in terms of the problem situation?

6. Describe how the width of the rectangle affects the length of the rectangle.

7. What is the ratio of the width to the length of the rectangles?

Problem 3   Bamboo Can Grow, Grow, Grow!

1. One species of bamboo can grow at an average rate of 60 centimeters per day. Assuming that the bamboo plant maintains the average rate of growth per day, how tall will the bamboo plant be if it grows for:

   a. 10 days?

   b. 30 days?

   c. one-half day?

Why do you think this problem says "average rate" instead of just rate?

2. Assuming that a bamboo plant maintains the average rate of growth over time, how long has it been growing if it is:

   a. 20 centimeters tall?

   b. 200 centimeters tall?

3. Complete the table using the given growth rate of the bamboo plant.

Time (days)	Height of Bamboo (cm)
10	
30	
$\frac{1}{2}$	
	20
	200

4. Complete the graph by plotting the quantities from the table you completed.

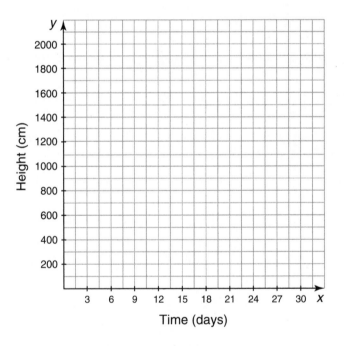

Time (days)

5. Draw a line to connect the points on this graph.

6. Describe the line you drew. Do all the points on your line make sense in terms of the problem situation?

7. Describe how the time affects the height of the bamboo plant.

8. What is the rate of the height of the bamboo plant to the time?

Talk the Talk

Go back and examine all the graphs in this lesson.

1. How are all the graphs that display ratios the same?

2. Sketch a graph that displays equivalent ratios.

Do you see a pattern?

Be prepared to share your solutions and methods.

2.3

KIDS JUST WANNA HAVE FUN!

Determining and Applying the Constant of Proportionality

2

Many organizations and businesses rely on market research and survey results to develop new products. For example, the music industry relies on survey chart listings to determine how well an artist's songs are selling and being played on radio stations. The higher the level on the album charts, the more the record company will try to get the songs used in television programs, movies, or even commercials.

Even the movie industry relies on surveys to determine which movie trailers should be shown at the beginning of certain movies. They also review weekly attendance reports a movie generates and how much money a movie generates through box office ticket sales. The greater the money amount, the more showings of the movie will air in theaters.

Can you think of other industries that routinely use survey results and market research for decision making of products?

Problem 1 Top of the Charts

Magic Music, a company that produces new recordings for artists, determines that 4 out of 5 girls will like the new recording artist, Sallie Pal.

1. If 4000 girls were surveyed, how many liked Sallie Pal? Explain how you determined your answer.

Remember, you can scale up a ratio or use proportions to determine the value of a ratio you're scaling up!

2. In one group of girls, 300 girls liked Sallie Pal. How many girls were in this group? Explain how you determined your answer.

3. Complete the table to show the number of girls who like Sallie Pal, and the total number of girls.

Number of Girls who Like Sallie Pal	Total Number of Girls	Ratio of Girls who Like Sallie Pal to Total Number of Girls
4	5	
	4000	
300		
120		
	1200	
248		

4. Determine the ratio between the number of girls who like Sallie Pal, and the total number of girls for each row in your table. Write each ratio in simplest form.

5. What do you notice about the ratios?

In a proportional relationship, the ratio between two values is always the same, or constant. This ratio is called the **constant of proportionality**. Generally, you can use the variable k to represent the constant of proportionality.

> Do you think the constant of proportionality is always a ratio?

6. What is the constant of proportionality, k, for the ratio between the number of girls who like Sallie Pal and the total number of girls?

Problem 2   Girls' Sports

Vista Middle School has determined that 5 out of 7 girls play sports at the school. The constant of proportionality, k, is $\frac{5}{7}$.

1. Write an equation showing the relationship between the number of girls who play sports, s, and the total number of girls, t, and the constant of proportionality.

2. Use the equation to solve each.

   a. If 175 girls play sports, how many total girls are there?

   b. There are 287 girls. How many play sports?

c. How many girls play sports if there are 784 girls at the school?

d. How many girls are there if 55 play sports?

3. Describe how the first equation shown was rewritten into the second equation.

$$\frac{y}{x} = k$$
$$y = kx$$

Problem 3   What Does the Constant
of Proportionality Represent?

There are 4 girls for every 3 boys enrolled in Sherman Middle School.

1. Set up proportions for each question. Then, solve each proportion to determine the unknown value. Use the information from the ratio given.

   a. If there are 15 boys enrolled in the school, how many girls are enrolled in the school?

   b. If there are 12 girls enrolled in the school, how many boys are enrolled in the school?

2. Define variables for the quantities that are changing in this situation.

3. Set up a proportion using the variables for the quantities to the ratio given for the enrollment of girls to boys enrolled in Sherman Middle School.

4. Use your proportion to write an equation for the number of girls enrolled at Sherman Middle School to the number of boys enrolled.

So, you want to isolate *g* because you're trying to write an equation for the number of girls.

5. What is the constant of proportionality in this equation?

6. What does the constant of proportionality represent in this problem situation?

7. Use your proportion to write an equation for the number of boys enrolled at Sherman Middle School to the number of girls enrolled.

This time, you want to isolate *b* because you're trying to write an equation for the number of boys.

8. What is the constant of proportionality in this equation?

9. What does the constant of proportionality represent in this problem situation?

10. What do you notice about the constant of proportionality in each situation?

11. Do you think each constant of proportionality makes sense in terms of the problem situation?

Sometimes, the constant of proportionality is not a whole number. The constant of proportionality can also be a decimal or a fraction. When the constant of proportionality involves whole items, like people, it may seem strange to think about the constant of proportionality in terms of a fraction. Instead, you can think of the constant of proportionality as a way to predict outcomes of a situation.

12. Use the given ratio about the boys and girls enrolled in Sherman Middle School.

   a. If there are 79 boys enrolled in the school, use the constant of proportionality to determine how many girls are enrolled at the school.

> Did you use the constant of proportionality for the girls or for the boys? Does it matter which constant of proportionality you use?

   b. If there are 113 girls enrolled in the school, how many boys are enrolled in the school?

Problem 4   Mixing *the* Perfect Lemonade

The following is the recipe to make 6 cups of Perfect Lemonade:

- 1 cup sugar
- 1 cup water (for the simple syrup)
- 1 cup lemon juice
- 4 cups cold water (to dilute)

1. Set up proportions and solve to answer each question.

    a. How many cups of sugar are needed for 24 cups of lemonade?

    b. How many cups of sugar are needed for 21 cups of lemonade?

2. Define variables for the quantities that are changing in this problem situation.

3. Set up a proportion using the variables of these quantities to the ratio of cups of sugar to glasses of lemonade.

4. Use your proportion to write an equation for the number of cups of lemonade based on the number of cups of sugar.

5. What is the constant of proportionality in this equation?

6. What does the constant of proportionality represent in this problem situation?

7. Use your proportion to write an equation for the number of cups of sugar based on the number of cups of lemonade.

8. What is the constant of proportionality in this equation?

Problem 5 Chemical Solutions for Chemical Experiments? Shouldn't That Be the Other Way Around?

A chemist must use a solution that is 30% of reagent and 70% of water for an experiment. A solution is a mixture of two or more liquids. A reagent is a substance used in a chemical reaction to produce other substances.

1. Define variables for the quantities that are changing in this problem situation.

2. Determine the constant of proportionality from the information given for creating the solution. Then, write an equation for the amount of water based on the amount of reagent.

So, do chemists usually use ratios and constants of proportionality in their work?

3. Use your equation to answer each question.

    a. If the chemist uses 6 liters of reagent, how many liters of water will she need to make her 30% solution?

    b. If the chemist uses 77 milliliters of water, how many milliliters of reagent will she need to make her 30% solution?

Problem 6 Fish-Inches

You are thinking of purchasing an aquarium for your parents. You contact Jim, a family friend who owns an aquarium store. You need to know how many fish to purchase for an aquarium, but first you must determine how big the aquarium will be. You ask Jim and he tells you his rule of thumb is to purchase "as many fish that measure 3 inches, or 3 fish-inches, for each 2 gallons of water in the aquarium."

1. Define variables for the quantities that are changing in this problem situation.

2. Write an equation for fish-inches based on the gallons of water.

3. Use your equation to answer each question.

    a. If an aquarium holds 10 gallons of water, how many fish inches should you purchase?

    b. If you want to purchase a 5-inch fish, two 2-inch fish, and three 3-inch fish, how many gallons of water should the aquarium hold?

Talk the Talk

1. Solve each using the equation for the constant of proportionality, $\frac{y}{x} = k$.

   a. $k = 0.7$ and $y = 4$

   b. $k = \frac{3}{11}$ and $x = 9$

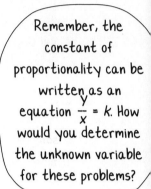

Remember, the constant of proportionality can be written as an equation $\frac{y}{x} = k$. How would you determine the unknown variable for these problems?

   c. $k = 5$ and $x = 1\frac{1}{2}$

   d. $k = \frac{1}{6}$ and $y = 3\frac{1}{3}$

Be prepared to share your solutions and methods.

STOP THAT SPEEDING SNAIL?

2.4

Using the Constant of Proportionality to Solve Proportions

Learning Goal

In this lesson, you will:

▶ Determine if there is a constant of proportionality between two variables.

What is one of the most interesting things you have ever eaten? Did you end up liking that interesting dish? Do you think eating snails would be an interesting dish?

While not as popular in the United States, it is common for French citizens to partake in these garden pests. Usually boiled and dipped in butter, escargot (pronounced es-car-go) is a delicacy. Of course, it also brings to mind about a funny joke about snails as well.

A snail went to buy a car. He asked the car dealer that he would buy a car only if they painted an "S" on the top of the car. Wanting the sale, the dealer agreed, but asked the snail, "Why do you want an "S" on the top of your new car?" The snail replied, "When I drive, I want people who are looking down on me say: Look at that S car go!" Maybe if the snail has a fast car, it won't become "escargot!"

Problem 1   Look at that "S" Car Go!

As a class assignment, your group records the distance in centimeters, that a snail traveled for a certain time in minutes. The results of this situation are recorded in the table shown.

Time (minutes)	Distance Traveled by Snail (cm)
2	11
5	27.5
12	66
15	82.5

1. Define variables for the quantities that are changing in this problem situation.

The table of values represents a proportional relationship.

2. How can you determine the constant of proportionality using the values in the table?

3. What is the constant of proportionality?

> Think about the rate: $\dfrac{distance}{time}$

4. Set up a proportion when the snail travels 2 minutes.

5. Use your proportion to write an equation for the distance the snail travels based on the time.

6. How far will the snail travel in 38 minutes? Assume that the snail will travel at a constant rate. Explain how you determined your answer.

7. How long will it take the snail to travel 144.5 centimeters? Assume the snail will travel at a constant rate. Explain how you determined your answer.

Problem 2   Is There a Constant of Proportionality?

So far, you have studied proportional relationships. However, not all relationships that involve two quantities are proportional. There are also non-proportional relationships between two quantities as well. For example, think about your height over time. You didn't grow at the same rate between the time you were born and your current height. Though there were two quantities, time and height, there was not a direct proportion between the two quantities because there wasn't a constant of proportionality.

1. Analyze each table to determine if the relationships are proportional. State a constant of proportionality if possible. Finally, explain how you determined your answer.

   a. The table shown is a survey of sixth graders who prefer to ride a skateboard or a bicycle. Is the relationship proportional?

Skateboard	Bicycle
2	4
30	32
40	60

b. There are 250 boys in 6th grade, and 75 are in the band. There are 200 girls in 6th grade, and 60 are in band. Is the relationship proportional?

6th Grade Class	Total	Band
Boys	250	75
Girls	200	60

c. A 30-minute television show has 8 minutes of commercials and 22 minutes of the show. A 120-minute television movie has 32 minutes of commercials and 88 minutes of the movie. Is the relationship proportional?

Television Show Total Length	Show Length (in minutes)	Commercial Length (in minutes)
30	22	8
120	88	32

d. Commuters in McKnight and Mitenridge either drive to work or take public transportation. Analyze the table to determine if there is a constant of proportionality.

Commuters	Drive to Work	Public Transportation to Work
McKnight	175	120
Mitenridge	525	300

e. Of the 250 middle-school boys who have a subscription to *Boys Noise*, 125 access the magazine through the website. Of the 280 middle-school girls who have a subscription to *Girls Rockstar*, 160 access the magazine through the website. Is there a constant of proportionality?

2.5 THE MAN WHO RAN FROM MARATHON TO ATHENS

Graphing Direct Proportions

Learning Goals

In this lesson, you will:

▶ Graph relationships that are directly proportional.

▶ Interpret the graphs of relationships that are directly proportional.

A marathon is a race that lasts for 26.2 miles. It has been a very popular race in various cities and at the Olympics. The term *marathon* dates back to around 492 B.C. during ancient Greece's war with Persia. As the story goes, a Greek messenger named Pheidippides (pronounced Fid-ip-i-deez) ran, without stopping, from the battlefield of Marathon to Athens to announce that the Greeks had defeated the Persians. After entering the Assembly, which was the political meeting place, he announced, "We have won!" He then reportedly collapsed and died.

Why do you think it was important for Pheidippides to announce to the Greeks that they had beaten the Persians? How else do you think messages were sent between people back in ancient times?

Problem 1   Running a Marathon

The distance (*d*) in miles a runner runs varies directly with the amount of time (*t*) in hours spent running. Suppose Antonio's constant of proportionality is 9.

1. Write an equation that represents the relationship between the distance ran, and the time spent running. Assume the runner can maintain the same rate of running.

2. Name the constant of proportionality and describe what it represents in this problem situation.

3. Complete the table to show the amount of time spent running and the distance run using the equation you wrote. Assume that Antonio's rate is constant.

Time (hours)	Distance (miles)
0	
0.25	
	4.5
0.75	
	9
1.25	
1.5	
	18

As you know, when two quantities vary in such a way that the ratio of the quantities is constant, the two quantities are directly proportional. You can also determine if two quantities are directly proportional by analyzing the plotted points on a coordinate plane.

4. Graph the values in the table you completed on the coordinate plane shown. Graph the values of *t* on the *x*-axis, and graph the values of *d* on the *y*-axis.

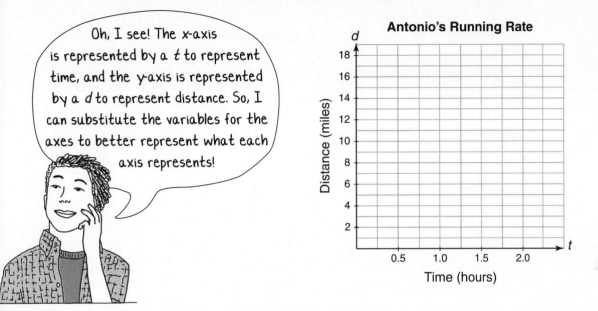

Oh, I see! The *x*-axis is represented by a *t* to represent time, and the *y*-axis is represented by a *d* to represent distance. So, I can substitute the variables for the axes to better represent what each axis represents!

a. What do you notice about the points on the graph?

b. Would it make sense to connect the points on the graph? Why or why not?

c. Interpret the meaning of the point (0, 0) for the graph.

d. Interpret the meaning of the point (1.5, 13.5) for the graph.

Remember, the graph of two variables that are directly proportional, or that vary directly, is a line that passes through the origin, (0, 0).

5. For each of the points on the graph, write a ratio in the form $\dfrac{y\text{-coordinate}}{x\text{-coordinate}}$ in the table. Then, simplify the ratio. What do you notice?

x-coordinate	*y*-coordinate	$\dfrac{y\text{-coordinate}}{x\text{-coordinate}}$
0.25	2.25	
0.5	4.5	
0.75	6.75	
1	9	
1.25	11.25	
1.5	13.5	
2	18	

6. Explain your conclusion from Question 5.

When analyzing the graph of two variables that are directly proportional, the ratio of the *y*-coordinate to the *x*-coordinate for any point is equivalent to the constant of proportionality, *k*.

7. Why do you think (0, 0) was not included in the table of ratios?

> Does this mean the graph doesn't really go through (0, 0)?

8. Locate the points (1, 9) and (1.5, 13.5) on your graph for Question 4.

   a. What is the horizontal distance (from left to right) from 1 to 1.5?

   b. What is the vertical distance from 9 to 13.5 on the graph?

   c. What is the ratio of the vertical distance to the horizontal distance?

2

9. Now locate the points (1.25, 11.25) and (2, 18) on the graph.

   a. What is the horizontal distance (from left to right) from 1.25 to 2?

   b. What is the vertical distance from 11.25 to 18 on the graph?

   c. What is the ratio of the vertical distance to the horizontal distance?

10. Choose two additional points from your graph for Question 4.

   a. What is the horizontal distance (from left to right) between the two points you chose?

   b. What is the vertical distance between the two points you chose?

   c. What is the ratio of the vertical distance to the horizontal distance?

11. What do you notice about the ratios?

Problem 2　Marathon Woman

The graph shown displays the relationship between the time and distance Ella runs.

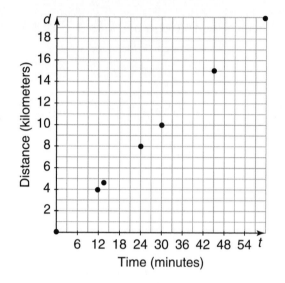

1. Does the distance Ella runs vary directly with the time? How do you know?

2. Determine the constant of proportionality. Explain how you determined k.

3. What does k represent in the problem situation?

4. Write an equation representing the relationship between Ella's distance and time.

5. Use your equation to answer each question.

    a. How far can Ella run in 15 minutes?

    b. How long does it take Ella to run 15 kilometers?

    c. How far can Ella run in one hour?

    d. Determine the constant of proportionality in kilometers per hour. Then, write another equation representing Ella's distance (*d*) is directly proportional to time (*t*).

    e. How is this equation the same as, and different from, the previous equation you wrote?

Problem 3   Proportional and Non-Proportional Relationships

Some beginning marathoners start out by training for a half-marathon, which is 13.1 miles. The table lists the recommended training workout for new marathoners training for a half-marathon.

10-Week Half-Marathon Training Schedule	
Week	Total Miles Run
1	13
2	15
3	16
4	19
5	21
6	24
7	26
8	22
9	18
10	21.1

1. Graph each point in the table on the coordinate plane shown. First, label the *x*-axis as the time (*t*), and the *y*-axis as the distance (*d*). Then, plot each ordered pair in the table. Finally, name your graph.

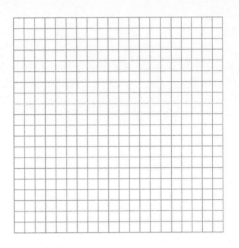

2

   a. What do you notice about the points you plotted?

   b. Determine if there is a constant of proportionality. Pick two points from the graph to form the ratio $\frac{y\text{-coordinate}}{x\text{-coordintate}}$.

Why not write the ratio as $\frac{x\text{-coordinate}}{y\text{-coordinate}}$? Is that wrong?

   c. How else can you determine if the relationship between two quantities is proportional or non-proportional?

Problem 4 Equations, Tables, and Graphs—Oh My!

1. Determine if each graph represents two quantities that vary directly. If possible, determine the constant of proportionality. Explain how you determined your answer.

2

a.

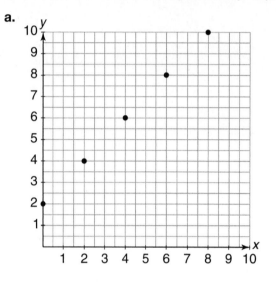

b.

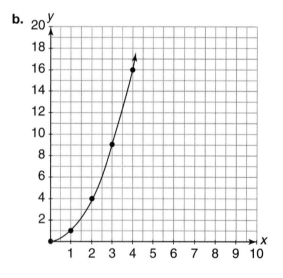

c.

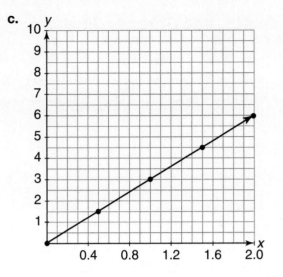

d.

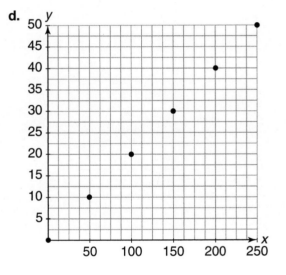

2. For each equation shown, first complete the table. Next, graph the data points on a graph. Then, determine if the graph is directly proportional.

a. $y = 3x$

x	y
0	
3	
7	
8	

b. $y = \frac{1}{3}x$

x	y
0	
1.5	
6	
9.6	

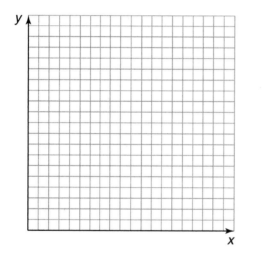

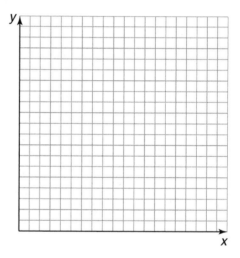

c. $y = \frac{18}{x}$

x	y
1	
2.25	
6.25	
10	

d. $y = x$

x	y
2	
10	
11.5	
15	

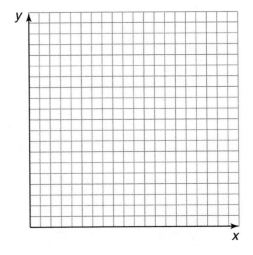

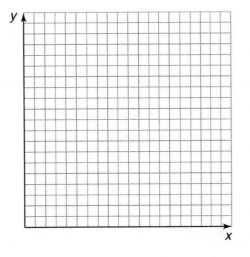

 Be prepared to share your solutions and methods.

2

2.6 RACING TO THE FINISH LINE!
Using Direct Proportions

Learning Goals

In this lesson, you will:

▶ Determine if two variables are directly proportional or vary directly.

▶ Interpret relationships that are direct proportions.

▶ Solve direct variation problems using the equation $y = kx$.

If someone asked you to run for 26.2 miles in one day, how would you train for such an activity? In fact, there are many different ways to train for a marathon, but one thing that most experts agree on is that setting a training pace is key to success. Most training-pace programs last between 16 and 26 weeks.

Generally, most marathon trainers strongly suggest not training for more than two days in a row, and that programs are designed to gradually build up the number of miles run per week. However, by the final weeks of training, most training programs actually have runners gradually run *fewer* miles instead of increasing the miles run.

Why do you think that training programs reduce the number of miles run in the final weeks of training?

Problem 1 Setting a Pace

The distance (d) in kilometers Carrie runs in a marathon varies directly with the amount of time (t) in hours spent running. Assume that Carrie's constant of proportionality is 23.

1. Write an equation representing the proportional relationship between d and t using the information given. Then, use your equation to answer each question.

a. If Carrie runs for $\frac{1}{4}$ of an hour, how far will she travel?

b. If Carrie runs $1\frac{1}{2}$ hours, how far will she travel?

c. If Carrie runs 57.5 kilometers, how long has she been running?

d. How long would it take Carrie to run 10 kilometers?

2. What do you think the constant of proportionality represents in this problem?

If y and x have a proportional relationship, then the constant of proportionality, k, can be expressed as $\frac{y}{x} = k$. This equation is equivalent to the equation $y = kx$, where k is the constant of proportionality.

Problem 2   Show Me the Money

Another example of direct proportion is the amount of hours a worker works and the wages earned in dollars, based on the hours worked.

The amount of money (m) Shaylah earns is directly proportional to the number of hours (h) she works. The equation describing this relationship is $m = 9.25h$.

1. Analyze the table shown. Complete the table showing the direct proportional relationship between the time Shaylah worked and her earnings based on the equation given.

Hours Worked	Earnings (dollars)
2	
7	
	101.75
40	
	189.63

2. What does the constant of proportionality represent in this problem?

3. During the summer, Fernando works as a movie attendant. The number of hours he works varies each week. Analyze the table shown. Complete the table using the constant of proportionality equation $m = kh$.

Hours Worked	Earnings (dollars)
3	26.88
15	
5.5	
	179.20
	161.28

4. What is the constant of proportionality? What does the constant of proportionality represent?

Problem 3   Me and My Shadow

Did you ever notice how the length of your shadow changes at different times of the day? At any given time of the day, the length of a shadow is directly proportional to, or varies directly with, the height of the object.

1. Corina and Drew want to determine the height of of a signpost that is next to their house. However, the signpost is too tall to measure. They decide to use their shadows and compare those shadows with the signpost's shadow.

   a. Write an equation representing the direct proportional relationship between the length of a shadow (*s*) and height (*h*).

   b. At 4:00 PM, Corina measures Drew's shadow to be 63 inches long. Drew is 54 inches tall. Drew then measures Corina's shadow. If Corina's shadow is 56 inches long, how tall is Corina? Explain your reasoning.

2

c. At 4:00 PM, Corina and Drew also measure the signpost's shadow. The signpost's shadow is 105 inches long. How tall is the signpost? Explain your reasoning.

2. At 11:00 AM, Corina's shadow is 40 inches long.

    a. How long is Drew's shadow? Explain your reasoning.

    b. How long is the signpost's shadow? Explain your reasoning.

3. The 6th graders at Shady Pine Middle School have been asked to determine the height of the telephone pole that is on the school grounds. The diagram shows the measurements they took. How tall is the telephone pole? Explain your reasoning.

shadow length
120 in.

60 in.

shadow length
64 in.

> Shadow lengths. Tip amounts. Wages. Are there other examples of direct variation you can think of?

Talk the Talk

1. Write an equation if *a* varies directly with *b*, and let *a* = 7, and *k* = 2. Use your equation to determine the value of *b*.

2. If *m* is directly proportional to *n*, and let *n* = 0.55, and *k* = 2.1, determine the value of *m*.

3. If *r* varies directly with *s*, and let *r* = 4, and *s* = 1.5, determine the value of *k*.

Be prepared to share your solutions and methods.

CONNECTING REPRESENTATIONS OF PROPORTIONAL RELATIONSHIPS

2.7

Interpreting Multiple Representations of Direct Proportions

2

Learning Goals

In this lesson, you will:

▶ Determine if relationships represented in words, tables, equations, or graphs are directly proportional.

▶ Interpret the meaning of direct proportions represented in words, tables, equations, and graphs.

▶ Determine and interpret the constant of proportionality for variables that are directly proportional and represented in words, tables, equations, and graphs.

In today's society, there are generally three ways most employees are paid. Some employees are paid by the number of hours they work. Also, in many states, if an employee works more than 40 hours in one week, then he or she can receive overtime pay. Generally, the employee will earn time and a half for every hour he or she works past 40 hours within a week.

Another type of worker is a salaried employee. These employees make a set amount of money per week whether they work more or less than 40 hours.

Finally, there are independent contractors who get paid for every hour they work. Usually, independent contractors do not receive overtime, so the amount per hour worked remains constant.

Out of these three examples, which type of employee is most likely to have a direct proportion between hours worked and the pay he or she receives?

Problem 1 Pay Day!

1. The amount a contractor gets paid (p) is directly proportional to the number of days worked (d).

a. Complete the table of values.

d	p (dollars)
	0
1	
2	500
3.5	

b. Determine the constant of proportionality and describe what it represents in this problem situation.

c. How many days would the contractor need to work to earn $2000? Explain your reasoning.

2. The graph shows Natasha's total number of free throw attempts (*a*), and the total number of free throws made (*m*).

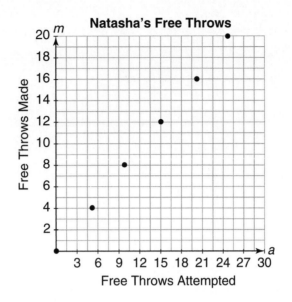

Natasha's Free Throws

a. Explain how you know the graph represents a relationship that is directly proportional.

b. Determine the constant of proportionality, and describe what it represents in this problem situation.

c. If Natasha attempted 30 shots, how many would she probably make? First, use your graph to determine the answer. Then, verify your answer by using an equation.

3. A painter needs 1.5 gallons of paint to cover every 180 square feet of wall space.

    a. Create a table of values showing the wall space covered varying directly with the amount of paint.

    b. Write an equation that represents the relationship between the amount of paint and the amount of wall space. Then, interpret k in terms of this problem.

c. How did you use the constant of proportionality to complete the table?

d. How much paint would it take to cover 1800 square feet?

e. How many square feet will 6.5 gallons of paint cover?

Problem 2   Representing Proportional Relationships in Multiple Ways

1. Suppose q varies directly as p. Write an equation representing the relationship between p and q.

2. Complete the table for variables p and q, where q varies directly as p. Explain how you determined your answers.

p	q	$\frac{q}{p} = k$
0		–
2	6	
4	12	
0.25		$\frac{0.75}{0.25} = 3$
	3	
1.5	4.5	

3. Write the equation that represents the relationship between p and q using the value of k you determined from the table.

4. Summarize how you can write the equation that represents the relationship between two variables that vary directly if you are given a ratio table.

5. Predict what a graph of the values in the table will look like.
Label p on the x-axis and q on the y-axis. Then, graph the values.

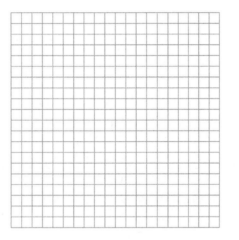

6. Use the graph two different ways to determine the constant of proportionality. Explain your reasoning.

7. Summarize how you can write the equation representing the relationship between two variables that are directly proportional if you are given a graph.

8. Make up a scenario for the graph you created. Then, interpret the meaning of the point (1.5, 4.5) for the graph using your scenario.

Talk the Talk

1. Suppose $a = 1.5b$. Explain the relationship between a and b using each phrase. To help you answer each question, you can have the variables represent different quantities in a problem situation.

> Can you write your own direct proportion situation and make a table and graph for it?

a. directly proportional

b. varies directly

c. using the equation given

2. Complete the table of values for *a* and *b* using the information from Question 1.

b	a
	0
	2
6	
10.5	
	1.5

3. Explain how you used the constant of proportionality to complete the table.

4. Determine if the graph shown represents a direct proportion between *a* and *b*. Explain why or why not.

a.

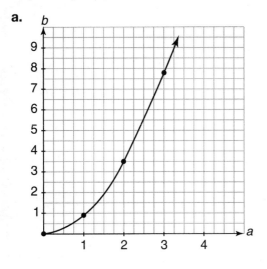

b.

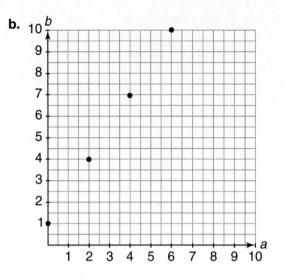

c.

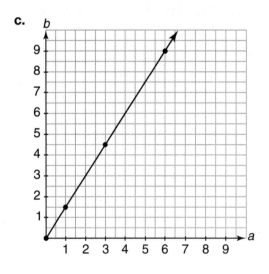

 Be prepared to share your solutions and methods.

Key Terms

▶ direct variation (2.1)

▶ origin (2.1)

▶ constant of proportionality (2.2)

2

2.1   Using Multiple Representations to Explore Variation

Data sets can either be discrete or continuous data. As quantitative data, discrete data can only have values that are counting numbers. Continuous data are measurements and can have values that fall between counting numbers. A function represents a direct variation if the ratio between the output values and input values is a constant. The two values are said to vary directly.

Example

A water tank initially containing 500 gallons of water begins leaking water at a rate of 20 gallons per hour. The table and the graph shown display the amount of water in the tank after the specified number of hours.

Water (gallons)	Time (hours)
500	0
480	1
400	5
300	10
100	20
0	25

Water in Tank

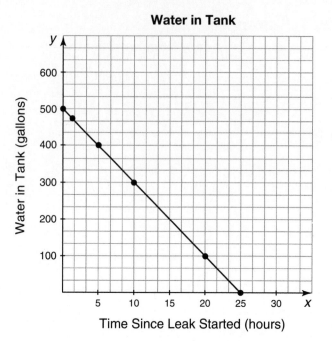

The points on the graph are connected by a line segment, because the data are continuous.

2.2 Determining if Data Points Represent Equivalent Ratios

For data points to represent equivalent ratios, the points must be in a straight line and pass through the origin of a graph.

1.
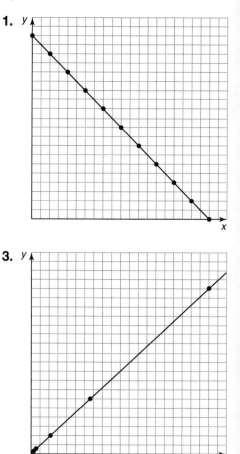

Example

The first graph and the second graph do not represent equivalent ratios.The third graph represents equivalent ratios because the points are in a straight line and pass through the origin.

2.
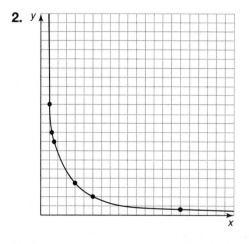

3.

2.3 Calculating Constants of Proportionality

The constant of proportionality, k, is the constant ratio between two corresponding values in a proportional relationship.

Example

The table shows the distance from Karen's house to each of three other locations and the number of gallons of gas needed to get to each location. Determine k for the ratio between the distance and the amount of gas needed.

Trip	Distance (in kilometers)	Gas (in gallons)
To Aunt's house	217	3.5
To beach	496	8
To camp	325.5	5.25

Divide any given distance by its corresponding gallons of gas.

$$\frac{217}{3.5} = 62$$

Because the ratio is 62, $k = 62$.

2.4 Determining Whether a Given Relationship is Proportional

When a relationship is proportional, the ratio of two corresponding values will be equal to the ratio of any other pair of corresponding values. In such cases, this ratio is the constant of proportionality.

Example

The data show the relationship between the number of boys and the number of girls in three different high schools.

School #	Number of Boys	Number of Girls
1	600	720
2	850	1020
3	900	1080

The ratio of girls to boys in school #1 is $\frac{720}{600}$ or $\frac{6}{5}$.

The ratio of girls to boys in school #2 is $\frac{1020}{850}$ or $\frac{6}{5}$.

The ratio of girls to boys in school #3 is $\frac{1080}{900}$ or $\frac{6}{5}$.

The relationship is proportional, because each data pair has the same constant of proportionality.

2.4 Graphing a Directly Proportional Relationship

The directly proportional relationship between two variables can be represented by a graph on a coordinate plane. When graphed correctly the data points lie on a straight line that passes through the origin.

Example

The number of days a bag of dog food lasts is directly proportional to the weight of the bag. The constant of proportionality is $\frac{4}{3}$. To graph the relationship between the number of days the dog food will last and the weight of the bag, follow the steps shown.

Step 1: Make a table to describe the relationship. Choose values for the weight and use k to determine the number of days.

Weight (pounds)	Days
12	16
15	20
30	40
45	60

Step 2: Plot the points. Connect the points because the weight and the number of days can be represented in fractions.

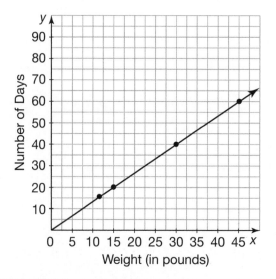

2.5 Determining *k* from the Graph of a Directly Proportional Relationship

There are two methods which can be used to determine the constant of proportionality, *k*, from the graph of a proportional relationship. The first method is to calculate the ratio of the *y*-coordinate to the *x*-coordinate for any given point on the graph. The second method is to choose two points on the graph and calculate the ratio of the vertical distance between the points to the horizontal distance between the points.

Example

The graph shows the relationship between the cost of carpet cleaning, and the area of the carpet. You can determine the constant of proportionality by using either method.

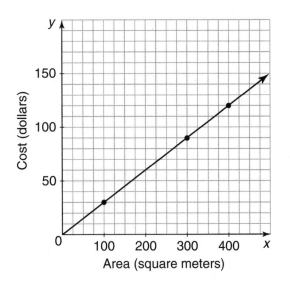

Method 1

Choose a point on the graph and write the ratio of the $\dfrac{y\text{-coordinate}}{x\text{-coordinate}}$.

$\dfrac{30}{100} = \dfrac{3}{10}$ or 0.3

Method 2

Choose two points on the graph.
(100, 30) and (300, 90)

Vertical distance changed
90 − 30 = 60

Horizontal distance changed
300 − 100 = 200

Write the ratio
$\dfrac{60}{200} = \dfrac{3}{10}$ or 0.3

The constant of proportionality is 0.3. The cost is $0.30 per square meter.

2.6 Solving a Problem with a Direct Variation Equation

To solve a problem involving a direct proportion when given a graph, a table, or words, you must first determine k. Then, write the equation using k and solve for the unknown value.

Example

The graph shows the relationship between the cups of flour and the tablespoons of salt needed in a recipe. You can determine how many cups of flour are needed when 4.5 tablespoons of salt are used.

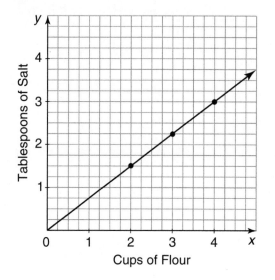

Let f represent flour, and let s represent salt.

Step 1: Calculate the value of k.

$$\frac{1.5}{2} = 0.75$$

Step 2: Write the equation.

$$s = 0.75f$$

Step 3: Solve for f when $s = 4.5$.

$$s = 0.75f$$
$$4.5 = 0.75f$$
$$\frac{4.5}{0.75} = f$$
$$6 = f$$

Six cups of flour are needed.

> Eating healthy is a great way to make your brain grow.

Determining Whether a Graph Represents a Directly Proportional Relationship

When the relationship between two variables is directly proportional, the data values plotted on a graph must be in a straight line which passes through the origin.

Example

This relationship shown is not directly proportional because the graph is not a straight line.

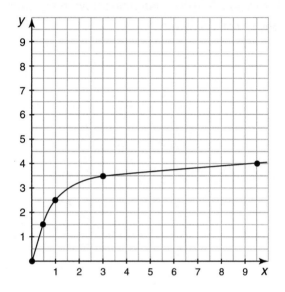

This relationship shown is not directly proportional because the graph does not pass through the origin.

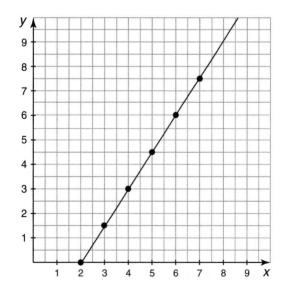

2.7

This relationship shown is directly proportional because the graph is a straight line and it passes through the origin.

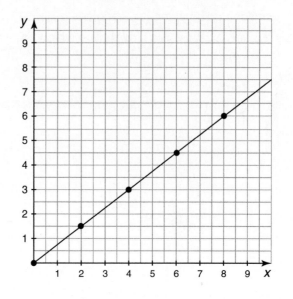

Did you get good service? If you did, it is common to leave a 15% or 20% tip for the waitress or waiter that served you. However, if the service is not good, it is customary to leave a penny tip!

3.1

GIVE ME A BALLPARK FIGURE OF THE COST

Estimating and Calculating with Percents and Rates

Learning Goals

In this lesson, you will:

▶ Estimate and calculate values using rates.

▶ Estimate and calculate the values of percents.

Have you ever wondered why discounts and coupons are always a multiple of 5 or 10 percent? Think about it: when was the last time you saw a discount of 17% off shoes? Or when was the last time you saw 38% off a flat screen television?

There are a few reasons for discounts that are multiples of 5 or 10 percent. One is that it is easier for customers to estimate the discount of an item that is 25% off the cost than an item that is 41%. Can you think of other reasons why multiples of 5 and 10 percent discounts are the most common discounts?

Problem 1   Ordering Flooring

A flooring company sells laminate, hardwood, and ceramic tile. For each different type of flooring there is a certain amount of waste material. The table shows the amounts of waste for each type of flooring.

Why do you think a flooring company would sell material that will end up being waste?

Flooring type	Laminate	Hardwood	Ceramic Tile
Waste	$\frac{1}{10}$	20%	25%

This means that when an order is placed, the amount of estimated waste material must be added to the order. For example, if an order is placed for 200 square feet of laminate, then one-tenth more laminate must be ordered to make sure that there is enough flooring to complete the job.

1. How much laminate flooring would be needed for a room of:

   a. 120 square feet?

   b. 200 square feet?

   c. 240 square meters?

   d. Explain how you determined each answer.

Remember that to determine a percent of a number, you can multiply just as you do to calculate a fraction of a number.

To determine 25% of 140, you can write the percent as a fraction or decimal and multiply:

As a Decimal   25% of 140 $(0.25)(140)$
$(0.25)(140) = 35$

As a Fraction   25% of 140 $\left(\frac{25}{100}\right)(140)$, or $\left(\frac{1}{4}\right)(140)$

$\left(\frac{1}{4}\right)(140) = \frac{1}{4} \cdot \overset{35}{\cancel{140}} = 35$

---

2. How much hardwood flooring would be needed for a room that is:

    a. 100 square feet?

    b. 180 square feet?

    c. 90 square meters?

    d. Explain how you determined each answer.

3

3. How much ceramic tile would be needed for a room that is:

    a. 300 square feet?

    b. 120 square feet?

Sometimes, changing the percent to a fraction first makes the calculation simpler.

    c. 108 square meters?

    d. Explain how you determined each answer.

Problem 2 Make Sure to Tip Your Waitresses and Waiters . . .

Most restaurant patrons add a tip to the final bill to show their appreciation for their wait staff. Usually, a patron will determine 15% or 20% of the bill, and then add that amount to the total. Many times, patrons will just round off the tip to the nearest dollar. For patrons tipping 20%, determining the amount of a tip is easier. Twenty percent is one-fifth, so to determine the tip, patrons only need to divide the rounded bill by 5.

For example, if the bill is $38.95, you would round to 40, and then divide by 5. The 20% tip should be about $8.

A patron is another word for a person who eats at a restaurant.

1. Estimate a 20% tip for each of the bills shown.

a. $89.45

b. $125

c. $12.45

A 15% tip can be estimated by first estimating 10% of the bill. Then, a patron would determine half of 10% of the bill which would be 5%. Finally, a patron would add the two percent values to calculate 15% of the bill.

> For example, if the bill is $23.53, first divide by 10 to get about $2.30. Then, you can determine half of that amount, or $1.15. Finally, add the two amounts together to get a 15% tip of $3.45, or approximately $3.50.

2. Estimate a 15% tip for each bill shown.

   a. $89.45

   b. $125

   c. $12.45

 Be prepared to share your solutions and methods.

3

3.2 ONE SIZE FITS ALL?
Solving Percent Problems

Learning Goal

In this lesson, you will:

▶ Solve problems involving percents.

3

Have you ever been told that there is only one right way to do something? Like, for example, tying your shoes? Mowing the lawn? Sometimes people assume that the best way to do certain things is to follow rules or procedures that only work for one situation. A challenge for trying to follow rules for certain situations is that it is very difficult to remember many different rules and when to apply which rule.

What examples of rules can you think of? Do you always follow these rules?

Problem 1 Percent Models

1. Three percent problems are shown. Each problem matches one of the models shown. Determine which model matches each problem.

- A test had 20 questions. If Tracey got 75% correct, how many questions did Tracey get correct?

- Twenty-eight students in a class took an algebra test. If 21 students passed the test, what percent did not pass?

- In a school, 25% of the teachers are math teachers. If there are 5 math teachers, how many teachers are there in the school?

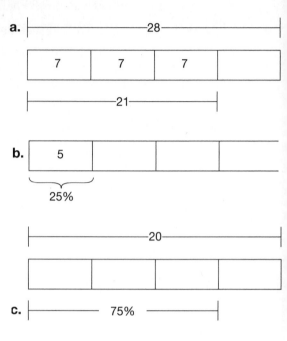

2. Use the appropriate model to solve each percent problem. Explain how you solved each.

Keisha writes three rules to solve percent problems:

Rule 1: If I want to calculate the percent of a number, I should multiply the percent as a decimal by the number.

Rule 2: If I want to calculate the percent, I should divide the part by the whole and change the decimal to a percent.

Rule 3: If I want to calculate the whole, I should divide the part by the percent written as a decimal.

3. Use each of Keisha's rules to solve the percent problems from Question 1. For each problem, list the rule you used and show your work.

Corinne says, "Wait. There is another way to do these problems that will always work and uses the same basic proportion. Remember, a percent is a ratio that is a 'part' to the 'whole' of 100. So I set up a proportion with one ratio as the part to whole with the percents, and the other ratio as the part to whole of the other two quantities. Then, I can solve this proportion for the unknown value.

Let me show you how this would work with the first two problems."

A test has 20 questions. If Tracey gets 75% correct, how many questions does Tracey get correct?

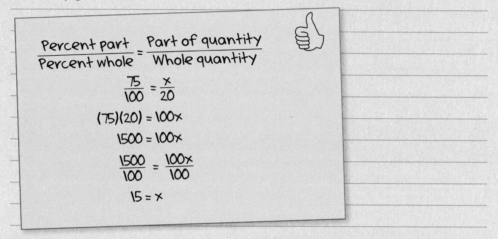

$$\frac{\text{Percent part}}{\text{Percent whole}} = \frac{\text{Part of quantity}}{\text{Whole quantity}}$$

$$\frac{75}{100} = \frac{x}{20}$$

$$(75)(20) = 100x$$

$$1500 = 100x$$

$$\frac{1500}{100} = \frac{100x}{100}$$

$$15 = x$$

Twenty-eight students in a class took an algebra test. If 21 students passed the test, what percent did not pass?

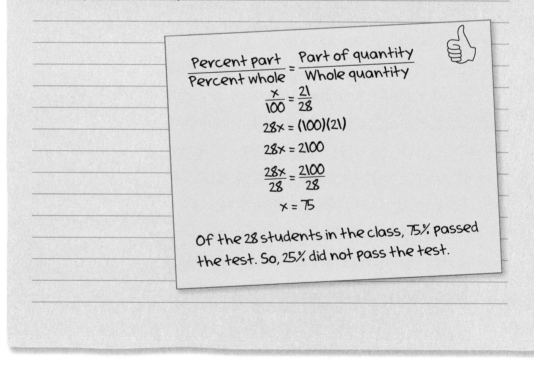

$$\frac{\text{Percent part}}{\text{Percent whole}} = \frac{\text{Part of quantity}}{\text{Whole quantity}}$$

$$\frac{x}{100} = \frac{21}{28}$$

$$28x = (100)(21)$$

$$28x = 2100$$

$$\frac{28x}{28} = \frac{2100}{28}$$

$$x = 75$$

Of the 28 students in the class, 75% passed the test. So, 25% did not pass the test.

4. Use Corinne's method to solve the third problem in Question 1.

In a school, 25% of the teachers teach algebra. If there are 5 math teachers, how many teachers are there in the school?

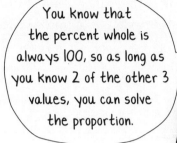

You know that the percent whole is always 100, so as long as you know 2 of the other 3 values, you can solve the proportion.

Problem 2   Or the Highway!

Solve each percent problem. Show your work.

1. The $199.99 game console Amy purchased was on sale for 10% off. What amount did Amy get off the price?

2. A computer is normally $899 but is discounted to $799. What percent of the original price does Shawn pay?

3. If Fernando paid $450 for a netbook that was 75% of the original price, what was the original price?

4. Herman once had 240 downloaded songs in his collection. He deleted some and now has 180. What percent of his original collection did he keep?

5. Dontrelle received 30% off when he purchased a rare book regularly priced at $96.50. How much did Dontrelle receive off the original price?

6. Brittany lost $450 on an investment, which was 45% of the money she invested. How much money did she invest?

Problem 3   Not Always?

Katie used Corinne's method to solve this problem:

1. Explain why Katie's answer is incorrect. Then, determine the correct answer.

> ## Katie
>
> My flight was $229.99 but I got 20% off because I booked it online. What did I pay?
>
> $$\frac{\text{Percent part}}{\text{Percent whole}} = \frac{\text{Part of quantity}}{\text{Whole quantity}}$$
>
> $$\frac{20}{100} = \frac{x}{229.99}$$
>
> $$\frac{4599.8}{100} = \frac{100x}{100}$$
>
> $$45.998 = x$$
>
> So, I paid about $46.

Vicki also used Corinne's method but, got the answer without having to subtract:

2. Explain why Vicki's method worked.

> ## Vicki
>
> My flight was $229.99 but I got 20% off because I booked it online. What did I pay?
>
> $$\frac{\text{Percent part}}{\text{Percent whole}} = \frac{\text{Part of quantity}}{\text{Whole quantity}}$$
>
> $$\frac{80}{100} = \frac{x}{229.99}$$
>
> $$\frac{18399.2}{100} = \frac{100x}{100}$$
>
> $$183.99 = x$$

> If I take 40% off $100, that's $100 – $40. That leaves me with $60, which is 100% – 40%, or 60%. Hmmmm . . .

3. Solve each problem.

a. Anita got 4 problems wrong on a test of 36 questions. What percent of the questions did she get correct?

b. Games that usually sell for $36.40 were on sale for $27.30. What percent off are they?

c. Jimmy's new cell phone cost him $49.99 when he signed a 2-year plan, which was 75% off the original price. What was the original price?

Be prepared to share your solutions and methods.

3.3 MATHEMATICS AND NUTRITION

Using Proportions and Percent Equations

3

Learning Goals

In this lesson, you will:

▶ Solve proportions.

▶ Solve percent equations.

Key Term

▶ percent equation

Which food is the healthiest in the world? Of course, fruits and vegetables are the healthiest, but which fruit or vegetable is the healthiest of them all? That's hard to say because it depends on which vitamins and minerals are being compared. However, in 1992, the Center for Science in the Public Interest tried to answer this question. They compared different fruits and vegetables, looking at the amounts of fiber, iron, calcium, protein, and vitamins A and C each offers. After completing their research, the center determined that the healthiest vegetable was none other than the sweet potato. Are you surprised by their conclusion?

Fruits and vegetables are important for a balanced diet, but what does it mean for a diet to be "balanced"? What things in mathematics are balanced or not balanced?

Problem 1 Calorie Counts

The average calorie requirement for an adult is about 2000 calories per day. The recommended distribution of calories is 57 percent from carbohydrates, 30 percent from fats, and 13 percent from protein.

You can use a proportion to determine the number of calories that should be from carbohydrates.

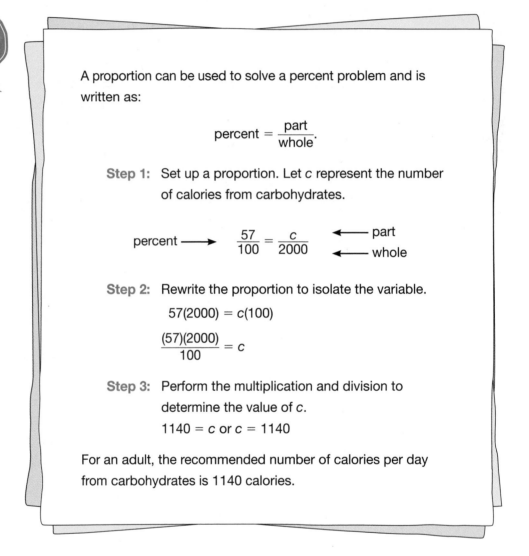

A proportion can be used to solve a percent problem and is written as:

$$\text{percent} = \frac{\text{part}}{\text{whole}}.$$

Step 1: Set up a proportion. Let c represent the number of calories from carbohydrates.

$$\text{percent} \longrightarrow \quad \frac{57}{100} = \frac{c}{2000} \quad \begin{array}{l}\longleftarrow \text{part} \\ \longleftarrow \text{whole}\end{array}$$

Step 2: Rewrite the proportion to isolate the variable.

$$57(2000) = c(100)$$

$$\frac{(57)(2000)}{100} = c$$

Step 3: Perform the multiplication and division to determine the value of c.

$$1140 = c \text{ or } c = 1140$$

For an adult, the recommended number of calories per day from carbohydrates is 1140 calories.

1. Use what you know about solving proportions to explain how the variable is isolated in Step 2.

You can also use a *percent equation* to determine the number of calories that should be from carbohydrates.

A **percent equation** can be written in the form percent × whole = part, where the percent is often written as a decimal.

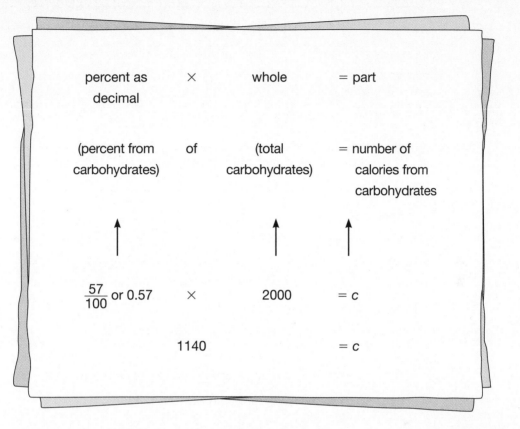

percent as decimal	×	whole	= part
(percent from carbohydrates)	of	(total carbohydrates)	= number of calories from carbohydrates
↑		↑	↑
$\frac{57}{100}$ or 0.57	×	2000	= c
	1140		= c

2. Explain how the variable is isolated. Then, describe how the number of calories from carbohydrates is calculated using the percent equation.

3. Use proportions and percent equations to calculate the number of calories from fat and protein that are recommended for an adult on a 2000-calorie diet. For each, isolate the variable first. Then, determine the number of calories from fat or protein recommended. Finally, write your answer in a complete sentence.

	Percent	Use a Proportion	Use a Percent Equation
Fat	30%		
Sentence			
Protein	13%		
Sentence			

4. Describe how the strategies you used to solve the proportions and the percent equations are similar.

5. Describe how the percent equation in the form percent $\times$ whole $=$ part is equivalent to a proportion in the form percent $= \dfrac{\text{part}}{\text{whole}}$.

6. Describe the strategy you can use to rewrite the percent equation as an equivalent proportion.

Problem 2   Determining the Percent of Calories for a Diet

A person on a 2000-calorie-per-day diet consumes 800 calories of fat. What percent of this diet comes from fat? You can use a proportion or a percent equation to determine the percent.

Use a Proportion	**Use a Percent Equation**
Step 1: Set up a proportion. $\dfrac{f}{100} = \dfrac{800}{2000}$	**Step 1:** Set up the percent equation. $f \times 2000 = 800$ $2000f = 800$
Step 2: Rewrite the proportion to isolate the variable. $f = \dfrac{(800)(100)}{2000}$	**Step 2:** Rewrite the equation to isolate the variable. $\dfrac{2000f}{2000} = \dfrac{800}{2000}$ $f = \dfrac{800}{2000}$
Step 3: Perform the operation(s) to determine the value of f. $f = 40$	**Step 3:** Perform the operation(s) to determine the value of f. $f = 0.4$

Fat makes up 40 percent of the person's 2000-calorie-per-day diet.

1. How was the variable isolated in Step 2 when the problem was solved using a proportion?

2. How was the variable isolated in Step 2 when the problem was solved using a percent equation?

3. How can you make the conclusion that 40 percent of the person's diet is from fat when the result from using the proportion is $f = 40$, and the result from using the percent equation is $f = 0.4$?

4. A person on a 2000-calorie-per-day diet consumes 1000 calories of carbohydrates and 200 calories of protein. What percent of the person's diet comes from carbohydrates? What percent comes from protein? Answer these questions by using both proportions and percent equations in the table shown. For each problem, isolate the variable first. Then, calculate the answer. Finally, write your answer in a complete sentence.

	Use a Proportion	**Use a Percent Equation**
Carbohydrates		
Sentence		
Protein		
Sentence		

> You can estimate to determine if your answer is reasonable. Fifty percent is the same as a half, twenty-five percent is the same as one-fourth, and so on.

5. Describe the strategies you used to solve each proportion and each percent equation in Question 4.

6. Determine each person's total caloric intake for the day given the percent of the calories consumed. Show your work, and then write a sentence to explain your answer in the table shown.

a. On Monday, 57 percent of the calories Johnny consumed were carbohydrates, which totaled 1425 calories. What was his total caloric intake?

> Total caloric intake is another way of saying how many total calories a person consumes for the day.

	Use a Proportion	**Write a Percent Equation**
Carbohydrates		
Sentence		

b. On Tuesday, 30 percent of the calories Brianna consumed were fat, which totaled 540 calories. What was her total caloric intake?

	Use a Proportion	**Write a Percent Equation**
Fat		
Sentence		

c. On Wednesday, 13 percent of the calories Cheyenne consumed were protein, which totaled 330 calories. What was her total caloric intake?

	Use a Proportion	Write a Percent Equation as a Proportion
Protein		
Sentence		

7. Crystal says that when she solved the proportion in Question 6, that she could set up her proportions in any way she wanted because ratios can be written in any way. Do you agree with Crystal's statement?

8. Describe how you solved each proportion and percent equation in Question 6.

 Be prepared to share your solutions and methods.

3.4

BE MINDFUL OF THE FEES!

Using Percents

Learning Goals

In this lesson, you will:

- Calculate simple interest.
- Calculate the percent of increase.
- Calculate the percent of decrease.
- Calculate discount of base price.
- Calculate tax on a purchase.
- Calculate depreciation.

Key Terms

- interest
- principal
- simple interest
- percent increase
- percent decrease
- depreciate

3

Credit cards are plastic cards that act as money. Generally, the credit card company will guarantee the purchase of an item based on a promise that the person making the purchase will pay the credit card company back, with the possibility of a charge and other fees being added to the purchase. It is a system that has been in use since the late 1800s, but it has changed dramatically over the years.

Why do you think credit card companies take the risk of paying for a purchase for its customers up front? Why do you think people use credit cards instead of cash?

Problem 1 Simple Interest

When you save money in a bank savings account, the bank pays you money each year and adds it to your account. This additional money is **interest,** and it is added to bank accounts because banks routinely use your money for other financial projects. They then pay interest for the money they borrow from you. An original amount of money in your account is called the **principal.** Interest is calculated as a percent of the principal.

One type of interest is **simple interest,** which is a fixed percent of the principal. Simple interest is paid over a specific period of time—either twice a year or once a year, for example.

The formula for simple interest is:

Interest rate (%)

$$I = P \times r \times t$$

Interest earned   Principal   Time that the money earns interest
(dollars)   (dollars)   (years)

For example, Kim deposits $300 into a savings account at a simple interest rate of 5% per year.

You can use the formula to calculate the interest she will have earned at the end of 3 years.

Interest = Principal $\times$ rate $\times$ time

Interest = (300)(0.05)(3)

= $45

Kim will have earned $45 in interest after 3 years.

1. Complete the table by using your knowledge of the formula for simple interest.

Principal Amount Saved (dollars)	Interest Rate	Time (years)	Interest Earned (dollars)
425	7%	5	
75	3%	1	
250	2%	8	
340	5%	2	
	4%	3	30.00
456	6%		109.44
500		4	120.00

In the same way that banks pay you interest when they use your money for financial projects, you too pay interest as well.

2. When you borrow money from a bank, the amount you borrow is the principal, and you pay the interest on that money to the bank. Complete the table shown.

Principal Borrowed (dollars)	Interest Rate	Time (years)	Interest Paid (dollars)
5000	6%	10	
450	5%	2	
1500	7%	3	
	2%	20	7200

Problem 2 Percent Increases and Decreases

You have used percents in many different situations, including tips, interest, and for construction projects. You can also use percents to describe a change in quantities.

A **percent increase** occurs when the new amount is greater than the original amount, such as when stores mark up the price they pay for an item in order to make a greater profit.

1. All That Glitters Jewelry Store marks up its prices so it can maximize its profits. What is the percent increase for each of these items? Use the formula shown to complete the table.

$$\text{Percent Increase} = \frac{\text{Amount of Increase}}{\text{Original Amount}}$$

All That Glitters Accounting Sheet				
Item	Cost (dollars)	Customer's Price (dollars)	Difference (dollars)	Percent Increase
Initial ring	60	90		
ID bracelet	120	240		
Earrings	25	50		
Pin	36	45		

A **percent decrease** occurs when the new amount is less than the original amount. An example of a percent decrease is the value of a car *depreciating* by 10 percent per year. **Depreciation** is the decrease in value of an item over time.

2. Cars depreciate at different rates, depending on the demand for the type of car, and the condition in which the car is kept. Use the formula shown to complete the table.

$$\text{Percent Decrease} = \frac{\text{Amount of Decrease}}{\text{Original Amount}}$$

Type of Car	Original Price (dollars)	Value after 1 Year (dollars)	Difference (dollars)	Percent Decrease
4-wheel drive	20,000	15,000		
Convertible	18,000	16,000		
Hybrid	25,000	20,000		
Sedan	12,000	9,000		

3. How do you know if the percent is a decrease or increase?

4. How would you describe a 100 percent increase?

Sometimes devices incorrectly use "200% increase" to mean a 100% increase.

5. How would you describe a 50 percent decrease?

6. Jake was doing a great job at work, so his boss gave him a 20 percent raise. But then he started coming to work late and missing days, so his boss gave him a 20 percent pay cut. Jake said, "That's okay. At least I'm back to where I started."

Do you think that Jake is correct in thinking he is making the same amount of money when he received a pay cut? If you agree, explain why he is correct. If you do not agree, explain to Jake what is incorrect with his thinking and determine what percent of his original salary he is making now.

Problem 3   Some Things Gain and Some Things Lose

Generally, things like homes and savings accounts gain value, or appreciate over time. Other things, like cars depreciate every year. New cars depreciate about 12% of their value each year.

1. How much would a new car depreciate the first year if it cost:

a. $35,000?

b. $45,000?

c. $20,000?

2. If a car lost $3600 in depreciation in the first year, what was the original cost of this car?

3. Complete the table to record the value of a car that costs $50,000 that depreciates at the rate of 12% per year for the first five years.

Time (years)	Value of the Car (dollars)
0	50,000
1	
2	
3	
4	
5	

4. Complete the graph.

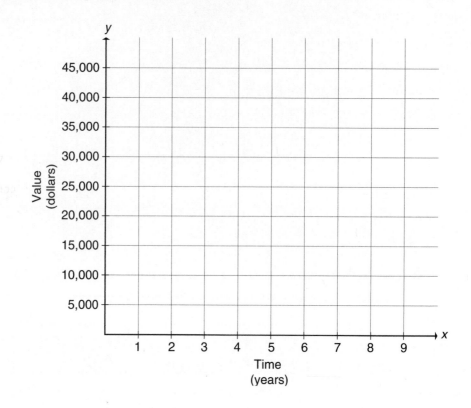

5. Would it make sense to connect the points on the graph? If so, connect the points. Explain your reasoning.

6. Describe how the value of the car decreases over time.

 Be prepared to share your solutions and methods.

3.5

SHOE SUPER STORE
Solving Percent Problems Involving Proportions

Learning Goals

In this lesson, you will:

▶ Solve percent problems using direct variation.

▶ Write equations to show the constant of proportionality.

Key Term

▶ commission

When you go shopping for food, does your family go to an individual store for each type of item you need? For example, do you go to a butcher shop for meat, or a grocer for fruits and vegetables? Chances are that you probably make these purchases at a supermarket. Supermarkets brought convenience of multiple food items under one roof. And supermarkets also can offer big savings to food items by offering items on sales, accepting coupons on items, and offering "rewards discounts" for loyal customers. In fact, most major supermarkets in the U.S. routinely offer discounts and sales on items weekly. How do you think supermarkets can continuously offer discounts and stay in business? Do you think supermarkets may be a reason that there are less specialized food stores that offer one type of food item?

Problem 1   Shoe Super Store

The Shoe Super Store sells name brand shoes at a price much less than most department stores. The chart hanging in the store displays the normal price of the shoes and the Shoe Super Store price.

Regular Department Store Price	Shoe Super Store Price
$20	$16
$25	$20
$30	$24
$35	$28
$40	$32
$50	$40

1. Do the Shoe Super Store prices vary directly with the regular department store price? Explain your reasoning.

2. Alfie claims that the relationship is not directly proportional because a $20 pair of shoes is only $4 cheaper, while a $50 pair of shoes is $10 cheaper at Shoe Super Store. Do you agree or disagree with Alfie? Explain your reasoning.

3. Define the variables and write an equation to represent the relationship between the department store price and Shoe Super Store price.

4. What is the constant of proportionality? Interpret the constant of proportionality for this problem situation.

5. What is the Shoe Super Store price for a pair of shoes that cost $28 at the department store? Explain your reasoning.

6. What is the department store price for a pair of shoes that cost $15 at Shoe Super Store? Explain your reasoning.

Problem 2   Car Commission

A car salesperson makes a 10% *commission* on each sale. A **commission** is an amount of money a salesperson earns after selling a product. Many times, the commission is a certain percent of the product.

1. Complete the table to show the relationship between the price of a car and the commission the salesperson receives.

Price (dollars)	Commission (dollars)
0	
9000	
15,000	
	1000
18,000	
	2000

2. Graph the relationship between the price of a car and the commission received.

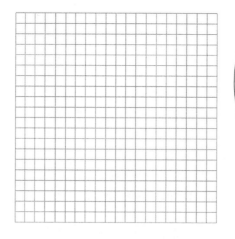

The constant of proportionality is constant, so you can use it to make all kinds of predictions in situations.

3. Define the variables and write the equation that represents the relationship between the price of a car and the commission received.

4. How much commission will the salesperson earn for selling a $25,000 car? Determine the commission using your equation.

5. If the salesperson earned a $1250 commission, what was the price of the car? Determine the price of the car using your equation.

Problem 3   Tips, Taxes, and Discounts

1. A waitress received a tip (t) that varies directly with the bill (b). Suppose that $t = 0.15b$.

   a. What percent tip does the waitress receive? How do you know?

   b. If the bill is $19, how much tip did she receive?

c. If the waitress receives a $2.10 tip, how much is the bill?

2. The amount a waiter or waitress gets tipped (t) varies directly with the amount of the restaurant bill (b).

    a. Write an equation representing the direct proportional relationship between the amount tipped and the restaurant bill. Let k represent the constant of proportionality.

    b. Omar receives a tip of $6 on a $30 restaurant bill. Determine the constant of proportionality.

    c. What does the constant of proportionality represent in this problem?

    d. What is the constant of proportionality?

3. Gourmet Eatery has a policy of automatically adding an 18% tip to every restaurant bill.

a. Write an equation representing the relationship between the tip (*t*) and the restaurant bill (*b*).

b. How much of a tip is added to a restaurant bill of $54? Use your equation to determine the amount of the tip.

c. Marie receives a tip of $12. How much is the restaurant bill? Use your equation to determine the amount of the restaurant bill.

d. A restaurant bill is $12. How much is the tip?

e. How much would a restaurant bill be if it had a tip of $3.20 added to it?

4. Many states charge a sales tax on products you buy. The table shows the price of several products and the amount of sales tax added to the price in Pennsylvania.

Cost of Product (dollars)	Sales Tax (dollars)
16	0.96
20	1.20
80	4.80

a. What percent is Pennsylvania's sales tax? How do you know?

b. How much sales tax would there be on a $750 flat screen TV? Show how you determined your answer.

c. If the sales tax on a lawn mower is $48, how much was the lawn mower? Let c represent the cost of the lawn mower.

5. Dexter's Department Store is having a sale with a 33% discount on all merchandise.

    a. Write the equation representing the relationship between the regular cost of merchandise and the discount received.

    b. What is the discount on a $50 pair of jeans?

    c. If a sweater has a discount of $9.90, what was the regular cost?

 Be prepared to share your solutions and methods.

3

Chapter 3 Summary

Key Terms

▶ percent equation (3.3)   ▶ percent increase (3.4)

▶ interest (3.4)   ▶ percent decrease (3.4)

▶ principal (3.4)   ▶ depreciation (3.4)

▶ simple interest (3.4)

3.1 Calculating Values Using Rates or Percents

To determine a percent of a number, write the percent as a fraction or decimal and multiply just like calculating a fraction of a number.

Example

A sale price of 75% or $\frac{3}{4}$ the original price of $36 is solved in two ways.

Decimal: $(0.75)(36) = 27$

Fraction:

$$\left(\frac{75}{100}\right)(36) = \left(\frac{3}{4}\right)(36)$$
$$= \frac{108}{4}$$
$$= 27$$

The sale price of the item is $27.

3

3.1 Estimating Values Using Rates or Percents

Often only an estimate of a percent or rate is needed, as in the case of tipping at a restaurant. To estimate, round the base amount and the percent or rate to numbers that are easy to work with before calculating.

Example

The bill for dinner was $38.29. If Sally wants to leave about a 20% tip, she can estimate the amount by rounding $38.29 to $40 and figuring 20% of that amount.

$(0.20)(40) = 8$

Sally should leave a tip of $8.

3

3.2 Solving Percent Problems

A percent problem involves three quantities: the part, the whole, and the percent. If you know two of the quantities, you can determine the third. Given the percent equation, $\frac{x}{100} = \frac{p}{w}$, p represents the part, w represents the whole, and $\frac{x}{100}$ represents the percent.

Examples

a. 16 is what percent of 25?

$$\frac{x}{100} = \frac{p}{w}$$

$$\frac{x}{100} \overset{\times 4}{\underset{\times 4}{=}} \frac{16}{25}$$

$$x = 64$$

So, 16 is 64% of 25.

b. 72% of what number is 54?

$$\frac{x}{100} = \frac{p}{w}$$

$$\frac{72}{100} = \frac{54}{w}$$

$$\frac{18}{25} \overset{\times 3}{\underset{\times 3}{=}} \frac{54}{w}$$

$$75 = w$$

So, 72% of 75 is 54.

3.3 Solving Proportions

A proportion that is used to solve a percent problem is often written in the form percent $= \dfrac{\text{part}}{\text{whole}}$, where the percent is written as a fraction. To solve a proportion, rewrite it to isolate the variable.

Example

A proportion is used to find 45% of 900.

$$\frac{45}{100} = \frac{n}{900}$$
$$\frac{45 \cdot 900}{100} = n$$
$$405 = n$$

405 is 45% of 900.

3.3 Solving Percent Equations

A percent problem can also be written as a percent equation. A percent equation can be written in the form percent $\times$ whole = part, where the percent is written as a decimal. To solve a percent equation, rewrite the equation to isolate the variable.

Example

The percent equation is used to calculate what percent 300 is of 1500.

$$n(1500) = 300$$
$$\frac{n(1500)}{1500} = \frac{300}{1500}$$
$$n = 0.2$$

300 is 20% of 1500.

3.4 Calculating Simple Interest

Simple interest is a fixed percentage of a principal balance paid over a specific time. The formula for simple interest is $I = P \times r \times t$, where I is the interest earned, P is the principal in dollars, r is the interest rate, and t is the time in years.

Example

Chen deposited $250 into a savings account at a simple interest rate of 4% per year and left his money there for 5 years.

$$I = P \times r \times t$$
$$= 250 \times 0.04 \times 5$$
$$= 50$$

Chen will earn $50 in interest in 5 years.

3.4 Calculating Percent Increase and Decrease

To determine the percent increase or decrease, divide the amount of increase or decrease by the original amount.

Example

In its first year, a store's sales were $93,570. The store's sales the second year were $149,765. The percent of increase between the two years is shown.

$$\text{Percent Increase} = \frac{\text{Amount of increase}}{\text{Original amount}}$$
$$= \frac{\$149,765 - \$93,570}{\$93,570}$$
$$= \frac{\$56,195}{\$93,570}$$
$$\approx 0.60$$
$$= 60\%$$

The percent of increase in sales for the store was 60%.

3.5 Solving Percent Problems Using Direct Variation

If two values vary directly, the ratio between the two values is always the same. This ratio is called the constant of proportionality. Because the constant of proportionality is constant, it can be used to write equations and make predictions in situations.

Example

Nathan bought a new video game during Game Town's grand opening celebration during which all stock was on sale at the same discount rate. His friend wanted to buy a game that's usually $30 and wanted to know how much that game would cost during the sale. Nathan couldn't remember what the discount was, but he knew that the game he bought for $15 usually sells for $20.

To determine how much the $30 game would be, first calculate the constant of proportionality.

$$15 = 20 - k(20)$$
$$k(20) = 5$$
$$k = \frac{5}{20}$$
$$k = 0.25$$

Next, apply the discount to the game price.

$$30 = (0.25)(30) = 30 - 7.5 = 22.5$$

Nathan's friend can expect to pay $22.50 for his game.

4 ADDITION AND SUBTRACTION WITH RATIONAL NUMBERS

Although baseball is considered America's national pastime, football attracts more television viewers in the U.S. The Super Bowl—the championship football game held at the end of the season—is not only the most watched sporting event but also the most watched television broadcast every year.

4

4.1

MATH FOOTBALL
Using Models to Understand Integers

Learning Goals

In this lesson, you will:

▶ Represent numbers as positive and negative integers.

▶ Use a model to represent the sum of a positive and a negative integer.

Golfers like negative numbers. This is because, in golf, the lower the score, the better the golfer is playing. Runners like negative numbers too. They often split the distances they have to run into two or more equal distances. If they are on pace to win, they will achieve what is called a negative split.

What about football? What are some ways in which negative numbers can be used in that sport?

4

Problem 1 Hut! Hut! Hike!

You and a partner are going to play "Math Football." You will take turns rolling two number cubes to determine how many yards you can advance the football toward your end zone.

Player 1 will be the Home Team and Player 2 will be the Visiting Team. In the first half, the Home Team will move toward the Home end zone, and the Visiting Team will move toward the Visiting end zone.

Rules:

Players both start at the zero yard line and take turns. On your turn, roll two number cubes, one red and one black. The number on each cube represents a number of yards. Move your football to the left the number of yards shown on the red cube. Move your football to the right the number of yards shown on the black cube. Start each of your next turns from the ending position of your previous turn.

(Nets are provided at the end of the lesson so you can cut out and construct your own number cubes. Don't forget to color the number cubes black and red.)

Scoring:

Each player must move the football the combined value of both number cubes to complete each turn and be eligible for points. When players reach their end zone, they score 6 points. If players reach their opponent's end zone, they lose 2 points. An end zone begins on either the $+10$ or -10 yard line.

Example:

	Player	Starting Position	Results of the Number Cubes Roll	Ending Position
First Turn	Home Team	0	Red 3 and Black 5	$+2$
	Visiting Team	0	Red 5 and Black 6	$+1$
Second Turn	Home Team	$+2$	Red 1 and Black 6	$+7$
	Visiting Team	$+1$	Red 6 and Black 2	-3

1. Read through the table. After two turns, which player is closest to their end zone?

2. Let's play Math Football. Begin by selecting the home or visiting team. Then, cut out your football. Set a time limit for playing a half. You will play two halves. Make sure to switch ends at half-time with the Home Team moving toward the Visiting end zone, and the Visiting Team moving toward the Home end zone.

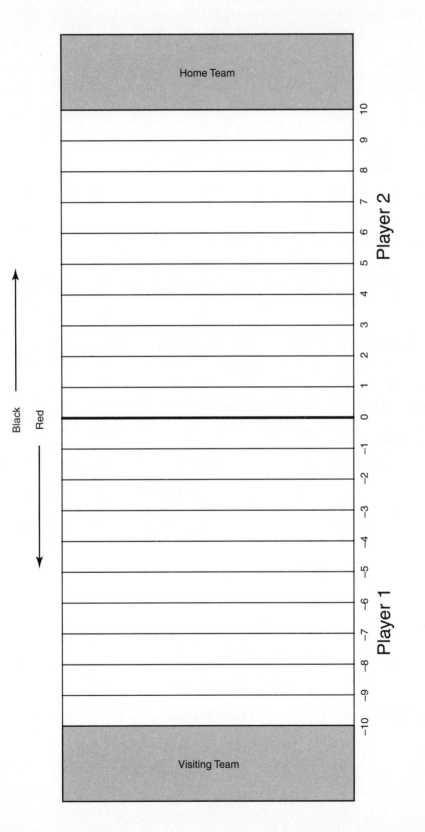

4

3. Answer each question based on your experiences playing Math Football.

   a. When you were trying to get to the Home end zone, which number cube did you want to show the greater value? Explain your reasoning.

   b. When you were trying to get to the Visiting end zone, which number cube did you want to show the greater value? Explain your reasoning.

   c. Did you ever find yourself back at the same position you ended on your previous turn? Describe the values shown on the cubes that would cause this to happen.

   d. Describe the roll that could cause you to move your football the greatest distance either left or right.

Problem 2   Writing Number Sentences

You can write number sentences to describe the results of number cube rolls. Think of the result of rolling the red number cube as a negative number and the result of rolling the black number cube as a positive number.

Consider the example from Problem 1. The number sentence for each turn has been included.

	Player	Starting Position	Results of the Number Cubes Roll	Ending Position	Number Sentence
First Turn	Home Team	0	Red 3 and Black 5	+2	$0 + (-3) + 5 = +2$
	Visiting Team	0	Red 5 and Black 6	+1	$0 + (-5) + 6 = +1$
Second Turn	Home Team	+2	Red 1 and Black 6	+7	$+2 + (-1) + 6 = +7$
	Visiting Team	+1	Red 6 and Black 2	-3	$+1 + (-6) + 2 = -3$

1. Describe each part of the number sentence for the second turn of the Visiting Team player.

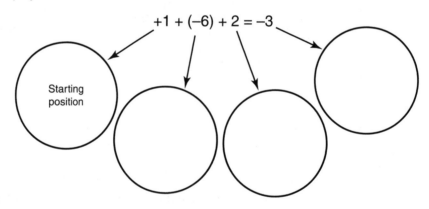

$+1 + (-6) + 2 = -3$

Starting position

2. Write a number sentence for each situation. Use the game board for help.

a. The Home Team player starts at the zero yard line and rolls a red 6 and a black 2. What is the ending position?

Number sentence _____

I calculated the result from the two cubes first and then added this to the starting number. Can I do that?

b. The Visiting Team player starts at the zero yard line and rolls a red 5 and a black 4. What is the ending position?

Number sentence _____

c. The Home Team player starts at the 5 yard line and rolls a red 2 and a black 2. What is the ending position?

Number sentence _____

d. The Visiting Team player starts at the −5 yard line and rolls a red 4 and a black 6. What is the ending position?

Number sentence _____

e. Suppose the Home Team player is at the +8 yard line. Complete the table and write two number sentences that will put the player into the Home end zone.

Starting Position	Roll of the Red Number Cube	Roll of the Black Number Cube	Number Sentence
+8			
+8			

f. Suppose the Visiting Team player is at the −8 yard line. Complete the table and write two number sentences that will put the player into the Visiting end zone.

Starting Position	Roll of the Red Number Cube	Roll of the Black Number Cube	Number Sentence
−8			
−8			

Be prepared to share your solutions and methods.

4

4

4.2 WALK THE LINE
Adding Integers, Part I

Learning Goals

In this lesson, you will:

▶ Model the addition of integers on a number line.

▶ Develop a rule for adding integers.

Corinne: "I'm thinking of a number between −20 and 20. What's my number?"

Benjamin: "Is it −5?"

Corinne: "Lower."

Benjamin: "−2?"

Corinne: "That's not lower than −5."

Benjamin: "Oh, right. How about −11?"

Corinne: "Higher."

Benjamin: "−8?"

Corinne: "Lower."

Benjamin: "−9?"

Corinne: "You got it!"

Try this game with a partner. See who can get the number with the fewest guesses.

Problem 1   Adding on Number Lines

1. Use the number line and determine the number described by each. Explain your reasoning.

```
◄──┼┼┼┼┼┼┼┼┼┼┼┼┼┼┼┼┼┼┼┼┼┼┼┼┼┼┼┼┼──►
    -15      -10      -5       0       5       10       15
```

a. the number that is 7 more than −9

b. the number that is 2 more than −6

c. the number that is 10 more than −8

d. the number that is 10 less than 6

e. the number that is 5 less than −4

f. the number that is 2 less than −4

A number line can be used to model integer addition.

When adding a positive integer, move to the right on a number line.

When adding a negative integer, move to the left on a number line.

Example 1: The number line shows how to determine $5 + 8$.

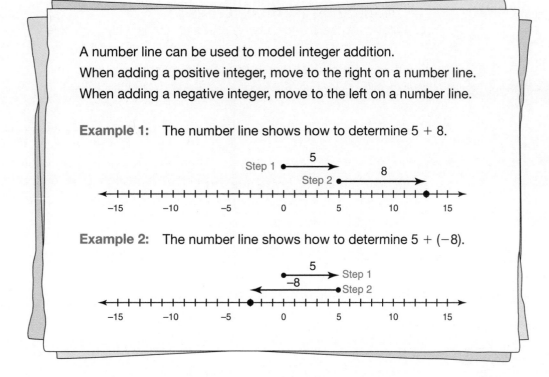

Example 2: The number line shows how to determine $5 + (-8)$.

2. Compare the first steps in each example.

   a. What distance is shown by the first term in each example?

   b. Describe the graphical representation of the first term. Where does it start and in which direction does it move? Why?

   c. What is the absolute value of the first term in each example?

Remember that the absolute value of a number is its distance from 0.

3. Compare the second steps in each example.

    a. What distance is shown by the second term in each example?

    b. Why did the graphical representation for the second terms both start at the endpoints of the first terms but then continue in opposite directions? Explain your reasoning.

    c. What are the absolute values of the second terms?

4. Use the number line to determine each sum. Show your work.

    a. $-3 + 7 =$ _____

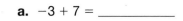

$$
\begin{array}{c}
\overset{\longleftarrow}{\underset{-15 \quad\quad -10 \quad\quad -5 \quad\quad 0 \quad\quad 5 \quad\quad 10 \quad\quad 15}{\rule{8cm}{0pt}}}
\end{array}
$$

    b. $3 + (-7) =$ _____

$$
\begin{array}{c}
\overset{\longleftarrow}{\underset{-15 \quad\quad -10 \quad\quad -5 \quad\quad 0 \quad\quad 5 \quad\quad 10 \quad\quad 15}{\rule{8cm}{0pt}}}
\end{array}
$$

c. $-3 + (-7) =$ _____

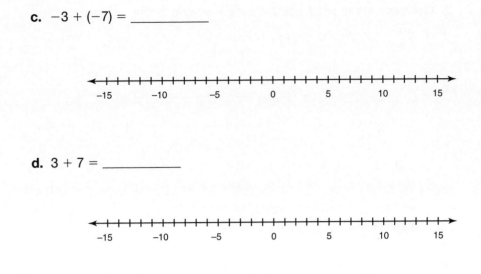

d. $3 + 7 =$ _____

Number line from −15 to 15.

5. Notice that the first term in each expression in parts (a) through (d) was either 3 or (−3).

   a. What do you notice about the distances shown by these terms on the number lines?

   b. What is the absolute value of each term?

6. Notice that the second term in each expression was either 7 or (−7).

   a. What do you notice about the distances shown by these terms on the number lines?

   b. What is the absolute value of each term?

7. Use the number line to determine each sum. Show your work.

a. $-9 + 5 =$ _____

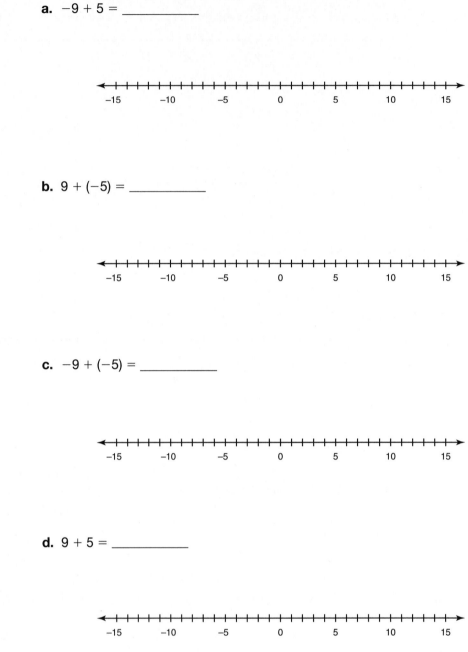

b. $9 + (-5) =$ _____

c. $-9 + (-5) =$ _____

d. $9 + 5 =$ _____

8. Notice that the first term in each expression in parts (a) through (d) was either 9 or (−9).

    a. What do you notice about the distances shown by these terms on the number lines?

    b. What is the absolute value of each term?

9. Notice that the second term in each expression was either 5 or (−5).

  a. What do you notice about the distances shown by these terms on the number lines?

    b. What is the absolute value of each term?

How is knowing the absolute value of each term important?

4

10. Use the number line to determine each sum. Show your work.

    a. $-8 + 2 =$ _____

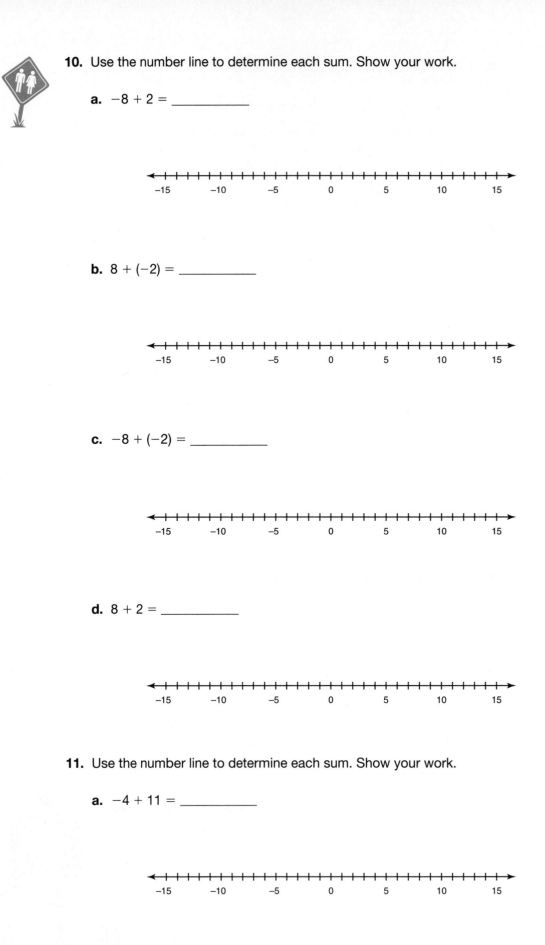

    b. $8 + (-2) =$ _____

    c. $-8 + (-2) =$ _____

    d. $8 + 2 =$ _____

11. Use the number line to determine each sum. Show your work.

    a. $-4 + 11 =$ _____

b. $4 + (-11) = $ _____

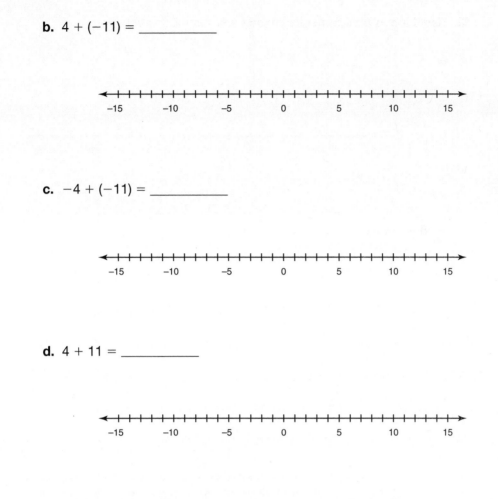

c. $-4 + (-11) = $ _____

d. $4 + 11 = $ _____

12. In Questions 4 through 11, what patterns do you notice when:

   a. you are adding two positive numbers?

   b. you are adding two negative numbers?

   c. you are adding a negative and a positive number?

Can you see how knowing the absolute value is important when adding and subtracting signed numbers?

13. Complete each number line model and number sentence.

a. 4 + _____ = 12

b. −3 + _____ = 2

c. 7 + _____ = −2

d. −6 + _____ = −11

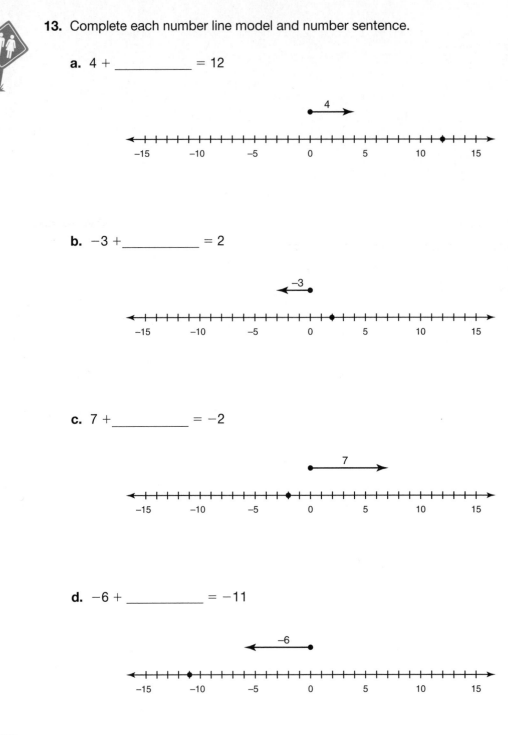

Be prepared to share your solutions and methods.

Learning Goals

In this lesson, you will:

▶ Model the addition of integers using two-color counters.

▶ Develop a rule for adding integers.

Key Term

▶ additive inverses

Opposites are all around us. If you move forward two spaces in a board game and then move back in the opposite direction two spaces, you're back where you started. In tug-of-war, if one team pulling on the rope pulls exactly as hard as the team on the opposite side, no one moves. If an element has the same number of positively charged protons as it does of negatively charged electrons, then the element has no charge.

In what ways have you worked with opposites in mathematics?

Problem 1 Two-Color Counters

1. Use the number line model to determine each sum.

a. $3 + (-3) =$ _____

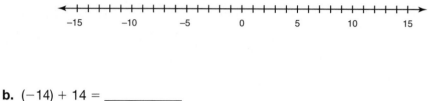

b. $(-14) + 14 =$ _____

c. $8 + (-8) =$ _____

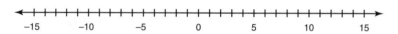

d. What pattern do you notice?

Two numbers with the sum of zero are called **additive inverses**.

Addition of integers can also be modeled using two-color counters that represent positive (+) charges and negative (−) charges. One color, usually red, represents the negative number, or negative charge. The other color, usually yellow, represents the positive number, or positive charge. In this book, gray shading will represent the negative number, and no shading will represent the positive number.

$$\bigodot = -1 \qquad \oplus = +1$$

You can model the expression $3 + (-3)$ in different ways using two-color counters:

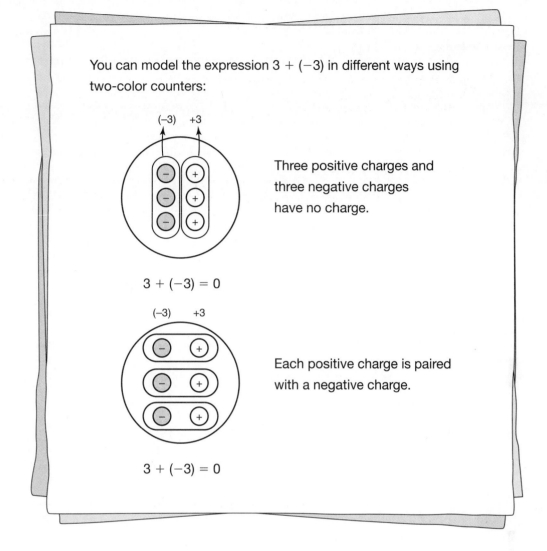

Three positive charges and three negative charges have no charge.

$3 + (-3) = 0$

Each positive charge is paired with a negative charge.

$3 + (-3) = 0$

2. What is the value of each ⊖ and ⊕ pair shown in the second model?

3. Describe how you can change the numbers of ⊖ and ⊕ counters in the model, but leave the sum unchanged.

Let's consider two examples where integers are added using two-color counters.

Example 1: 5 + 8

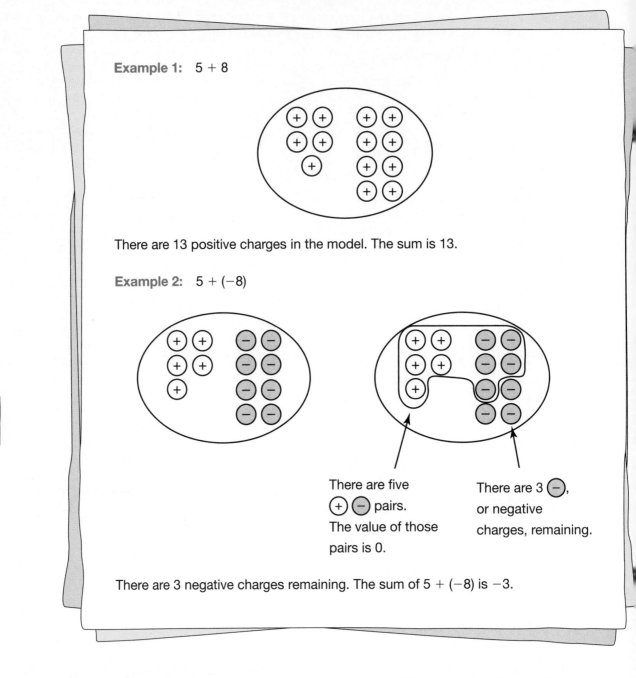

There are 13 positive charges in the model. The sum is 13.

Example 2: 5 + (−8)

There are five
(+)(−) pairs.
The value of those
pairs is 0.

There are 3 (−),
or negative
charges, remaining.

There are 3 negative charges remaining. The sum of 5 + (−8) is −3.

4. Create another model to represent a sum of −3. Write the appropriate number sentence.

5. Share your model with your classmates. How are they the same? How are they different?

6. Write a number sentence to represent each model.

a.
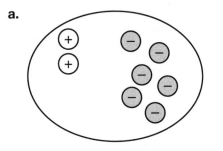

b.
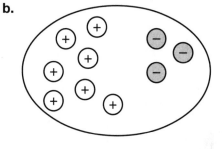

c.
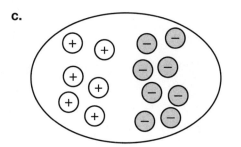

d.
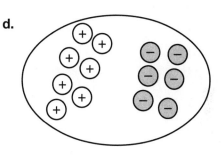

e.
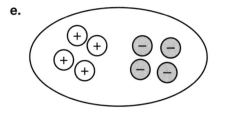

f.
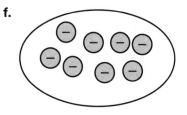

7. Does the order in which you wrote the integers in your number sentence matter? How do you know?

8. Write each number sentence in Question 6 a second way.

9. Draw a model for each, and then complete the number sentence.

    a. $-9 + (-4) =$ _____   **b.** $-9 + 4 =$ _____

    c. $9 + (-4) =$ _____   **d.** $9 + 4 =$ _____

10. Complete the model to determine the unknown integer.

a. 1 + _____ = −4

b. −3 + _____ = 7

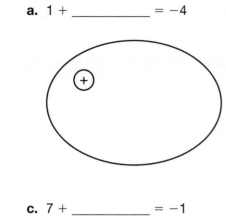

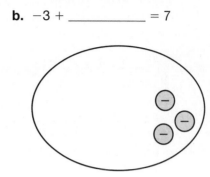

c. 7 + _____ = −1

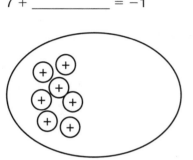

11. Describe the set of integers that makes each sentence true.

a. What integer(s) when added to −7 give a sum greater than 0?

b. What integer(s) when added to −7 give a sum of less than 0?

c. What integer(s) when added to −7 give a sum of 0?

> Consider drawing a number line model or a two-color counter model to help you answer each question.

4

12. When adding two integers, what will the sign of the sum be if:

    a. both integers are positive?

    b. both integers are negative?

    c. one integer is negative and one integer is positive?

> What happens when you add a negative and a positive integer and they both have the same absolute value?

13. Write a rule that states how to determine the sum of any two integers that have the same sign.

14. Write a rule that states how to determine the sum of any two integers that have opposite signs.

15. Use your rule to determine each sum.

    a. $-58 + (24) =$ **b.** $-35 + (-15) =$

    c. $-33 + (-12) =$ **d.** $-48 + 60 =$

    e. $26 + (-13) =$ **f.** $-67 + 67 =$

    g. $105 + (-25) =$ **h.** $153 + (-37) =$

16. Determine each unknown addend.

    a. _____ $+ (-25) = 34$ **b.** _____ $+ 26 = 12$

    c. $8 +$ _____ $= -24$ **d.** $-12 +$ _____ $= -24$

    e. $-15 +$ _____ $= -28$ **f.** _____ $+ 18 = -3$

Talk the Talk

Represent the sum of additive inverses in the graphic organizer provided. First, write a number sentence. Then, represent your number sentence in words, using a number line model, and using a two-color counter model.

Be prepared to share your solutions and methods.

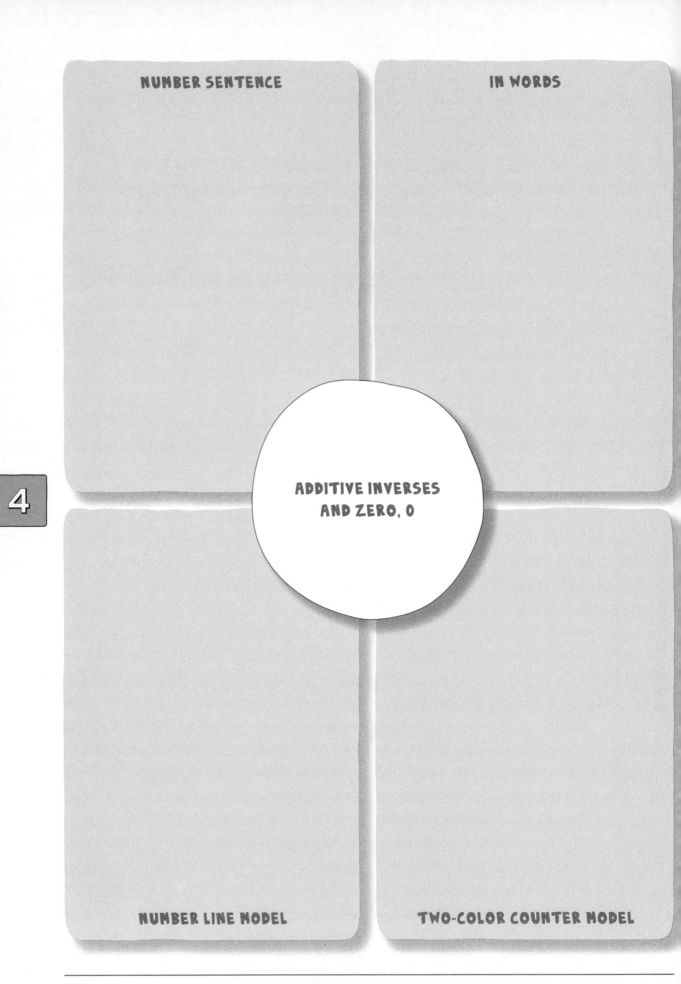

NUMBER SENTENCE

IN WORDS

ADDITIVE INVERSES
AND ZERO, 0

NUMBER LINE MODEL

TWO-COLOR COUNTER MODEL

4.4

WHAT'S THE DIFFERENCE?
Subtracting Integers

Learning Goals

In this lesson, you will:

▶ Model subtraction of integers using two-color counters.

▶ Model subtraction of integers on a number line.

▶ Develop a rule for subtracting integers.

Key Term

▶ zero pair

"I don't want nothing!" "We don't need no education." "I can't get no satisfaction." You may have heard—or even said—these phrases before. In proper English writing, however, these kinds of phrases should be avoided because they contain double negatives, which can make your writing confusing.

For example, the phrase "I don't need none" contains two "negatives": the word "don't" and the word "none." The sentence should be rewritten as "I don't need any." In mathematics, double negatives can be confusing as well, but it's perfectly okay to use them!

In this lesson, you will learn about subtracting integers, which sometimes involves double negatives.

4

Problem 1   Temperatures

1. Complete the table to determine the difference between the maximum and minimum temperatures in each row.

> Subtract the minimum temperature from the maximum temperature, not the other way around.

United States Extreme Record Temperatures and Differences			
State	Maximum Temp. (°F)	Minimum Temp. (°F)	Difference (°F)
Georgia	112	−17	
Hawaii	100	12	
Florida	109	−2	
Alaska	100	−80	
California	134	−35	
North Carolina	110	−34	
Arizona	128	−40	
Texas	120	−23	

a. Which state shows the least difference between the maximum and minimum temperature?

b. Which state shows the greatest difference between the maximum and minimum temperature?

2. You overheard a radio announcer report that from 12:00 PM to 3:00 PM the temperature went from −5°F to −10°F. He said, "It is getting warmer." Was he correct? Explain your reasoning.

Problem 2   Models for Subtracting Integers

Subtraction can mean to "take away" objects from a set. Subtraction can also mean a comparison of two numbers, or the "difference between them."

The number line model and the two-color counter model used in the addition of integers can also be used to investigate the subtraction of integers.

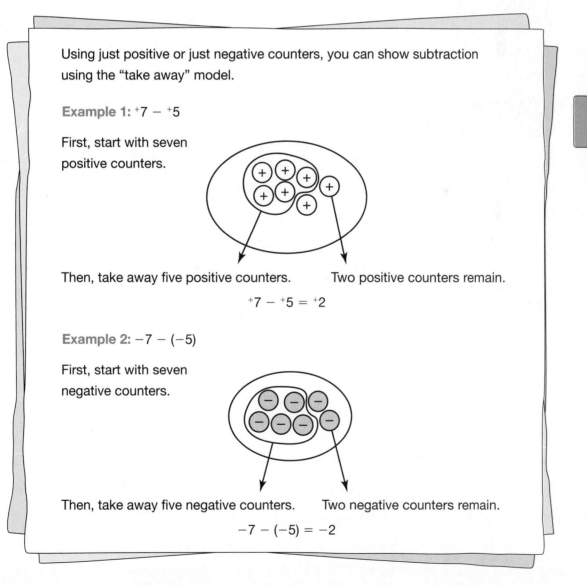

Using just positive or just negative counters, you can show subtraction using the "take away" model.

Example 1: $^+7 - {}^+5$

First, start with seven positive counters.

Then, take away five positive counters.   Two positive counters remain.

$$^+7 - {}^+5 = {}^+2$$

Example 2: $-7 - (-5)$

First, start with seven negative counters.

Then, take away five negative counters.   Two negative counters remain.

$$-7 - (-5) = -2$$

1. How are Examples 1 and 2 similar? How are these examples different?

To subtract integers using both positive and negative counters, you will need to use *zero pairs*.

$$ \oplus + \ominus = 0 $$

Recall that the value of a $\ominus$ and $\oplus$ pair is zero. So, together they form a **zero pair**. You can add as many pairs as you need and not change the value.

Example 3: $^+7 - (-5)$

Start with seven positive counters.

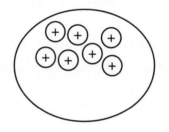

The expression says to subtract five negative counters, but there are no negative counters in the first model. Insert five negative counters into the model. So that you don't change the value, you must also insert five positive counters.

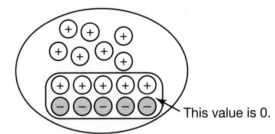

This value is 0.

Now, you can subtract, or take away, the five negative counters.

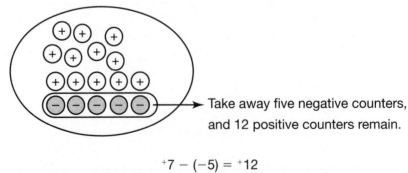

Take away five negative counters, and 12 positive counters remain.

$$ ^+7 - (-5) = {^+}12 $$

Example 4: $-7 - {}^{+}5$

Start with seven negative counters.

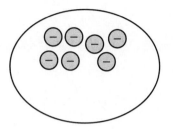

2. The expression says to subtract five positive counters, but there are no positive counters in the first model.

   a. How can you insert positive counters into the model and not change the value?

   b. Complete the model.

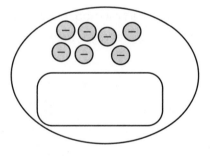

   c. Now, subtract, or take away, the five positive counters. Sketch the model to show that $-7 - {}^{+}5 = -12$.

This is a little bit like regrouping in subtraction.

3. Draw a representation for each subtraction problem. Then, calculate the difference.

  a. $4 - (-5)$

  b. $-4 - (-5)$

  c. $-4 - {}^+5$

d. $4 - 5$

4. How could you model $0 - (-7)$?

    a. Draw a sketch of your model. Finally, determine the difference.

    b. In part (a), would it matter how many zero pairs you add? Explain your reasoning.

5. Does the order in which you subtract two numbers matter? Does $5 - 3$ have the same answer as $3 - 5$? Draw models to explain your reasoning.

6. Write a rule for subtracting positive and negative integers.

Problem 3   Subtracting on a Number Line

Cara thought of subtraction of integers another way. She said, "Subtraction means to back up, or move in the opposite direction. Like in football when a team is penalized or loses yardage, they have to move back."

Analyze Cara's examples.

Example 1: $-6 - (+2)$

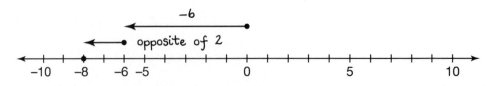

First, I moved from zero to -6, and then I went in the opposite direction of the $+2$ because I am subtracting. So, I went two units to the left and ended up at -8.

$-6 - (+2) = -8$

Example 2: −6 − (−2)

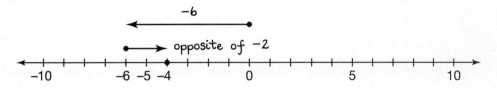

In this problem, I went from zero to −6. Because I am subtracting (−2), I went in the opposite direction of the −2, or right two units, and ended up at −4.

−6 − (−2) = −4

Example 3: 6 − (−2)

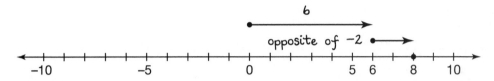

1. Explain the model Cara created in Example 3.

Example 4: 6 − (+2)

2. Explain the model Cara created in Example 4.

3. Use the number line to complete each number sentence.

> Use Cara's examples for help.

a. $-4 - (-3) =$ _____

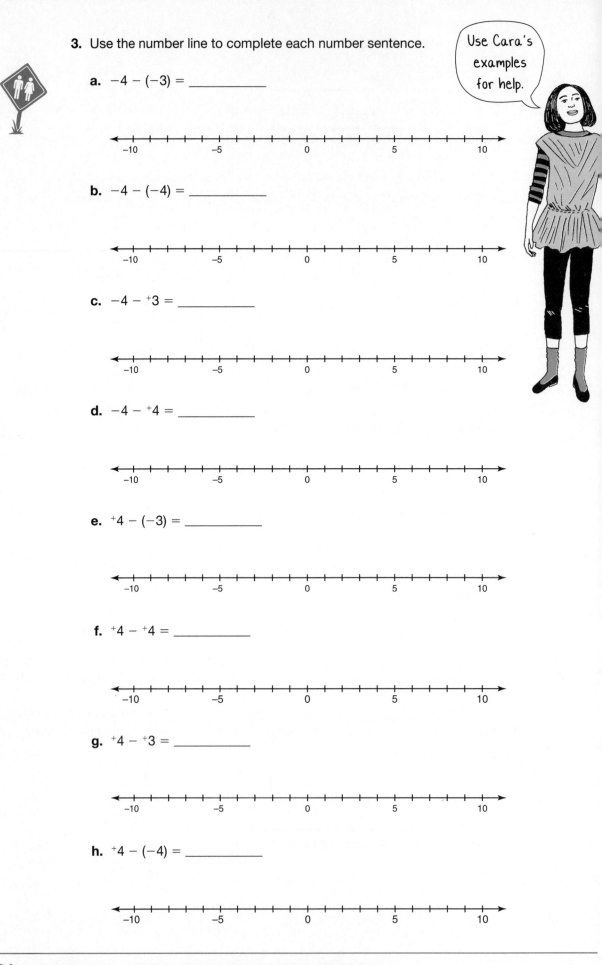

b. $-4 - (-4) =$ _____

c. $-4 - {}^+3 =$ _____

d. $-4 - {}^+4 =$ _____

e. ${}^+4 - (-3) =$ _____

f. ${}^+4 - {}^+4 =$ _____

g. ${}^+4 - {}^+3 =$ _____

h. ${}^+4 - (-4) =$ _____

4. What patterns did you notice when subtracting the integers in Question 3?

    a. Subtracting two negative integers is similar to

    _____

    b. Subtracting two positive integers is similar to

    _____

    c. Subtracting a positive integer from a negative integer is similar to

    _____

    d. Subtracting a negative integer from a positive integer is similar to

    _____

5. Analyze the number sentences shown.

    ● $-8 - 5 = -13$ ● $-8 - 4 = -12$

    ● $-8 - 3 = -11$ ● $-8 - 2 = -10$

    ● $-8 - 1 = -9$ ● $-8 - 0 = -8$

    a. What patterns do you see? What happens as the integer subtracted
    from -8 decreases?

    b. From your pattern, predict the answer to $-8 - (-1)$.

For a subtraction expression, such as $-8 - (-2)$, Cara's method is to start at zero and go to -8, and then go two spaces in the opposite direction of -2 to get -6.

Dava says, "I see another pattern. Since subtraction is the inverse of addition, you can think of subtraction as adding the opposite number. That matches with Cara's method of going in the opposite direction."

$-8 - (-2)$ is the same as $-8 + -(-2)$
$-8 + 2 = -6$

opposite of $-2 = -(-2)$

```
 ←——+——+——+——+——+——◆——+——+——+——+——+——+——+——+——+——+——+——+——+——+——+——→
   -10    -8    -6 -5              0              5             10
```

An example of Dava's method is shown.

$$^+10 - (^-4) =$$
$$10 + -(^-4)$$
$$10 + 4 = 14$$

6. Apply Dava's method to determine each difference.

a. $-9 - (-2) =$

b. $-3 - (-3) =$

c. $-7 - {}^+5 =$

d. $^+24 - {}^+8 =$

e. $-4 - {}^+2 =$

f. $^+5 - {}^+9 =$

So, I can change any subtraction problem to show addition if I take the opposite of the number that follows the subtraction sign.

g. $-20 - (-30) =$

h. $-10 - {}^+18 =$

7. Determine the unknown integer in each number sentence.

a. $^+3 +$ _____ $= {}^+7$

b. $^+2 +$ _____ $= -7$

c. _____ $+ -20 = -10$

d. _____ $- {}^+5 = {}^+40$

e. _____ $- (-5) = {}^+40$

f. _____ $+ {}^+5 = {}^+40$

g. $^+6 +$ _____ $= {}^+52$

h. $-6 +$ _____ $= {}^+52$

i. $-6 +$ _____ $= -52$

8. Determine each absolute value.

    a. $|-7 - (-3)|$ **b.** $|-7 - {}^{+}3|$

    c. $|7 - {}^{+}3|$ **d.** $|7 - (-3)|$

9. How does the absolute value relate to the distance between the two numbers in Question 8, parts (a) through (d)?

10. Is $|8 - 6|$ equal to $|6 - 8|$? Is $|4 - 6|$ equal to $|6 - 4|$? Explain your thinking.

Talk the Talk

1. Tell whether these subtraction sentences are always true, sometimes true, or never true. Give examples to explain your thinking.

    a. positive − positive = positive

    b. negative − positive = negative

    c. positive − negative = negative

    d. negative − negative = negative

2. If you subtract two negative integers, will the answer be greater than or less than the number you started with? Explain your thinking.

3. What happens when a positive number is subtracted from zero?

4. What happens when a negative number is subtracted from zero?

5. Just by looking at the problem, how do you know if the sum of two integers is positive, negative, or zero?

6. How are addition and subtraction of integers related?

Be prepared to share your solutions and methods.

WHAT DO WE DO NOW?

4.5

Adding and Subtracting Rational Numbers

Learning Goal

In this lesson, you will:

▶ Add and subtract rational numbers.

You might think that as you go deeper below the Earth's surface, it would get colder. But this is not the case.

Drill down past the Earth's crust, and you reach a layer called the mantle, which extends to a depth of about −1800 miles. The temperature in this region is approximately +1600°F. Next stop is the outer core, which extends to a depth of about −3200 miles and has a temperature of approximately +8000°F. The last stop is the very center, the inner core. At approximately −4000 miles, the inner core may have a temperature as high as 12,000°F−as high as the temperature on the surface of the Sun!

What do you think makes the temperature increase as elevation decreases?

Problem 1   Adding Rational Numbers

Previously, you learned how to add and subtract with positive and negative integers. In this lesson, you will apply what you know about your work with integers to the set of rational numbers.

Consider this problem and the two methods shown.

$$-3\frac{3}{4} + 4\frac{1}{4} = \,?$$

Kaitlin's Method

Omar's Method

1. Describe each method and the correct answer.

2. Now, consider this problem:

$$12\tfrac{1}{3} + \left(-23\tfrac{3}{4}\right) = ?$$

a. Why might it be difficult to use either a number line or counters to solve this problem?

b. What is the rule for adding signed numbers with different signs?

c. What will be the sign of the sum for this problem? Explain your reasoning.

4

Now that I am working with fractions, I need to remember to find a common denominator first.

d. Calculate the sum.

$$12\tfrac{1}{3} + \left(-23\tfrac{3}{4}\right) =$$

3. What is the rule for adding signed numbers with the same sign?

4. Determine each sum. Show your work.

    a. $-5\frac{3}{5} + 6\frac{1}{3} =$

    b. $-3\frac{2}{3} + \left(-4\frac{2}{3}\right) =$

    c. $-7.34 + 10.6 =$

    d. $17\frac{2}{3} + 11\frac{1}{6} =$

> Remember that when you add or subtract with decimals, you should first align the decimal points.

    e. $-104\frac{3}{4} + 88\frac{1}{6} =$

    f. $-27 + 16.127 =$

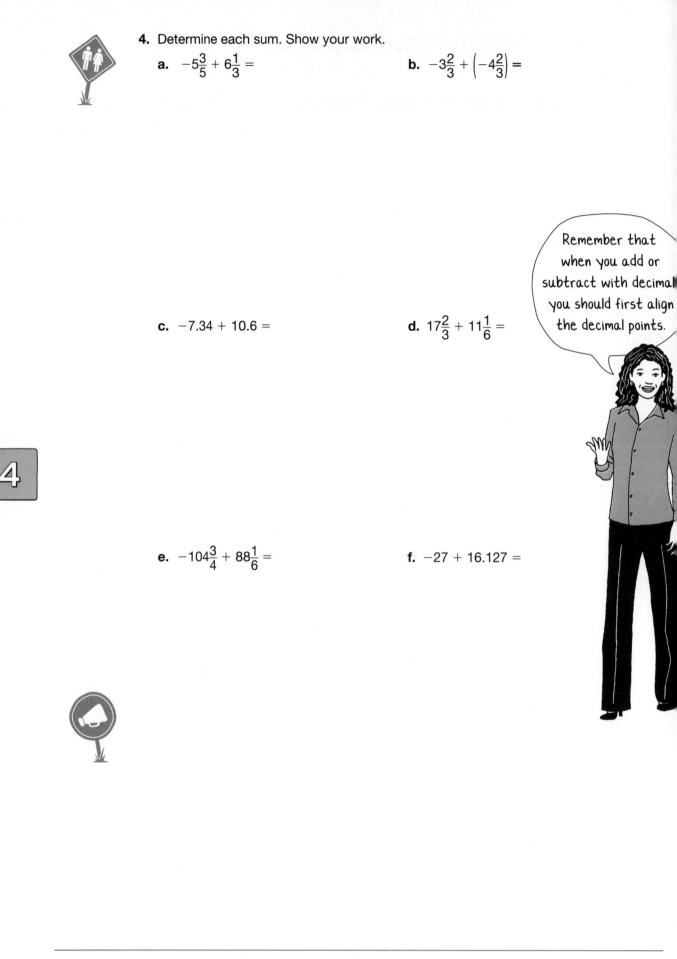

Problem 2   Subtracting Rational Numbers

1. What is the rule for subtracting signed numbers?

2. Determine each difference. Show your work.

   a. $-5\frac{1}{5} - 6\frac{2}{3} =$

   b. $8\frac{1}{4} - \left(-5\frac{1}{3}\right) =$

   c. $-7\frac{3}{4} - \left(-4\frac{7}{8}\right) =$

   d. $-11\frac{1}{2} - 12\frac{1}{5} =$

   e. $-24.15 - (13.7) =$

   f. $-6.775 - (-1.7) =$

Problem 3 Adding and Subtracting with an Algorithm

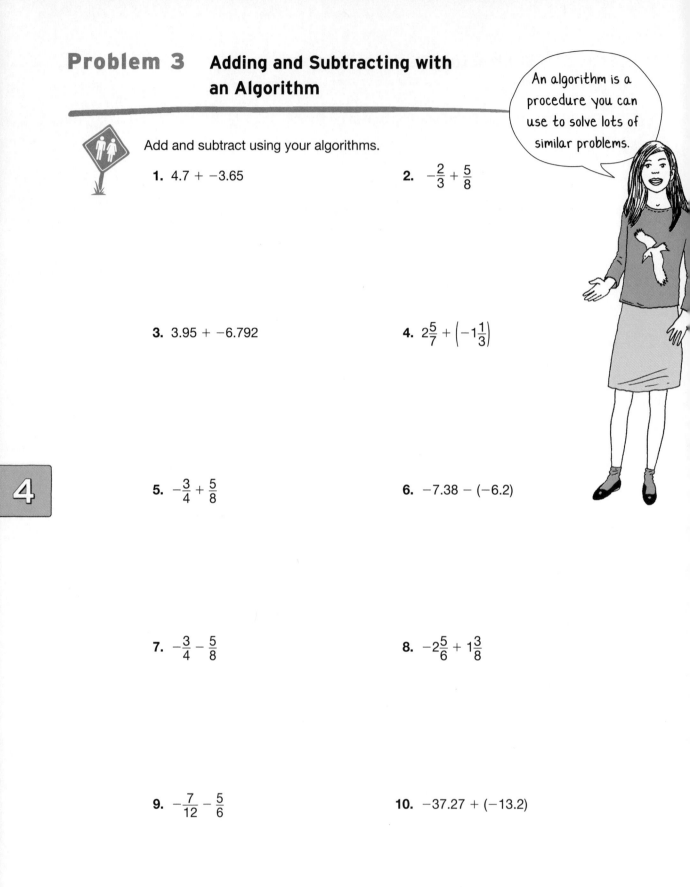

An algorithm is a procedure you can use to solve lots of similar problems.

Add and subtract using your algorithms.

1. $4.7 + -3.65$

2. $-\dfrac{2}{3} + \dfrac{5}{8}$

3. $3.95 + -6.792$

4. $2\dfrac{5}{7} + \left(-1\dfrac{1}{3}\right)$

5. $-\dfrac{3}{4} + \dfrac{5}{8}$

6. $-7.38 - (-6.2)$

7. $-\dfrac{3}{4} - \dfrac{5}{8}$

8. $-2\dfrac{5}{6} + 1\dfrac{3}{8}$

9. $-\dfrac{7}{12} - \dfrac{5}{6}$

10. $-37.27 + (-13.2)$

11. $-0.8 - (-0.6)$

12. $2\frac{3}{7} + -1\frac{3}{4}$

13. $0.67 + (-0.33)$

14. $-42.65 - (-16.3)$

15. $-7300 + 2100$

16. $-3\frac{5}{8} - \left(-2\frac{1}{3}\right)$

17. $-4.7 + 3.16$

18. $26.9 - (-3.1)$

19. $-325 + (-775)$

20. $-2\frac{1}{5} - 1\frac{3}{10}$

 Be prepared to share your solutions and methods.

4

Chapter 4   Summary

Key Terms

▶ additive inverses (4.3)

▶ zero pair (4.4)

4.1 Writing Number Sentences to Represent the Sum of Positive and Negative Integers

Integers are useful for representing some sort of progress from a starting quantity or position. Sequential events can often be modeled by a number sentence involving both positive and negative integers.

Example

During a model boat race, a boat is in the lead by two boat lengths at the halfway point of the race. However, during the second half of the race, the boat loses five boat lengths to the eventual winner. The boat's progress in relation to the boat race winner is shown through the additional sentence.

$(+2) + (-5) = -3$

4.2 Modeling Integer Addition on a Number Line

A number line can be used to model integer addition. When adding a positive integer, move to the right on the number line. When adding a negative integer, move to the left on the number line.

Example

$-8 + 3$

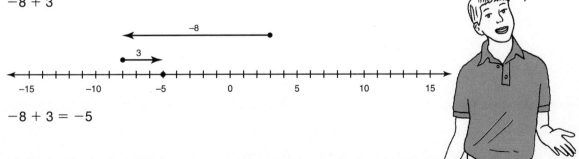

$-8 + 3 = -5$

4

4.3 Modeling Integer Addition Using Two-Color Counters

Let a red counter represent -1 and a yellow counter represent $+1$. Each pair of positive and negative counters has a value of zero.

Example

A model representing $7 + (-4)$ using two-color counters is shown. The zero pairs are circled showing the sum.

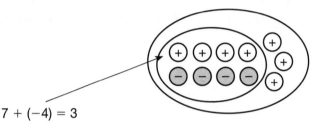

$7 + (-4) = 3$

4.3 Adding Integers

When adding two integers with the same sign, add the integers and keep the sign. When adding integers with opposite signs, subtract the integers and keep the sign of the integer with the greater absolute value.

Example

$-9 + (-12)$ $7 + (-15)$
$= -(9 + 12)$ $= -8$
$= -21$

4.4 Modeling Integer Subtraction Using Two-Color Counters

Subtraction can be modeled by "taking away" objects of a set. Positive and negative counters can be used to represent this "take away" model. Because a pair of positive and negative counters has a value of zero, as many zero pairs as are needed can be added without changing the value.

Example

Two-color counters can be used to model subtraction. Begin by adding the number of counters to represent the first term, and then add enough zero pairs to be able to subtract the second term.

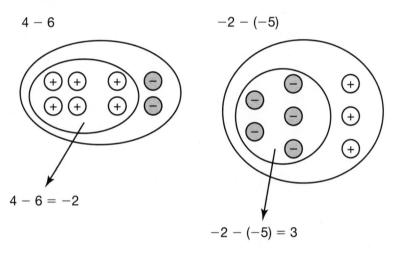

$4 - 6$

$-2 - (-5)$

$4 - 6 = -2$

$-2 - (-5) = 3$

4

4.4 Modeling Integer Subtraction on a Number Line

A number line can be used to model integer subtraction. Subtraction means to move in the opposite direction on the number line. When subtracting a positive integer, move to the left on the number line. When subtracting a negative integer, move to the right on the number line.

Example

$-10 - (-6)$

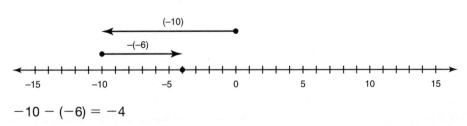

$-10 - (-6) = -4$

4.4 Subtracting Integers

Because subtraction is the inverse of addition, it is the same as adding the opposite number.

Examples

$$-7 - 19 = -7 + (-19)$$
$$= -26$$

$$12 - 21 = 12 + (-21)$$
$$= -9$$

4.5 Adding Rational Numbers

When adding positive and negative rational numbers, follow the same rules as when adding integers. When adding rational numbers with the same sign, add the numbers and keep the sign. When the rational numbers have different signs, subtract the numbers and keep the sign of the number with the greater absolute value.

Examples

$$-8.54 + (-3.4)$$
$$= -(8.54 + 3.4)$$
$$= -11.94$$

$$5\frac{1}{2} + (-10\frac{3}{4})$$
$$= 10\frac{3}{4} - 5\frac{2}{4}$$
$$= -5\frac{1}{4}$$

4.5 Subtracting Rational Numbers

When subtracting positive and negative rational numbers, follow the same rules as when subtracting integers. Because subtraction is the inverse of addition, it is the same as adding the opposite number.

Examples

$$-7\frac{1}{4} - (-10\frac{5}{8})$$
$$= -7\frac{2}{8} + (+10\frac{5}{8})$$
$$= 3\frac{3}{8}$$

$$-8.5 - 3.4$$
$$= -8.5 + (-3.4)$$
$$= -11.9$$

5

MULTIPLICATION AND DIVISION WITH RATIONAL NUMBERS

> Kitty Hawk, North Carolina, is famous for being the place where the first airplane flight took place. The brothers who flew these first flights grew up in Ohio, but they chose Kitty Hawk for its steady winds, soft landings, and privacy.

5

5

5.1

EQUAL GROUPS

Multiplying and Dividing Integers

Learning Goals

In this lesson, you will:

▶ Multiply integers.

▶ Divide integers.

Pick any positive integer. If the integer is even, divide it by 2. If it is odd, multiply it by 3 and then add 1. Repeat this process with your result.

No matter what number you start with, eventually you will have a result of 1. This is known as the Collatz Conjecture—a conjecture in mathematics that no one has yet proven or disproven. How do you think it works?

5

Problem 1 Multiply Integers

When you multiply integers, you can think of multiplication as repeated addition.

Consider the expression $3 \times (-4)$.

As repeated addition, it means $(-4) + (-4) + (-4) = -12$.

You can think of $3 \times (-4)$ as three groups of (-4).

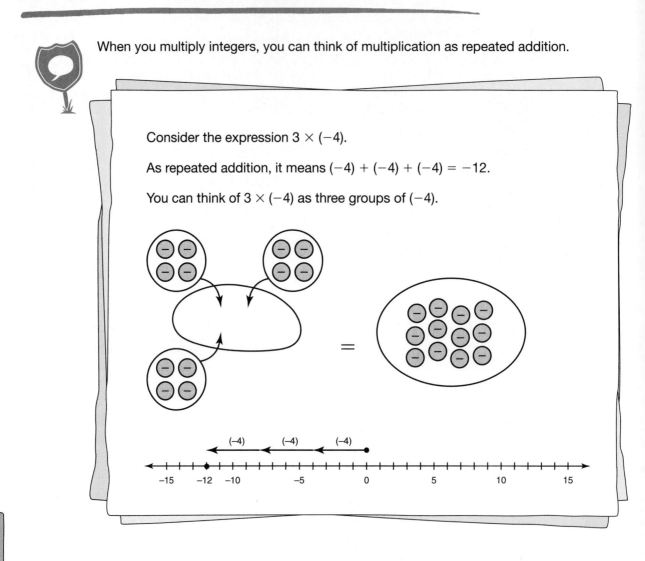

Here is another example: $4 \times (-3)$.

You can think of this as four sets of (-3), or $(-3) + (-3) + (-3) + (-3) = -12$.

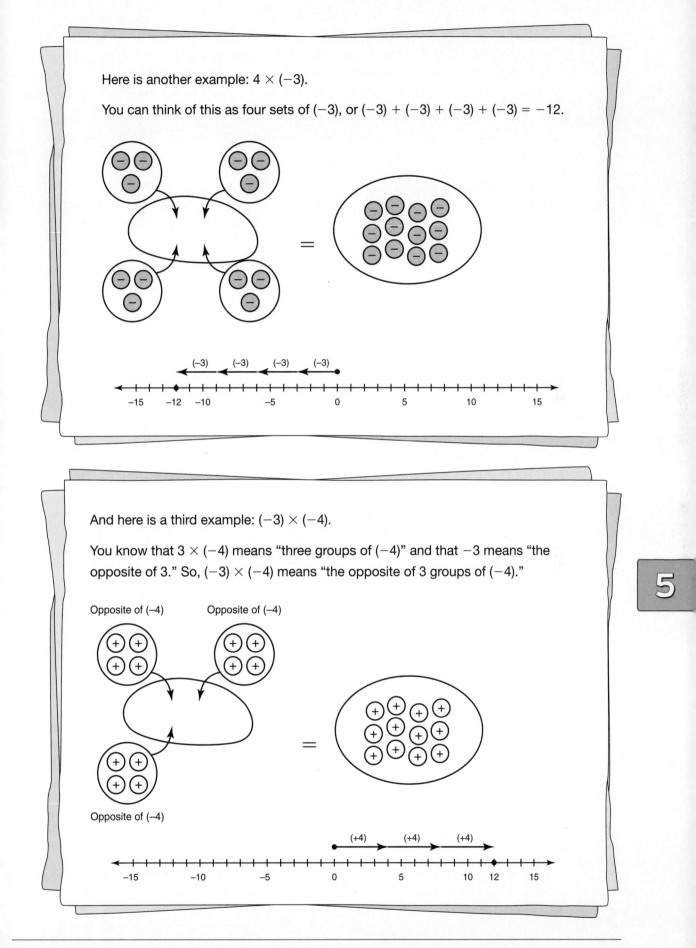

And here is a third example: $(-3) \times (-4)$.

You know that $3 \times (-4)$ means "three groups of (-4)" and that -3 means "the opposite of 3." So, $(-3) \times (-4)$ means "the opposite of 3 groups of (-4)."

1. Draw either a number line representation or a two-color counter model to determine each product. Describe the expression in words.

Use the examples if you need help.

a. 2×3

b. $2 \times (-3)$

c. $(-2) \times 3$

5

d. $(-2) \times (-3)$

2. Complete the table.

Expression	Description	Addition Sentence	Product
3×5	Three groups of 5	$5 + 5 + 5 = 15$	15
$(-3) \times 5$			
$3 \times (-5)$			
$(-3) \times (-5)$			

3. Analyze each number sentence.

$$4 \times 5 = 20$$
$$4 \times 4 = 16$$
$$4 \times 3 = 12$$
$$4 \times 2 = 8$$
$$4 \times 1 = 4$$
$$4 \times 0 = 0$$

What pattern do you notice in the products as the numbers multiplied by 4 decrease?

4. Determine each product. Describe the pattern.

    a. $4 \times (-1) = $ _____

    b. $4 \times (-2) = $ _____

    c. $4 \times (-3) = $ _____

5. Write the next three number sentences that extend this pattern.

$$-5 \times 5 = -25$$
$$-5 \times 4 = -20$$
$$-5 \times 3 = -15$$
$$-5 \times 2 = -10$$
$$-5 \times 1 = -5$$
$$-5 \times 0 = 0$$

6. How do these products change as the numbers multiplied by -5 decrease?

7. Determine each product.

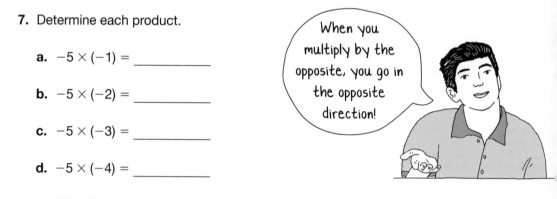

When you multiply by the opposite, you go in the opposite direction!

a. $-5 \times (-1) = $ _____

b. $-5 \times (-2) = $ _____

c. $-5 \times (-3) = $ _____

d. $-5 \times (-4) = $ _____

e. Write the next three number sentences that extend this pattern.

8. What is the sign of the product of two integers when:

a. they are both positive?　　　　b. they are both negative?

c. one is positive and one is negative?　　d. one is zero?

9. If you know that the product of two integers is negative, what can you say about the two integers? Give examples.

10. Describe an algorithm that will help you multiply any two integers.

11. Use your algorithm to simplify these expressions.

a. 6×5
    $6 \times (-5)$
    -6×5
    $-6 \times (-5)$

b. -8×7
    $-8 \times (-7)$
    $8 \times (-7)$
    8×7

c. $-3 \times 2 \times (-4)$
    $-3 \times (-2) \times (-4)$
    $3 \times (-2) \times 4$
    $-3 \times (-2) \times 4$
    $3 \times 2 \times (-4)$
    $-3 \times 2 \times 4$

12. Determine the single-digit integers that make each number sentence true.

a. _____ $\times$ _____ $= -42$

b. _____ $\times$ _____ $= 56$

c. _____ $\times (-9) = 63$

d. _____ $\times$ _____ $= -48$

13. Describe the sign of each product and how you know.

    a. the product of three negative integers

    b. the product of four negative integers

    c. the product of seven negative integers

    d. the product of ten negative integers

14. What is the sign of the product of any odd number of negative integers? Explain your reasoning.

15. What is the sign of the product of three positive integers and five negative integers? Explain your reasoning.

Problem 2   Division of Integers

When you studied division in elementary school, you learned that multiplication and division were inverse operations. For every multiplication fact, you can write a corresponding division fact.

The example shown is a fact family for 4, 5, and 20.

Fact Family

$5 \times 4 = 20$

$4 \times 5 = 20$

$20 \div 4 = 5$

$20 \div 5 = 4$

Similarly, you can write fact families for integer multiplication and division.

Examples:

$-7 \times 3 = -21$ $-8 \times (-4) = 32$

$3 \times (-7) = -21$ $-4 \times (-8) = 32$

$-21 \div (-7) = 3$ $32 \div (-8) = -4$

$-21 \div 3 = -7$ $32 \div (-4) = -8$

1. What pattern(s) do you notice in each fact family?

2. Write a fact family for −6, 8, and −48.

3. Fill in the unknown numbers to make each number sentence true.

a. $56 \div (-8) =$ _____

b. $28 \div (-4) =$ _____

c. $-63 \div$ _____ $= -7$

d. $24 \div$ _____ $= -8$

e. _____ $\div (-8) = -4$

f. $-105 \div$ _____ $= -5$

g. _____ $\div (-8) = 0$

h. $-26 \div$ _____ $= -1$

Talk the Talk

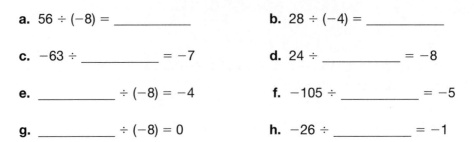

1. What is the sign of the quotient of two integers when

    a. both integers are positive?

    b. one integer is positive and one integer is negative?

    c. both integers are negative?

    d. the dividend is zero?

2. How do the answers to Question 1 compare to the answers to the same questions about the multiplication of two integers? Explain your reasoning.

Be prepared to share your solutions and methods.

WHAT'S MY PRODUCT OR QUOTIENT?

Multiplying and Dividing Rational Numbers

Learning Goals

In this lesson, you will:

▶ Multiply rational numbers.

▶ Divide rational numbers.

Look at these models. The top model shows $\frac{6}{8}$, and the bottom model shows $\frac{3}{8}$.

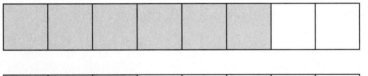

To determine $\frac{6}{8} \div \frac{3}{8}$, you can ask, "How many $\frac{3}{8}$ go into $\frac{6}{8}$?" You can see that the answer, or quotient, is just $6 \div 3$, or 2.

So, if you are dividing two fractions with the same denominators, can you always just divide the numerators to determine the quotient?

Try it out and see!

5

Problem 1   From Integer to Rational

In this lesson, you will apply what you learned about multiplying and dividing with integers to multiply and divide with rational numbers.

1. Consider this multiplication sentence:

$$-2\frac{1}{2} \times 3\frac{1}{5} = ?$$

    a. What is the rule for multiplying signed numbers?

When you convert a mixed number to an improper fraction, ignore the sign at first. Put it back in when you have finished converting.

    b. Use the rule to calculate the product. Show your work.

2. Calculate each product and show your work.

    a. $-5\frac{1}{3} \times -4\frac{1}{4} =$

    b. $5.02 \times -3.1 =$

It doesn't matter what numbers I have. The rules for the signs are the same.

    c. $2\frac{1}{6} \times -7\frac{1}{5} =$

    d. $-20.1 \times -19.02 =$

e. $-4\frac{1}{2} \times -3\frac{2}{3} =$

f. $-2\frac{1}{2} \times 3\frac{1}{5} \times -1\frac{2}{3} =$

Problem 2 And On to Dividing

1. Consider this division sentence:

$$-3\frac{1}{3} \div 2\frac{1}{2} = ?$$

a. What is the rule for dividing signed numbers?

b. Use the rule to calculate the quotient. Show your work.

2. Calculate each quotient and show your work.

a. $-2\frac{1}{8} \div -4\frac{1}{4} =$

b. $4.03 \div -3.1 =$

c. $-\frac{5}{6} \div -2\frac{1}{7} =$

d. $-20.582 \div -4.1 =$

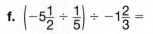

e. $-11 \div \frac{2}{3} =$

f. $\left(-5\frac{1}{2} \div \frac{1}{5}\right) \div -1\frac{2}{3} =$

Talk the Talk

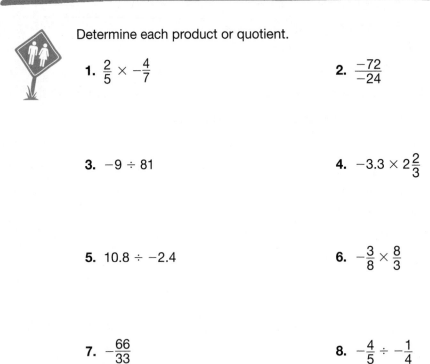

Determine each product or quotient.

1. $\frac{2}{5} \times -\frac{4}{7}$

2. $\frac{-72}{-24}$

3. $-9 \div 81$

4. $-3.3 \times 2\frac{2}{3}$

5. $10.8 \div -2.4$

6. $-\frac{3}{8} \times \frac{8}{3}$

7. $-\frac{66}{33}$

8. $-\frac{4}{5} \div -\frac{1}{4}$

Be prepared to share your solutions and methods.

5.3 PROPERTIES SCHMOPERTIES

Simplifying Arithmetic Expressions with Rational Numbers

Learning Goal

In this lesson, you will:

▶ Simply arithmetic expressions using the number properties and the order of operations.

Suppose you didn't know that a negative times a negative is equal to a positive. How could you prove it? One way is to use properties—in this case, the Zero Property and the Distributive Property.

The Zero Property tells us that any number times 0 is equal to 0, and the Distributive Property tells us that something like $4 \times (2 + 3)$ is equal to $(4 \times 2) + (4 \times 3)$. We want these properties to be true for negative numbers too.

So, start with this:

$$-5 \times 0 = 0$$

That's the Zero Property. We want that to be true. Now, let's replace the first 0 with an expression that equals 0:

$$-5 \times (5 + -5) = 0$$

Using the Distributive Property, we can rewrite that as

$$(-5 \times 5) + (-5 \times -5) = 0$$

$$\downarrow \qquad\qquad \downarrow$$

$$-25 \quad + \quad ? \quad = 0$$

For the properties to be true, -5×-5 has to equal *positive* 25! What other number properties do you remember learning about?

> Hey, did you hear what Zero said to Eight? "Nice belt."

Problem 1 Properties and Operations

1. For each equation, identify the number property or operation used.

Equation	Number Property/Operation
a. $3\frac{1}{2} + 2\frac{1}{4} = 5\frac{3}{4}$	
b. $-3\frac{1}{2} + 2\frac{1}{4} = 2\frac{1}{4} + \left(-3\frac{1}{2}\right)$	
c. $\left(3\frac{1}{2} \times 2\frac{1}{4}\right) \times 5\frac{3}{4} = 3\frac{1}{2} \times \left(2\frac{1}{4} \times 5\frac{3}{4}\right)$	
d. $-3\frac{1}{2} \div 2\frac{1}{4} = -1\frac{5}{9}$	
e. $-3\frac{1}{2} + \left(-2\frac{1}{4} + 5\frac{3}{4}\right) = \left(-3\frac{1}{2} + \left(-2\frac{1}{4}\right)\right) + 5\frac{3}{4}$	
f. $2\frac{1}{4} \times 5\frac{3}{5} = 12\frac{3}{5}$	
g. $-3\frac{1}{2} - 2\frac{1}{4} = -5\frac{3}{4}$	
h. $\left(-3\frac{1}{2} + 2\frac{1}{4}\right)1\frac{5}{9} = \left(-3\frac{1}{2}\right)1\frac{5}{9} + \left(2\frac{1}{4}\right)1\frac{5}{9}$	
i. $\dfrac{-3\frac{1}{2}-2\frac{1}{4}}{4} = \dfrac{-3\frac{1}{2}}{4} - \dfrac{2\frac{1}{4}}{4}$	
j. $(-7.02)(-3.42) = (-3.42)(-7.02)$	

2. For each step of the simplification of the expression, identify the operation or property applied.

Number Property/Operation

a. $3\frac{1}{2} + 5\frac{3}{4} + 2\frac{1}{2} =$

$3\frac{1}{2} + 2\frac{1}{2} + 5\frac{3}{4} =$ _____

$6 + 5\frac{3}{4} =$ _____

$11\frac{3}{4}$ _____

b. $\left(-3\frac{1}{5} + 5\frac{3}{4}\right) + 3\frac{1}{4} =$

$-3\frac{1}{5} + \left(5\frac{3}{4} + 3\frac{1}{4}\right) =$ _____

$-3\frac{1}{5} + 9 =$ _____

$5\frac{4}{5}$ _____

c. $-3\frac{1}{3}\left(-3\frac{1}{5} + 5\frac{3}{5}\right) =$

$-3\frac{1}{3}\left(2\frac{2}{5}\right) =$ _____

-8 _____

d. $-3\frac{1}{3}\left(-3\frac{1}{5} + 5\frac{3}{5}\right) =$

$\left(-3\frac{1}{3}\right)\left(-3\frac{1}{5}\right) + \left(-3\frac{1}{3}\right)\left(+5\frac{3}{5}\right) =$ _____

$\frac{32}{3} + -\frac{56}{3} =$ _____

-8 _____

3. Supply the next step in each simplification using the operation or property provided.

	Number Property/Operation
a. $3\frac{3}{4} + \left(-5\frac{2}{5}\right) + 7\frac{1}{4} =$	
	Commutative Property of Addition
	Addition
	Addition
b. $\left(5\frac{1}{6} + -3\frac{3}{4}\right) + -3\frac{1}{4} =$	
	Associative Property of Addition
	Addition
	Addition
c. $-5.2(-93.7 + 3.7) =$	
	Addition
	Multiplication

d. $-5.1(70 + 3) =$	
	Distributive Property of Multiplication over Addition
	Multiplication
	Addition
e. $\left(-3\frac{1}{4}\right)\left(5\frac{1}{6}\right) + \left(-3\frac{1}{4}\right)\left(2\frac{5}{6}\right) =$	
	Distributive Property of Multiplication over Addition
	Addition
	Multiplication

Problem 2   On Your Own

Simplify each expression step by step, listing the property or operation(s) used.

1. $5\left(-3\frac{1}{4}\right) + 5\left(-6\frac{3}{4}\right) =$

Number Property/Operation

2. $\left(-3\dfrac{1}{4} - 2\dfrac{1}{5}\right) + \left(-6\dfrac{3}{5}\right) =$

Number Property/Operation

3. $\dfrac{7}{8} \times \left(-\dfrac{4}{5}\right) \times \left(-\dfrac{8}{7}\right) =$

Number Property/Operation

4. $\dfrac{\dfrac{8}{9} + -\dfrac{4}{5}}{4} =$

Number Property/Operation

5. $-3.1(90.7 - (-4.3)) =$

Number Property/Operation

6. $(-11.4)(6.4) + (-11.4)(-12.4) =$

Number Property/Operation

Be prepared to share your solutions and methods.

BUILDING A WRIGHT BROTHERS' FLYER
Evaluating Expressions with Rational Numbers

5.4

Learning Goals

In this lesson, you will:

▶ Model a situation with an expression using rational numbers.

▶ Evaluate rational expressions.

On December 17, 1903, two brothers—Orville and Wilbur Wright—became the first two people to make a controlled flight in a powered plane. They made four flights that day, the longest covering only 852 feet and lasting just 59 seconds.

Human flight progressed amazingly quickly after those first flights. In the year before Orville died, Chuck Yeager had already piloted the first flight that broke the sound barrier!

5

Problem 1   Building a Wright Brothers' Flyer

In order to build a balsa wood model of the Wright brothers' plane, you would need to cut long lengths of wood spindles into shorter lengths for the wing stays, the vertical poles that support and connect the two wings. Each stay for the main wings of the model needs to be cut $3\frac{1}{4}$ inches long.

Show your work and explain your reasoning.

1. If the wood spindles are each 10 inches long, how many stays could you cut from one spindle?

2. How many inches of the spindle would be left over?

3. If the wood spindles are each 12 inches long, how many stays could you cut from one spindle?

4. How many inches of the spindle would be left over?

You also need to cut vertical stays for the smaller wing that are each $1\frac{5}{8}$ inches long.

5. If the wood spindles are each 10 inches long, how many of these stays could you cut from one spindle?

5

6. How many inches of the spindle would be left over?

7. If the wood spindles are each 12 inches long, how many stays could you cut from one spindle?

5

8. How many inches of the spindle would be left over?

9. Which length of spindle should be used to cut each of the different stays so that there is the least amount wasted?

5

Problem 2   Building a Wright Brothers' Flyer Redux

There are longer spindles that measure 36 inches.

1. How much of a 36-inch-long spindle would be left over if you cut one of the stays from it?

Remember, a stay is $3\frac{1}{4}$ inch.

Show your work and explain your reasoning.

2. How much of this spindle would be left over if you cut two of the stays from it?

3. Define variables for the number of $3\frac{1}{4}$ inch stays and the amount of the 36-inch-long spindle that is left over.

4. Write an equation for the relationship between these variables.

5. Use your equation to calculate the amount of the spindle left over after cutting 10 stays.

6. Use your equation to calculate the amount of the spindle left over after cutting 13 stays.

Problem 3   Evaluating Expressions

1. Evaluate the expression $-12\frac{1}{2}-\left(3\frac{1}{3}\right)v$ for:

   a. $v = -5$

   To evaluate an expression, substitute the values for the variables and then perform the operations.

   b. $v = 3$

   c. $v = -\frac{6}{7}$

   d. $v = 2\frac{2}{5}$

5

2. Evaluate the expression $\left(-1\frac{1}{4}\right)x - 8\frac{7}{8}$ for:

   a. $x = -\frac{2}{5}$

   b. $x = -2$

 Be prepared to share your solutions and methods.

5

5

5.5 REPEAT OR NOT? THAT IS THE QUESTION!

Exact Decimal Representations of Fractions

Learning Goals

In this lesson, you will:

▶ Use decimals and fractions to evaluate arithmetic expressions.

▶ Convert fractions to decimals.

▶ Represent fractions as repeating decimals.

Key Terms

▶ terminating decimals

▶ non-terminating decimals

▶ repeating decimals

▶ non-repeating decimals

▶ bar notation

Sometimes calculating an exact answer is very important. For example, making sure that all the parts of an airplane fit exactly is very important to keep the plane in the air. Can you think of other examples where very exact answers are necessary?

5

Problem 1   Not More Homework!

Jayme was complaining to her brother about having to do homework problems with fractions like this:

$$2\frac{1}{2} + \left(-3\frac{3}{4}\right) + 5\frac{2}{5} = ?$$

Jayme said, "I have to find the least common denominator, convert the fractions to equivalent fractions with the least common denominator, and then calculate the answer!"

Her brother said, "Whoa! Why don't you just use decimals?"

1. Calculate the answer using Jayme's method.

2. Convert each mixed number to a decimal and calculate the sum.

3. In this case, which method do you think works best?

Jayme said: "That's okay for that problem, but what about this next one?"

$$5\frac{1}{3} + \left(-4\frac{1}{6}\right) + \left(-2\frac{1}{2}\right) =$$

4. Calculate the answer using Jayme's method.

5. Will Jayme's brother's method work for the second problem? Why or why not?

Problem 2   Analyzing Decimals

1. Convert each fraction to a decimal.

    a. $\dfrac{11}{25}$ **b.** $\dfrac{1}{6}$

    c. $\dfrac{27}{50}$ **d.** $\dfrac{15}{64}$

e. $\frac{7}{9}$

f. $\frac{5}{11}$

g. $\frac{7}{22}$

h. $\frac{5}{8}$

i. $\frac{3}{7}$

j. $\frac{39}{60}$

Decimals can be classified in four different ways:

- *terminating,*
- *non-terminating,*
- *repeating,*
- *or non-repeating.*

A **terminating decimal** has a finite number of digits,
meaning that the decimal will end, or terminate.

A **non-terminating** decimal is a decimal that continues without end.

A **repeating decimal** is a decimal in which a digit, or a group of digits,
repeat(s) without end.

A **non-repeating decimal** neither terminates nor repeats.

Bar notation is used for repeating decimals. Consider the example
shown. The sequence 142857 repeats. The numbers that lie underneath
the bar are those numbers that repeat.

$$\frac{1}{7} = 0.142857142857... = 0.\overline{142857}$$

> The bar is called a vinculum.

2. Classify each decimal in Question 1, parts (a) through (j) as terminating, non-terminating, repeating, or non-repeating. If the decimal repeats, rewrite it using bar notation.

3. Can all fractions be represented as either terminating or repeating decimals? Write some examples to explain your answer.

4. Complete the graphic organizer.
   - Describe each decimal in words.
   - Show examples.

Be prepared to share your solutions and methods.

TERMINATING

NON-TERMINATING

DECIMALS

π is a well-known non-repeating decimal. You will learn more when you study circles later in this course.

5

REPEATING

NON-REPEATING

5.1   Multiplying Integers

When multiplying integers, multiplication can be thought of as repeated addition. Two-color counter models and number lines can be used to represent multiplication of integers.

Example

Consider the expression $3 \times (-3)$. As repeated addition, it means $(-3) + (-3) + (-3) = -9$. The expression $3 \times (-3)$ can be thought of as three groups of (-3).

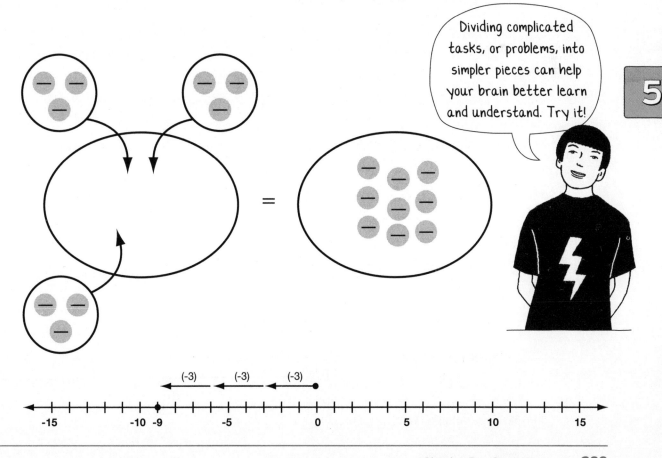

Dividing complicated tasks, or problems, into simpler pieces can help your brain better learn and understand. Try it!

5

5.1 Dividing Integers

Multiplication and division are inverse operations. For every multiplication fact, there is a corresponding division fact.

Example

This is a fact family for 3, 8, and 24.

$$3 \times 8 = 24$$
$$8 \times 3 = 24$$
$$24 \div 8 = 3$$
$$24 \div 8 = 8$$

5.1 Determining the Sign of a Product or Quotient

The sign of a product or quotient of two integers depends on the signs of the two integers being multiplied or divided. The product or quotient will be positive when both integers have the same sign. The product or quotient will be negative when one integer is positive and the other is negative.

Example

Notice the sign of each product or quotient.

$$5 \times 7 = 35 \qquad\qquad 35 \div 5 = 7$$
$$-5 \times 7 = -35 \qquad\qquad -35 \div 5 = -7$$
$$-5 \times -7 = -35 \qquad\qquad 35 \div -5 = -7$$
$$-5 \times -7 = 35 \qquad\qquad -35 \div -5 = 7$$

5.2 Multiplying and Dividing Rational Numbers

The rules used to determine the sign of a product or quotient of two integers also apply when multiplying and dividing rational numbers.

Example

The product or quotient of each are shown following the rules for determining the sign for each.

$$3\frac{1}{4} \times 5\frac{1}{3} = \frac{13}{4} \times \frac{\overset{4}{\cancel{16}}}{3} = \frac{13}{1} \times \frac{4}{3} = \frac{52}{3} = 17\frac{1}{3}$$

$$12.1 \times -5.6 = -67.76$$

$$-6\frac{3}{4} \div 1\frac{7}{8} = -\frac{27}{4} \div \frac{15}{8} = -\frac{\overset{9}{\cancel{27}}}{\underset{1}{\cancel{4}}} \times \frac{\overset{2}{\cancel{8}}}{\underset{5}{\cancel{15}}} = -\frac{9}{1} \times \frac{2}{5} = -\frac{18}{5} = -3\frac{3}{5}$$

$$-58.75 \div -6.25 = 9.40$$

5.3 Simplifying Expressions with Rational Numbers

When simplifying arithmetic expressions involving rational numbers, it is often helpful to identify and use the number properties or operations that make the simplification easier.

Example

The steps for simplifying the expression are shown.

$$2\frac{3}{4}\left(5\frac{1}{2}\right) + 2\frac{3}{4}\left(2\frac{1}{2}\right) = \qquad \text{Number Property/Operation}$$

$$2\frac{3}{4}\left(5\frac{1}{2} + 2\frac{1}{2}\right) = \qquad \text{Distributive Property of Multiplication over Addition}$$

$$2\frac{3}{4}(8) = \qquad \text{Addition}$$

$$22 \qquad \text{Multiplication}$$

5.4 Evaluating Expressions with Rational Numbers

To evaluate an expression containing variables, substitute the values for the variables and then perform the necessary operations.

Example

The evaluation of the expression $8\frac{3}{4}\left(m - 6\frac{1}{5}\right)$ when $m = 7$ is shown.

$$8\frac{3}{4}\left(7 - 6\frac{1}{5}\right) = 8\frac{3}{4}\left(\frac{4}{5}\right)$$

$$= \frac{35}{4}\left(\frac{4}{5}\right)$$

$$= \frac{7}{1}\left(\frac{1}{1}\right)$$

$$= 7$$

5

5.5 Representing Fractions as Decimals

To convert a fraction to a decimal, divide the numerator of the fraction by the denominator. A terminating decimal has a finite number of digits, meaning that the decimal will end or terminate. A non-terminating decimal is a decimal that continues without end. A repeating decimal is a decimal in which a digit, or a group of digits, repeats without end. When writing a repeating decimal, bar notation is used to indicate the digits that repeat. A non-repeating decimal neither terminates nor repeats.

Example

The fraction $\frac{3}{4}$ is a terminating decimal. The decimal equivalent of $\frac{3}{4}$ is 0.75.

The fraction $\frac{2}{11}$ is a non-terminating, repeating decimal. The decimal equivalent of $\frac{2}{11}$ is 0.181818... Using bar notation, $\frac{2}{11}$ is written as $0.\overline{18}$.

6 NUMERICAL AND ALGEBRAIC EXPRESSIONS AND EQUATIONS

Sometimes it's hard to tell how a person is feeling when you're not talking to them face to face. People use emoticons in emails and chat messages to show different facial expressions. Each expression shows a different kind of emotion. But you probably already knew that. ;)

6

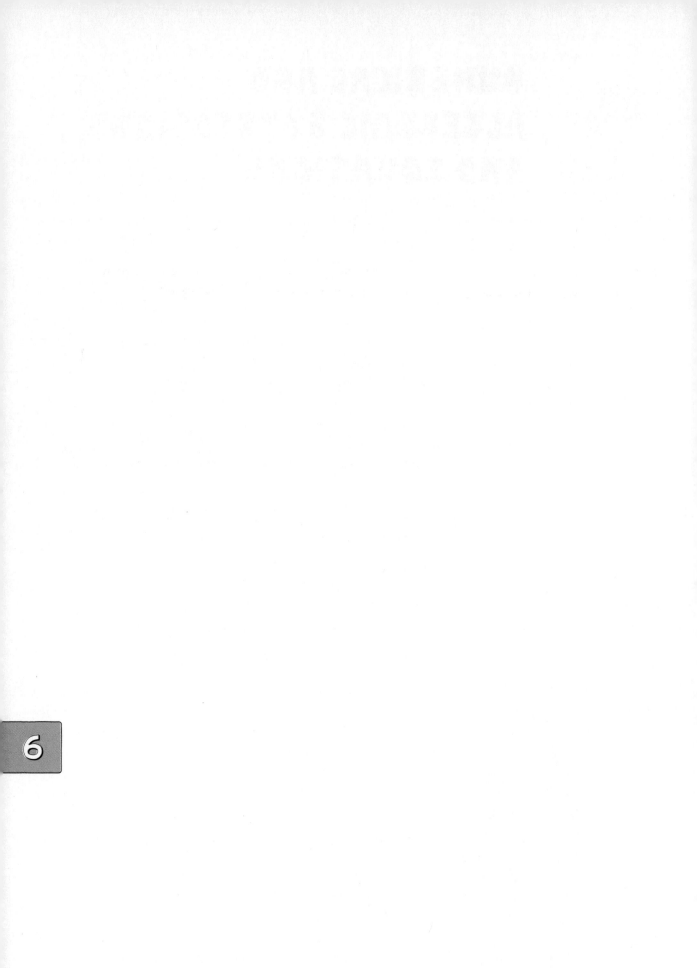

6

6.1 WHAT'S IT REALLY SAYING?
Evaluating Algebraic Expressions

Learning Goal

In this lesson, you will:

▶ Evaluate algebraic expressions.

Key Terms

▶ variable
▶ algebraic expression
▶ evaluate an algebraic expression

Do you have all your ducks in a row? That's just a drop in the bucket! That's a piece of cake!

What do each of these statements have in common? Well, they are all idioms. Idioms are expressions that have meanings which are completely different from their literal meanings. For example, the "ducks in a row" idiom refers to asking if someone is organized and ready to start a task. A person who uses this idiom is not literally asking if you have ducks that are all lined up.

For people just learning a language, idioms can be very challenging to understand. Usually if someone struggles with an idiom's meaning, a person will say "that's just an expression," and explain its meaning in a different way. Can you think of other idioms? What does your idiom mean?

6

Problem 1 Game Day Special

You volunteer to help out in the concession stand at your middle-school football game. You must create a poster to display the Game Day Special: a hot dog, a bag of chips, and a drink for $3.75.

1. Complete the poster by multiplying the number of specials by the cost of the special.

Game Day Special 1 hot dog, 1 bag of chips, and a drink for $3.75	
Number of Specials	Cost
1 2 3 4 5 6	

In algebra, a **variable** is a letter or symbol that is used to represent a quantity. An **algebraic expression** is a mathematical phrase that has at least one variable, and it can contain numbers and operation symbols.

Whenever you perform the same mathematical process over and over again, an algebraic expression is often used to represent the situation.

2. What algebraic expression did you use to represent the total cost on your poster? Let *s* represent the number of Game Day Specials.

3. The cheerleading coach wants to purchase a Game Day Special for every student on the squad. Use your algebraic expression to calculate the total cost of purchasing 18 Game Day Specials.

Problem 2   Planning a Graduation Party

Your aunt is planning to host your cousin's high school graduation party at Lattanzi's Restaurant and Reception Hall. Lattanzi's has a flyer that describes the Deluxe Graduation Reception.

> **Deluxe Graduation Reception**
>
> Includes:
> One salad (chef or Caesar)
> One entree (chicken, beef, or seafood)
> Two side dishes
> One dessert
>
> Fee:
> $105 for the reception hall plus $40 per guest

1. Write an algebraic expression to determine the cost of the graduation party. Let g represent the number of guests attending the party.

> So, an equation has an equals sign. An expression does not.

2. Determine the cost of the party for each number of attendees. Show your work.

   a. 8 guests attend

   b. 10 guests attend

   c. 12 guests attend

Problem 3   Evaluating Expressions

In Problems 1 and 2, you worked with two expressions, 3.75s and (105 + 40g). You evaluated those expressions for different values of the variable. To **evaluate an algebraic expression**, you replace each variable in the expression with a number or numerical expression and then perform all possible mathematical operations.

1. Evaluate each algebraic expression.

   a. $x - 7$
   - for $x = -8$
   - for $x = -11$
   - for $x = 16$

   b. $-6y$
   - for $y = -3$
   - for $y = 0$
   - for $y = 7$

   c. $3b - 5$
   - for $b = -2$
   - for $b = 3$
   - for $b = 9$

   d. $-1.6 + 5.3n$
   - for $n = -5$
   - for $n = 0$
   - for $n = 4$

Use parentheses to show multiplication like -6(-3).

6

Sometimes, it is more convenient to use a table to record the results when evaluating the same expression with multiple values.

2. Complete each table.

a.

h	−2h − 7
2	
−1	
8	
−7	

b.

a	−12	−10	−4	0
$\frac{a}{4} + 6$				

c.

x	x² − 5
1	
3	
6	
−2	

d.

y	−5	−1	0	15
$-\frac{1}{5}y + 3\frac{2}{5}$				

Problem 4   Evaluating Algebraic Expressions Using Given Values

1. Evaluate each algebraic expression for $x = 2$, -3, 0.5, and $-2\frac{1}{3}$.

    a. $-3x$

    b. $5x + 10$

    c. $6 - 3x$

> Using tables may help you evaluate these expressions.

    d. $8x + 75$

2. Evaluate each algebraic expression for $x = -7$, 5, 1.5, and $-1\frac{1}{6}$.

a. $5x$

b. $2x + 3x$

c. $8x - 3x$

I'm noticing something similar about all of these expressions. What is it?

3. Evaluate each algebraic expression for $x = 23.76$ and $-21\frac{5}{6}$.

a. $2.67x - 31.85$

b. $11\frac{3}{4}x + 56\frac{3}{8}$

Talk the Talk

1. Describe your basic strategy for evaluating any algebraic expression.

2. How are tables helpful when evaluating expressions?

Be prepared to share your solutions and methods.

Learning Goals

In this lesson, you will:

▶ Write and use the distributive properties.

▶ Use distributive properties to simplify expressions.

Key Terms

▶ Distributive Property of Multiplication over Addition

▶ Distributive Property of Multiplication over Subtraction

▶ Distributive Property of Division over Addition

▶ Distributive Property of Division over Subtraction

It once started out with camping out the night before the sale. Then, it evolved to handing out wrist bands to prevent camping out. Now, it's all about the Internet. What do these three activities have in common?

For concerts, movie premieres, and highly-anticipated sporting events, the distribution and sale of tickets have changed with computer technology. Generally, hopeful ticket buyers log into a Web site and hope to get a chance to buy tickets. What are other ways to distribute tickets? What are other things that routinely get distributed to people?

6

Problem 1   Fastest Math in the Wild West

Dominique and Sarah are checking each other's math homework. Sarah tells Dominique that she has a quick and easy way to multiply a one-digit number by any other number in her head. Dominique decides to test Sarah by asking her to multiply 7 by 230.

1. Calculate the product 7 × 230.

Sarah is able to correctly multiply 7 by 230 in her head. She explains her method to Dominique.

> ## Sarah
> ### 230 × 7
> First, break 230 into the sum of 200 and 30. Then, multiply 7 × 200 to get a product of 1400 and 7 × 30 to get a product of 210. Finally, add 1400 and 210 together to get 1610.

2. Write an expression that shows the mathematical steps Sarah performed to calculate the product.

Dominique makes the connection between Sarah's quick mental calculation and calculating the area of a rectangle. She draws the models shown to represent Sarah's thinking in a different way.

> ## Dominique
> Calculating 230 × 7 is the same as determining the area of a rectangle by multiplying the length by the width.
>
> But I can also divide the rectangle into two smaller rectangles and calculate the area of each rectangle. I can then add the two areas to get the total.

6

3. First, use Dominique's method and sketch a model for each. Then, write an expression that shows Sarah's method and calculate.

   a. 9(48)

   b. 6(73)

   c. 4(460)

> I can draw at least two different models to determine 4(460).

Sarah's and Dominique's methods are both examples of the **Distributive Property of Multiplication over Addition,** which states that if a, b, and c are any real numbers, then
$a \cdot (b + c) = a \cdot b + a \cdot c$.

Including the Distributive Property of Multiplication over Addition, there are a total of *four* different forms of the Distributive Property. Another Distributive Property is the **Distributive Property of Multiplication over Subtraction,** which states that if a, b, and c are any real numbers, then $a \cdot (b - c) = a \cdot b - a \cdot c$.

The Distributive Property also holds true for division over addition and division over subtraction as well.

The **Distributive Property of Division over Addition** states that if a, b, and c are real numbers and $c \neq 0$, then $\frac{a + b}{c} = \frac{a}{c} + \frac{b}{c}$.

The **Distributive Property of Division over Subtraction** states that if a, b, and c are real numbers and $c \neq 0$, then $\frac{a - b}{c} = \frac{a}{c} - \frac{b}{c}$.

4. Draw a model for each expression, and then simplify.

    a. $6(x + 9)$ **b.** $7(2b - 5)$

    c. $-2(4a + 1)$ **d.** $\frac{x + 15}{5}$

> Dividing by 5 is the same as multiplying by what number?

5. Use one of the Distributive Properties to rewrite each expression in an equivalent form.

    a. $3y(4y + 2)$ **b.** $12(x + 3)$

    c. $-4a(3b - 5)$ **d.** $-7y(2y - 3x + 9)$

    e. $\frac{6m + 12}{-2}$ **f.** $\frac{22 - 4x}{2}$

Problem 2   Simplifying and Evaluating

1. Simplify each expression. Show your work.

    a. $-6(3x + (-4y))$

    b. $-4(-3x - 8) - 34$

    c. $\dfrac{-7.2 - 6.4x}{-0.8}$

    d. $\left(-2\frac{1}{2}\right)\left(3\frac{1}{4}\right) + \left(-2\frac{1}{2}\right)\left(-2\frac{1}{4}\right)$

    e. $\dfrac{\left(-7\frac{1}{2}\right) + 5y}{2\frac{1}{2}}$

6

2. Evaluate each expression for the given value. Then, use properties to simplify the original expression. Finally, evaluate the simplified expression.

    a. $2x(-3x + 7)$ for $x = -1\frac{2}{3}$

    b. $\dfrac{4.2x - 7}{1.4}$ for $x = 1.26$

    c. Which form—simplified or not simplified—did you prefer to evaluate? Why?

 Be prepared to share your solutions and methods.

6.3 REVERSE DISTRIBUTION
Factoring Algebraic Expressions

Learning Goals

In this lesson, you will:

▶ Use the distributive properties to factor expressions.

▶ Combine like terms to simplify expressions.

Key Terms

▶ factor
▶ common factor
▶ greatest common factor (GCF)
▶ coefficient
▶ like terms
▶ combining like terms

Many beginning drivers have difficulty with driving in reverse. They think that they must turn the wheel in the opposite direction of where they want the back end to go. But actually, the *reverse*, is true. To turn the back end of the car to the left, turn the steering wheel to the left. To turn the back end to the right, turn the wheel to the right.

Even after mastering reversing, most people would have difficulty driving that way all the time. But not Rajagopal Kawendar. In 2010, Kawendar set a world record for driving in reverse—over 600 miles at about 40 miles per hour!

6

Problem 1   Factoring

You can use the Distributive Property in reverse. Consider the expression:

$$7(26) + 7(14)$$

Since both 26 and 14 are being multiplied by the same number, 7, the Distributive Property says you can add the multiplicands together first, and then multiply their sum by 7 just once.

$$7(26) + 7(14) = 7(26 + 14)$$

You have *factored* the original expression. To **factor** an expression means to rewrite the expression as a product of factors.

The number 7 is a *common factor* of both 7(26) and 7(14). A **common factor** is a number or an algebraic expression that is a factor of two or more numbers or algebraic expressions.

1. Factor each expression using a Distributive Property.

    a. $4(33) - 4(28)$ **b.** $16(17) + 16(13)$

The Distributive Properties can also be used in reverse to factor algebraic expressions. For example, the expression $3x + 15$ can be written as $3(x) + 3(5)$, or $3(x + 5)$. The factor, 3, is the *greatest common factor* to both terms. The **greatest common factor** (GCF) is the largest factor that two or more numbers or terms have in common.

When factoring algebraic expressions, you can factor out the greatest common factor from all the terms.

Consider the expression $12x + 42$. The greatest common factor of $12x$ and 42 is 6. Therefore, you can rewrite the expression as $6(2x + 7)$.

It is important to pay attention to negative numbers. When factoring an expression that contains a negative leading *coefficient*, or first term, it is preferred to factor out the negative sign. A **coefficient** is the number that is multiplied by a variable in an algebraic expression.

6

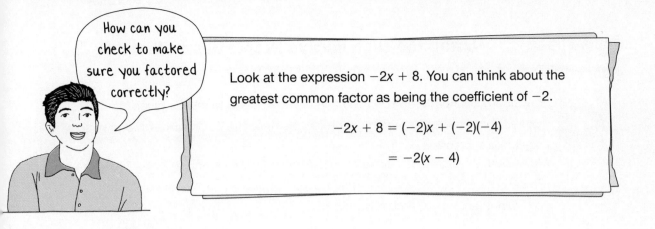

How can you check to make sure you factored correctly?

Look at the expression $-2x + 8$. You can think about the greatest common factor as being the coefficient of -2.

$$-2x + 8 = (-2)x + (-2)(-4)$$
$$= -2(x - 4)$$

2. Rewrite each expression by factoring out the greatest common factor.

a. $7x + 14$

b. $9x - 27$

c. $10y - 25$

d. $8n + 28$

e. $3x^2 - 21x$

f. $24a^2 + 18a$

g. $15mn - 35n$

h. $-3x - 27$

i. $-6x + 30$

So, when you factor out a negative number all the signs will change.

6

Problem 2   Using the Distributive Properties to Simplify

So far, the Distributive Properties have provided ways to rewrite given algebraic expressions in equivalent forms. You can also use the Distributive Properties to simplify algebraic expressions.

Consider the algebraic expression $5x + 11x$.

1. What factors do the terms have in common?

2. Rewrite $5x + 11x$ using the Distributive Property.

3. Simplify your expression.

The terms $5x$ and $11x$ are called **like terms**, meaning that their variable portions are the same. When you add $5x$ and $11x$ together, you are **combining like terms**.

4. Simplify each expression by combining like terms.

   a. $5ab + 22ab$ b. $32x^2 - 44x^2$

5. Simplify each algebraic expression by combining like terms. If the expression is already simplified, state how you know.

   a. $6x + 9x$ b. $-13y - 34y$

   c. $14mn - 19mn$ d. $8mn - 5m$

   e. $6x^2 + 12x^2 - 7x^2$ f. $6x^2 + 12x^2 - 7x$

   g. $-3z - 8z - 7$ h. $5x + 5y$

1. Factor each expression.

   a. $-24x + 16y =$

   b. $-4.4 - 1.21z =$

   c. $-27x - 33 =$

   d. $-2x - 9y =$

   e. $4x + (-5xy) - 3x =$

2. Evaluate each expression for the given value. Then factor the expression and evaluate the factored expression for the given value.

   a. $-4x + 16$ for $x = 2\frac{1}{2}$ **b.** $30x - 140$ for $x = 5.63$

   c. Which form—simplified or not simplified—did you prefer to evaluate? Why?

Problem 4 Combining Like Terms and Evaluating

1. Simplify each expression by combining like terms.

   a. $30x - 140 - 23x =$

   b. $-5(-2x - 13) - 7x =$

   c. $-4x - 5(2x - y) - 3y =$

   d. $7.6x - 3.2(3.1x - 2.4) =$

   e. $3\frac{2}{3}x - 1\frac{3}{4}\left(4x - 2\frac{1}{7}\right) =$

2. Evaluate each expression for the given value. Then combine the like terms in each expression and evaluate the simplified expression for the given value.

   a. $-5x - 12 + 3x$ for $x = 2.4$

b. $-2\frac{1}{2}x - 1\frac{2}{3}\left(6x + 2\frac{2}{5}\right)$ for $x = -1\frac{1}{4}$

Why doesn't it change the answer when I simplify first?

6

Be prepared to share your solutions and methods.

ARE THEY THE SAME OR DIFFERENT?
Verifying That Expressions Are Equivalent

Learning Goals

In this lesson, you will:

▶ Simplify algebraic expressions.

▶ Verify that algebraic expressions are equivalent by graphing, simplifying, and evaluating expressions.

Bart and Lisa are competing to see who can get the highest grades. But they are in different classes. In the first week, Lisa took a quiz and got 9 out of 10 correct for a 90%. Bart took a test and got 70 out of 100 for a 70%. Looks like Lisa won the first week!

The next week, Lisa took a test and got 35 out of 100 correct for a 35%. Bart took a quiz and got 2 out of 10 correct for a 20%. Lisa won the second week also!

Over the two weeks, it looks like Lisa was the winner. But look at the total number of questions and the total each of them got correct: Lisa answered a total of 110 questions and got a total of 34 correct for about a 31%. Bart answered a total of 110 questions and got a total of 72 correct for a 65%! Is Bart the real winner?

This surprising result is known as Simpson's Paradox. Can you see how it works?

6

Problem 1 Are They Equivalent?

Consider this equation:

$$-4(3.2x - 5.4) = 12.8x + 21.6$$

Keegan says that to tell if the expressions in an equation are equivalent (not just equal), you just need to evaluate each expression for the same value of x.

So, *equivalent* is not the same as *equal*? What's the difference?

1. Evaluate the expression on each side of the equals sign for $x = 2$.

2. Are these expressions equivalent? Explain your reasoning.

Jasmine

Keegan's method can prove that two expressions are not equivalent, but it can't prove that they are equivalent.

3. Explain why Jasmine is correct. Provide an example of two expressions that verify your answer.

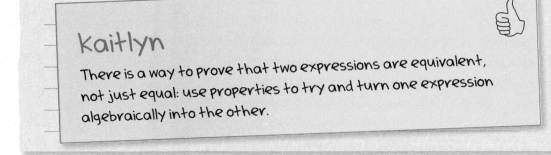

Kaitlyn

There is a way to prove that two expressions are equivalent, not just equal: use properties to try and turn one expression algebraically into the other.

4. Reconsider again the equation $-4(3.2x - 5.4) = 12.8x + 21.6$. Use the distributive properties to simplify the left side and to factor the right side to try to determine if these expressions are equivalent.

5. Are the expressions equivalent? Explain your reasoning.

6. Will Kaitlyn's method always work? Explain your reasoning.

Jason

There is another method to verify the equivalence of expressions: graph them, and if their graphs are the same, then the expressions must be equivalent.

7. Graph each expression on your graphics calculator or other graphing technology. Sketch the graphs.

If you are using your graphing calculator, don't forget to set your bounds.

8. Are the expressions equivalent? Explain your reasoning.

9. Which method is more efficient for this problem? Explain your reasoning.

Problem 2   Are These Equivalent?

Determine whether the expressions are equivalent using the specified method.

1. $3.1(-2.3x - 8.4) + 3.5x = -3.63x + (-26.04)$ by evaluating for $x = 1$.

> Remember, evaluating can only prove that two expressions are not equivalent.

2. $3\frac{1}{3}\left(-3x - 2\frac{1}{10}\right) + 4\frac{3}{4} = -2\frac{1}{2}\left(4x + \frac{2}{5}\right) - 1\frac{1}{4}$ by simplifying each side.

3. Graph each expression using graphing technology to determine if these are equivalent expressions. Sketch the graphs.

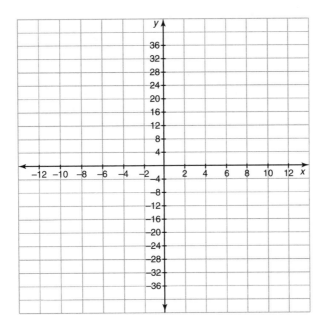

Problem 3   What About These? Are They Equivalent?

For each equation, verify whether the expressions are equivalent using any of these methods. Identify the method and show your work.

1. $3\frac{1}{3}\left(6x - 2\frac{1}{5}\right) + 5\frac{1}{3} = -6\frac{2}{3}\left(-3x + 1\frac{6}{5}\right) + 12\frac{2}{3}$

2. $4.2(-3.2x - 8.2) - 7.6x = -15.02x + 3(4.1 - 3x)$

3. $-2\left(-3\frac{1}{2}x - 2\frac{1}{10}\right) = 10x - 3(x + 1) + 7.2$

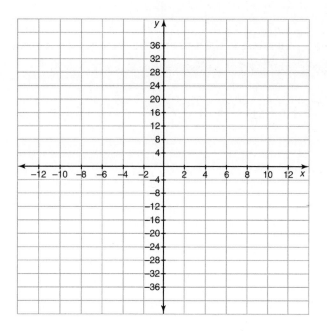

Be prepared to share your solutions and methods.

6

6.5

IT IS TIME TO JUSTIFY!

Simplifying Algebraic Expressions Using Operations and Their Properties

Learning Goal

In this lesson, you will:

▶ Simplify algebraic expressions using operations and their properties.

Have you ever been asked to give reasons for something that you did? When did this occur? Were your reasons accepted or rejected? Is it always important to have reasons for doing something or believing something?

6

Problem 1 Justifying!!

One method for verifying that algebraic expressions are equivalent is to simplify the expressions into two identical expressions.

For this equation, the left side is simplified completely to show that the two expressions are equivalent.

$$-2\frac{1}{2}\left(1\frac{1}{3}x - \frac{2}{5}\right) + 2 = -3\frac{1}{3}x + 3$$

Step	Justification
$-2\frac{1}{2}\left(1\frac{1}{3}x - \frac{2}{5}\right) + 2 =$	Given
$\left(-\frac{5}{2}\right)\left(\frac{4}{3}x\right) + \left(-\frac{5}{2}\right)\left(-\frac{2}{5}\right) + 2 =$	Distributive Property of Multiplication over Subtraction
$-\frac{10}{3}x + 1 + 2 =$	Multiplication
$-3\frac{1}{3}x + 3$	Addition Yes, they are equivalent.

1. Use an operation or a property to justify each step and indicate if the expressions are equivalent.

   a. $-4(-3x - 8) - 4x + 8 = -8x + 40$

Step	Justification
$-4(-3x - 8) - 4x + 8 =$	
$12x + 32 + (-4x) + 8 =$	
$12x + (-4x) + 32 + 8 =$	
$-8x + 40 =$	

   b. $-2.1(-3.2x - 4) + 1.2(2x - 5) = 9.16x + 3.4$

Step	Justification
$-2.1(-3.2x - 4) + 1.2(2x - 5) =$	
$6.72x + 8.4 + 2.4x + (-6) =$	
$6.72x + 2.4x + 8.4 + (-6) =$	
$9.16x + 2.4 =$	

c. $\dfrac{-4x - 9}{2} + \dfrac{-3x + 7}{3} = -3x + \left(-\dfrac{13}{6}\right)$

Step	Justification
$\dfrac{-4x - 9}{2} + \dfrac{-3x + 7}{3} =$	
$\dfrac{-4x}{2} + \left(-\dfrac{9}{2}\right) + \dfrac{-3x}{3} + \dfrac{7}{3} =$	
$-2x + \left(-\dfrac{9}{2}\right) + (-x) + \dfrac{7}{3} =$	
$-2x + (-x) + \left(-\dfrac{9}{2}\right) + \dfrac{7}{3} =$	
$-3x + \left(-\dfrac{27}{6}\right) + \dfrac{14}{6} =$	
$-3x + \left(-\dfrac{13}{6}\right) =$	

6

2. For each equation, simplify the left side completely using the given operation or property that justifies each step and indicate if the expressions are equivalent.

a. $-4x - \dfrac{6x - 7}{5} = -\dfrac{26}{5}x + \dfrac{7}{5}$

Step	Justification
	Given
	Distributive Property of Division over Subtraction
	Division
	Addition of Like Terms Yes, they are equivalent.

b. $-4x - 3(3x - 6) + 8(2.5x + 3.5) = 7x + 46$

Step	Justification
	Given
	Distributive Property of Multiplication over Addition
	Addition
	Commutative Property of Addition
	Addition of Like Terms Yes, they are equivalent.

6

Problem 2   Simplify and Justify!

For each equation, simplify the left side completely to determine if the two expressions are equivalent. Use an operation or a property to justify each step and indicate if the expressions are equivalent.

1. $-4x + 3(-7x + 3) - 2(-3x + 4) = -19x + 1$

Step	Justification

I think it's easier to simplify first and then come up with the reasons when I'm done. What do you think?

2. $-5(x + 4.3) - 5(x + 4.3) = -10x - 43$

Step	Justification

For each equation, simplify the left side and the right side completely to determine if the two expressions are equivalent. Use an operation or a property to justify each step and indicate if the expressions are equivalent.

3. $-3(-x + 17) + 7(-x + 30) -8x = -6x + 3(-x + 50) + 9$

Left side

Step	Justification

Right side

Step	Justification

4. $-3\frac{1}{2}(4x + 6) + 1\frac{1}{3}(-6x - 3) - 4x = -5\frac{1}{2}x - 13 + 2\frac{1}{2}(-6x + 1) - 5\frac{1}{2}x - 14\frac{1}{2}$

Left side

Step	Justification

Right side

Step	Justification

 Be prepared to share your solutions and methods.

Key Terms

- variable (6.1)
- algebraic expression (6.1)
- evaluate an algebraic expression (6.1)
- Distributive Property of Multiplication over Addition (6.2)
- Distributive Property of Multiplication over Subtraction (6.2)
- Distributive Property of Division over Addition (6.2)
- Distributive Property of Division over Subtraction (6.2)
- factor (6.3)
- common factor (6.3)
- greatest common factor (GCF) (6.3)
- coefficient (6.3)
- like terms (6.3)
- combining like terms (6.3)

6.1 Writing Algebraic Expressions

When a mathematical process is repeated over and over, a mathematical phrase, called an algebraic expression, can be used to represent the situation. An algebraic expression is a mathematical phrase involving at least one variable and sometimes numbers and operation symbols.

Example

The algebraic expression $2.49p$ represents the cost of p pounds of apples.

One pound of apples costs 2.49(1), or $2.49. Two pounds of apples costs 2.49(2), or $4.98.

Having trouble remembering something new? Your brain learns by association so create a mnemonic, a song, or a story about the information and it will be easier to remember!

6.1 Evaluating Algebraic Expressions

To evaluate an algebraic expression, replace each variable in the expression with a number or numerical expression and then perform all possible mathematical operations.

Example

The expression $2x - 7$ has been evaluated for these values of x: 9, 2, -3, and 4.5.

$$
\begin{array}{llll}
2(9) - 7 = 18 - 7 & 2(2) - 7 = 4 - 7 & 2(-3) - 7 = -6 - 7 & 2(4.5) - 7 = 9 - 7 \\
\qquad\quad = 11 & \qquad\quad = -3 & \qquad\qquad = -13 & \qquad\qquad = 2
\end{array}
$$

6.2 Using the Distributive Property of Multiplication over Addition to Simplify Numerical Expressions

The Distributive Property of Multiplication over Addition states that if a, b, and c are any real numbers, then $a \bullet (b + c) = a \bullet b + a \bullet c$.

Example

A model is drawn and an expression written to show how the Distributive Property of Multiplication over Addition can be used to solve a multiplication problem.

6(820)   800   20

6	4800	120

$$
\begin{aligned}
& 6(800 + 20) \\
= & 6(800) + 6(20) \\
= & 4800 + 120 \\
= & 4920
\end{aligned}
$$

6

6.2 Using the Distributive Properties to Simplify and Evaluate Algebraic Expressions

Including the Distributive Property of Multiplication over Addition, there are a total of four different forms of the Distributive Property.

Another Distributive Property is the Distributive Property of Multiplication over Subtraction, which states that if a, b, and c are any real numbers, then $a \cdot (b - c) = a \cdot b - a \cdot c$.

The Distributive Property of Division over Addition states that if a, b, and c are real numbers and $c \neq 0$, then $\frac{a + b}{c} = \frac{a}{c} + \frac{b}{c}$.

The Distributive Property of Division over Subtraction states that if a, b, and c are real numbers and $c \neq 0$, then $\frac{a - b}{c} = \frac{a}{c} - \frac{b}{c}$.

Example

The Distributive Properties have been used to simplify the algebraic expression. The simplified expression is then evaluated for $x = 2$.

$$\frac{4(6x - 7) + 10}{3} = \frac{24x - 28 + 10}{3}$$

$$= \frac{24x - 18}{3} \qquad\qquad 8x - 6 = 8(2) - 6$$

$$= \frac{24x}{3} - \frac{18}{3} \qquad\qquad\qquad = 16 - 6$$

$$= 8x - 6 \qquad\qquad\qquad\qquad = 10$$

6.3 Using the Distributive Properties to Factor Expressions

The Distributive Properties can be used in reverse to rewrite an expression as a product of factors. When factoring expressions, it is important to factor out the greatest common factor from all the terms. The greatest common factor (GCF) is the largest factor that two or more numbers or terms have in common.

Example

The expression has been rewritten by factoring out the greatest common factor.

$$24x^3 + 3x^2 - 9x = 3x(8x^2) + 3x(x) - 3x(3)$$
$$= 3x(8x^2 + x - 3)$$

6

6.3 Combining Like Terms to Simplify Expressions

Like terms are terms whose variable portions are the same. When you add like terms together, you are combining like terms. You can combine like terms to simplify algebraic expressions to make them easier to evaluate.

Example

Like terms have been combined to simplify the algebraic expression. The simplified expression is then evaluated for $x = 5$.

$$7x - 2(3x - 4) = 7x - 6x + 8 \qquad x + 8 = 5 + 8$$
$$= x + 8 \qquad\qquad\qquad = 13$$

6.4 Determining If Expressions Are Equivalent by Evaluating

Evaluate the expression on each side of the equal sign for the same value of x. If the results are the same, then the expressions are equivalent.

Example

The expressions are equivalent.

$$(x + 12) + (4x - 9) = 5x + 3 \text{ for } x = 1$$

$$(1 + 12) + (4 \cdot 1 - 9) \stackrel{?}{=} 5 \cdot 1 + 3$$
$$13 + (-5) \stackrel{?}{=} 5 + 3$$
$$8 = 8$$

6.4 Determining If Expressions Are Equivalent by Simplifying

The Distributive Properties and factoring can be used to determine if the expressions on each side of the equal sign are equivalent.

Example

The expressions are equivalent.

$$5\left(-3x - \frac{2}{5}\right) = -\frac{1}{3}(45x + 6)$$
$$-15x - 2 = -15x - 2$$

6.4 Determining If Two Expressions Are Equivalent by Graphing

Expressions can be graphed to determine if the expressions are equivalent. If the graph of each expression is the same, then the expressions are equal.

Example

$3(x + 3) - x = 3x + 3$ is not true because the graph of each expression is not the same.

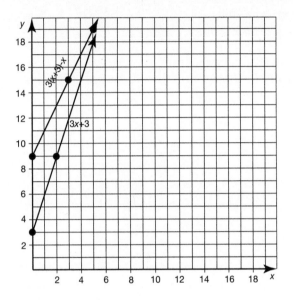

6.5 Simplifying Algebraic Expressions Using Operations and Their Properties

Simplify each side completely to determine if the two expressions are equivalent. Use an operation or a property to justify each step and indicate if the expressions are equivalent.

Example

$-3(-2x - 9) - 3x - 7 = 3x + 20$

Step	Justification
$-3(-2x +(-9)) - 3x - 7 =$	Given
$6x + 27 + (-3x) + (-7) =$	Distributive Property of Multiplication over Addition
$6x + (-3x) + 27 + (-7) =$	Commutative Property of Addition
$3x + 20 =$	Addition of Like Terms Yes, they are equivalent.

6

7 SOLVING EQUATIONS AND INEQUALITIES

Rock balancing is a serious art for some people. Rock balance artists take rocks they find nearby and balance them in formations that seem impossible. And these artists don't use any tools—just their hands!

7

7

7.1 PICTURE THIS
Picture Algebra

Learning Goals

In this lesson, you will:

▶ Use drawings to represent daily life situations.

▶ Develop different methods to represent daily life situations mathematically.

Key Term

▶ equation

Have you ever made a model of an airplane or a doll house or a car? Well, did you know that there are some people whose job it is to create models? It's true! These professional model builders create scale models of all sorts of buildings, bridges, parks, cars—well almost anything you can think of.

Many times, designers and architects employ model builders to create scale models from their blueprints for presentations. Why do you think scale models are helpful for presentations?

7

Problem 1   A Typical Day in a Small Town

1. There are two main sections in a small town called the Hill Section and the Lake Section. The town has a population of 3496 people. The number of people who live in the Hill Section is 295 more than twice the number of people who live in the Lake Section. How many people live in each section of town?

One method to solve this type of problem is to draw a "picture" that models the situation. In the "picture," you can draw a rectangle or box to represent an unknown quantity.

a. In the situation given, one unknown quantity is the number of people living in the Lake Section. Draw a box to represent this quantity and label it with a p.

Lake Section:

Hill Section:

b. Next, draw three boxes to represent the people who live in the Hill Section. Label these boxes, p, p, and 295. Why do you think these boxes are labeled this way?

> Try to draw the same size box to represent p each time.

c. Use your picture to calculate how many people live in each section of town.

Number of people in the Lake Section:

Number of people in the Hill Section:

You can represent the picture you drew as a mathematical sentence using operations and an equals sign. An **equation** is a mathematical sentence you create by placing an equals sign, =, between two expressions.

One way to write an equation is to think about writing it with words.

One equation you can write for the population in a small town situation is:

| Number of people in the Lake Section | + | Number of people in the Hill Section | = 3496 |

Now that you have written the situation in words, let's think about how to write an equation.

d. First, write an expression to represent the number of people in the Lake Section. Let p represent the number of people in the Lake Section.

e. Next, write an expression to represent the number of people in the Hill Section.

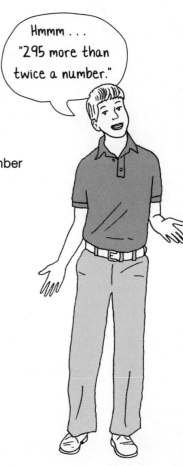

Hmmm . . . "295 more than twice a number."

f. Finally, write an equation to represent the total number of people in the small town.

7

2. One of the farms outside of town uses a water tank for irrigation. The water tank holds a total of 5600 gallons, and the tank has three pipes through which water drains to irrigate three different areas of the field. When water is drained from the tank, Pipe B drains twice as much water as Pipe A. Pipe C drains 65 gallons more than Pipe B. Assume that the tank is drained completely before it is refilled. How many gallons of water does each pipe drain?

a. Draw a picture to represent the water tank situation. Label the unknown parts with variables and the known parts with their values.

Pipe A:

Pipe B:

Pipe C:

b. Use your picture to determine the number of gallons of water each pipe drains. Explain your reasoning.

Gallons drained by Pipe A:

Gallons drained by Pipe B:

Gallons drained by Pipe C:

c. Write an expression for each part. Let a represent the number of gallons drained by Pipe A.

The number of gallons drained by Pipe A:

The number of gallons drained by Pipe B:

The number of gallons drained by Pipe C:

d. Write an equation to represent the water tank situation.

3. The members of a small town's local arts council are selling raffle tickets. The art council decides that the top three raffle ticket sellers will share a portion of the profits. The second-place seller will receive twice as much as the third-place seller. The first-place seller will receive $20 more than second-place seller. How much will each of the top three sellers receive if the profit portion they will share is $200?

> This problem doesn't tell me anything about the 3rd-place seller. Should I start there?

a. Draw a picture to represent the art raffle situation. Label the unknown parts with variables and the known parts with their values.

First-Place Seller:

Second-Place Seller:

Third-Place Seller:

b. Use your picture to determine the cash prize each of the top three sellers will receive. Explain your reasoning.

Prize for First-Place Seller:

Prize for Second-Place Seller:

Prize for Third-Place Seller:

c. Write an expression for each part. Let p represent the cash prize for the third-place seller.

Prize for the First-Place Seller:

Prize for the Second-Place Seller:

Prize for the Third-Place Seller:

d. Write an equation to represent this situation.

7

4. During the summer, Matthew and Devan started their own business mowing lawns for people in the Lake Section. Before starting any work, Matthew spent $15 to fill up the gas tank for the lawnmower. The boys agreed that each person would earn the same amount after Matthew was reimbursed the money he spent for gas. After a week of work, the boys were paid a total of $243. Matthew filled up the gas tank just once. How much did each boy earn?

a. Draw a picture to represent the situation. Label the unknown parts with variables and the known parts with their values.

Matthew's earnings:

Devan's earnings:

b. Use your picture to determine the earnings each boy received. Explain your reasoning.

Matthew's earnings:

Devan's earnings:

c. Write an expression for each part. Let *m* represent the earnings.

Matthew's earnings:

Devan's earnings:

d. Write an equation to represent this situation.

7

 Be prepared to share your solutions and methods.

7.2 MAINTAINING A BALANCE
Solving Equations

Learning Goals

In this lesson, you will:

▶ Develop an understanding of equality.

▶ Use properties of equality to solve equations represented with algebra tiles.

▶ Solve one-step equations.

Key Term

▶ Properties of Equality

A balance is an instrument used to measure the weight and mass of an object. No one is quite sure who invented the balance, but there have been models found in Mesopotamia and Egypt that suggest the machine has been around since 5000 B.C. The balance consists of a lever and two pans.

The way the balance works is that a known weight is placed on one side, while the object being weighed is placed in the pan on the other side of the lever. When the weight and the object being weighed are the same, the lever remains "balanced" in a horizontal position.

What other scales or balances have you seen? Have you seen scales or balances in the nurse's office or supermarket?

7

Problem 1   Equal or Not

1. Each representation shows a balance. What will balance one rectangle 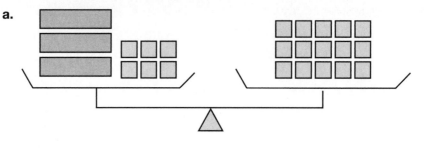 in each problem? Adjustments can be made in each pan as long as the balance is maintained. Describe your strategies.

a.

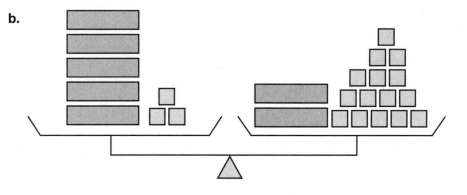

Strategies:

What will balance one rectangle?

b.

Strategies:

What will balance one rectangle?

c.

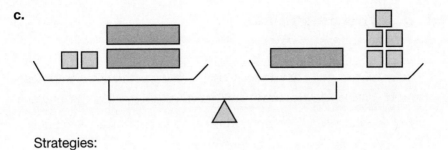

Strategies:

What will balance one rectangle?

2. Generalize the strategies for maintaining balance. Complete each sentence.

   a. To maintain balance when you subtract a quantity from one side, you must

   _____

   b. To maintain balance when you add a quantity to one side, you must

   _____

   c. To maintain balance when you multiply a quantity by one side, you must

   _____

   d. To maintain balance when you divide a quantity by one side, you must

   _____

7

Problem 2   Two Steps Back

1. Rewrite Problem 1, Question 1, part (a) using variables and numbers.

   Let [   ] = x and [ ] = 1 unit.

   a. Describe how the strategies you used to determine what balanced 1 rectangle can apply to the equation. Determine what balances x.

   b. Substitute the value of x back into the original equation. Does the value of x maintain balance in the original equation? Show your work.

   You just solved a two-step equation.

   c. Describe the Order of Operations you used in the original equation.

   d. Compare the way you solved the equation to the order of the operations in the original equation.

When you "undo" operations, it is often simpler to undo them in the reverse of the order of operations. In other words, the operation that comes *last* in the original equation should be undone *first*.

2. Write a sentence to describe how to apply inverse operations to solve each equation. Then, solve each equation and verify your solution.

   a. $4x - 15 = 61$

   b. $2 + 7x = 16$

   c. $5 + \dfrac{x}{2} = 16$

   d. $17 = 2x + 8$

3. Solve each riddle. Show your work.

    a. What is a number that when you multiply it by 3 and subtract 5 from the product, you get 28? Let *x* represent the number you are trying to determine.

    b. What is a number that when you multiply it by 4 and add 15 to the product, you get 79?

    c. Make a number riddle for your partner to solve.

I've got one. What is a number that when you multiply it by 5 and add 6 to the product, you get 31?

Talk the Talk

The **Properties of Equality** allow you to balance and solve equations involving any number.

Properties of Equality	For all numbers *a*, *b*, and *c*, . . .
Addition Property of Equality	If $a = b$, then $a + c = b + c$.
Subtraction Property of Equality	If $a = b$, then $a - c = b - c$.
Multiplication Property of Equality	If $a = b$, then $ac = bc$.
Division Property of Equality	If $a = b$ and $c \neq 0$, then $\frac{a}{c} = \frac{b}{c}$.

Complete the graphic organizer on the next page. Show examples for each Property of Equality using models and equations.

Be prepared to share your solutions and methods.

7

ADDITION PROPERTY OF EQUALITY

MULTIPLICATION PROPERTY
OF EQUALITY

PROPERTIES OF EQUALITY

SUBTRACTION PROPERTY OF EQUALITY

DIVISION PROPERTY OF EQUALITY

7.3

PLANNING A GRADUATION PARTY

Solving Two-Step Equations

Learning Goals

In this lesson, you will:

▶ Write two-step equations.

▶ Solve two-step equations.

▶ Check solutions algebraically.

▶ Verify solutions within a problem context.

Key Term

▶ two-step equation

How do you get invited to a friend's party, club events, or even practices? For many events, people now use e-invitations that are sent via email. However, there still seems to be two events that people like to send out invitations through regular mail: weddings and graduations. It appears that people like the personal touch of receiving an "old-fashioned" invitation with fancy script writing, and elegant colors. Can you think of other items or acts that are "old-fashioned," but are still popular with people?

7

Problem 1 Ordering Invitations

1. Shelly is throwing a graduation party. She wants to send nice invitations to all of her guests. She found a company that will send her a 10-pack of personalized invitations for $6 each, plus a $5 shipping fee for the entire order no matter how large or small.

   a. What is the cost of Shelly's order if she buys three 10-packs of invitations?

   b. What is the cost of Shelly's order if she buys five 10-packs of invitations?

   c. Describe how you calculated the cost of each order.

   d. Write an algebraic expression that represents the total cost of any order. Let p represent the number of 10-pack invitations that were ordered.

   e. How many 10-packs were ordered if the total cost of the order was $53?

7

f. How many 10-packs were ordered if the total cost of the order was $29?

g. Write a sentence to describe how you calculated the number of 10-pack invitations ordered for any order amount.

h. Write an equation to describe this situation. Let *p* represent the number of 10-packs of invitations ordered and *c* represent the total cost of the order.

i. Use your equation to determine how many 10-pack invitations Shelly ordered if her total cost was $47.

7

Problem 2 How Does It Work?

In Problem 1, you wrote and solved a *two-step equation*. A **two-step equation** requires two inverse operations to be performed in order to isolate the variable.

When you calculated the number of 10-pack invitations ordered in Question 1, parts (e) and (f), you were solving a two-step equation.

> So, I "undo" operations just like I balanced the scales.

Suppose that Shelly paid $101 for her invitations, and you want to know how many 10-packs of invitations she ordered. You can use the equation you wrote in part (h) and substitute 101 for c, the total cost of the order.

$$6p + 5 = 101$$

This equation is a two-step equation because it requires two steps to solve it. To solve this equation, you need to perform steps that "undo" the steps in the original equation.

1. What operations are given in the equation $6p + 5 = 101$?

2. In what order would you perform the operations using the Order of Operation rules?

Remember that when you "undo" operations, it is often simpler to undo them in the reverse of the Order of Operations.

3. In what order would you perform the inverse operations for $6p + 5 = 101$?

4. Solve $6p + 5 = 101$ for p.

5. What does this solution mean in terms of the problem situation?

6. Write a sentence to describe how to apply inverse operations to solve each equation. Then, solve each equation and verify your solution.

a. $5x - 3 = 2$

b. $1 + 2x = 19$

c. $\dfrac{x}{5} + 2 = 9$

7

d. $1 = 3x - 11$

e. $7x + 2 = -12$

 f. $-38 = -6x - 14$

Get in the habit of checking your answers. It will help you avoid mistakes.

7

Problem 3   Using Two-Step Equations to Solve Problems

1. Pete's Garage charges $45 per hour for labor when performing auto repairs. The mechanics filled in partial details for their job tickets. The office manager must have the cost of parts and the hours of each job ticket to complete the bills for the customers.

   a. Complete the table shown to help the office manager.

Customer	Cost of Parts (in dollars)	Length of Job (in hours)	Total Cost of Repair Bill (in dollars)
Hadley	79.00	2.5	
Burns	225.00	5.75	
Mask	167.00		358.25
Christian	160.10		250.10
Snyder		0.5	25.00
Lewis		3	135.00

   b. Write an equation to represent this problem situation. Define your variables.

   c. Hadley turned in one more incomplete job ticket for Ms. Jones. The total bill was $269.75, and the cost of the parts was $101. Use your equation to determine how many hours Hadley worked on this job.

7

Be prepared to show your solutions and methods.

7.4 SOLVING IN BIG-TIME STYLE

Using Two-Step Equations

Learning Goals

In this lesson, you will:

▶ Write two-step equations.

▶ Solve two-step equations.

▶ Verify solutions within a problem context.

Have you ever heard of the term "business plan"? A business plan is a way for a company or business owner to conduct research on competition, determine costs for running the business, and set financial goals in terms of profits for the company. Many times, businesses will create 1-, 3-, and 5-year business plans.

Why do you think businesses would create multiple business plans?

7

Problem 1 Learning the Limo Business

Katie is starting her own limousine rental company. She wisely decides to check her competitors' pricing plans before setting her own plan. The table shows the fees from two rival limousine rental companies.

Number of Hours Rented	Limousines by Lilly (in dollars)	Transportation with Class (in dollars)
1	99.99	89.99
2	123.74	126.54
3	147.49	163.09
4	171.24	199.64
5	194.99	236.19

1. Use the table to answer each question.

a. What is the difference in price to rent a limousine from Limousines by Lilly for two hours compared to one hour?

> So, a 2 hour rental is about $125 and a 1 hour rental is about $100, the difference will be about $25.

b. What is the difference in price to rent a limousine from Limousines by Lilly for three hours compared to two hours?

c. What is the difference in price to rent a limousine from Limousines by Lilly for four hours compared to three hours?

d. What is the difference in price to rent a limousine from Limousines by Lilly for five hours compared to four hours?

e. How does the total cost of a Limousines by Lilly rental change when the rental time increases by one hour (except the first hour)?

f. What does the first hour of a rental from Limousines by Lilly cost?

g. What does each rental hour cost from Limousines by Lilly after the first hour?

h. What would it cost to rent a limo from Limousines by Lilly for ten hours? Explain your reasoning.

Do you have an estimate in mind for the cost to rent from Lilly for 10 hours?

i. What would it cost to rent a limo from Limousines by Lilly for thirteen hours? Explain your reasoning.

7

2. Let h represent the total number of rental hours from Limousines by Lilly. Write an expression to calculate the number of hours that cost $23.75.

3. Write an equation you could solve to find the number of hours a limousine is rented from Limousines by Lilly if the total rental cost is $266.24.

The equation you wrote in Question 3 can be simplified before it can be solved. In previous lessons, you learned to simplify algebraic expressions using a variety of strategies.

4. Name the strategies necessary to simplify the equation you wrote.

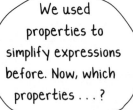

We used properties to simplify expressions before. Now, which properties . . . ?

5. Simplify the equation you wrote in Question 3. Does it look like the two-step equations you solved in previous lessons? Why or why not?

6. Solve your equation from Question 5. What does your solution mean in terms of the problem situation?

7. Use the table above Question 1 to answer each question.

    a. What is the difference in price to rent a limousine from Transportation with Class for two hours compared to one hour?

    b. What is the difference in price to rent a limousine from Transportation with Class for five hours compared to four hours?

    c. How does the total cost of the Transportation with Class rental change when the rental time increases by one hour (except the first hour)?

    d. What does the first hour of a rental from Transportation with Class cost?

7

8. Let h represent the total number of rental hours from Transportation with Class. Write an expression to find the number of hours that cost $36.55.

9. Write and solve an equation to determine the number of hours a limousine is rented from Transportation with Class if the total rental cost is $309.29.

10. After how many hours would the cost to rent a limousine be the same for each limo rental company? Write an equation and explain your reasoning.

11. What suggestions would you provide to Katie on the fees she should charge for her limo rental business? Explain your reasoning.

12. Solve each equation.

a. $4(x - 7) + 12 = 20$

b. $-5 = -3(x + 11) - 17$

Pay attention to negative signs!

c. $8(x + 6) - 3x = 18$

d. $\frac{1}{2}(5 - x) = \frac{1}{4}$

e. $2(3x + 4) = 19$

f. $6.4 = 1.2(4 + 2x)$

Problem 2   Business Extras

As part of her research, Katie discovers that she must charge sales tax to her customers in addition to her rental fees. In her county, the sales tax is 7%. That means that she must charge an additional 7% of her rental fee to be paid as tax.

1. Write a percent equation that would tell Katie how much tax to collect for any amount of rental fee. Let x represent the rental fee and y represent the sales tax.

Katie also discovers that most limousine rental companies collect a flat gratuity from customers in addition to the rental fee. Katie decides to collect a gratuity of $35 from her customers.

2. Write an equation that represents the total amount of additional money to be collected for tax and gratuity, t, in terms of the rental fee, x.

   a. Use your equation to calculate the amount of tax and gratuity Katie should collect if the rental fee is $220.

   b. Use your equation to calculate the amount of tax and gratuity Katie should collect if the rental fee is $365.

7

c. Use your equation to calculate the rental fee if Katie collected $65.66 in tax and gratuity.

d. Use your equation to calculate the rental fee if Katie collected $46.34 in tax and gratuity.

7

3. After completing her research, Katie decides to charge customers $75 for the first hour and $39 each additional hour. She continues to collect the 7% sales tax, and the $35 gratuity from each customer in addition to the rental fee.

If the amount of tax and gratuity that Katie collected from a customer is $62.09, how many hours did the customer rent a limousine from Katie?

Be prepared to show your solutions and methods.

WE'RE SHIPPING OUT!
Solving and Graphing Inequalities in One Variable

Learning Goals

In this lesson, you will:

▶ Write simple inequalities.

▶ Graph one-variable inequalities.

▶ Solve one-variable inequalities.

Key Term

▶ solve an inequality

Listening to music too loud can cause permanent hearing damage. Do not operate heavy equipment after taking a sleeping pill. This product is intended for external use—ingesting it can cause sickness or even death. Have you seen statements like this on products?

It seems that warning labels are all around. Despite the thought that warning labels are a relatively new thing, in fact warning labels have been around since 1938. That year, Congress required companies to print the ingredients of products and foods on a label. Then, in 1973, Congress enacted a law that required companies to disclose if a product contained toxic materials.

Probably the most famous or most infamous story involving warning labels—or lack of warning labels—occurred in 1992, when Stella Liebeck won a lawsuit after a cup of coffee spilled on her leg resulting in third degree burns to her body. Following this, warning labels got much more attention—and more frequent on products. In fact, it became the subject matter of a few television shows in the 1990s. Do you think warning labels are helpful? Do you notice warning labels on products? Have warning labels ever caused you to think twice about using a product?

7

Problem 1   Solving Inequalities

1. Aaron wants to buy new football pads that cost $55.00 at GoodSportsBuys.com. The online store charges $11 for shipping on orders less than $75. He is also considering buying ski gloves, but he does not want to pay more than the $11.00 shipping fee. Write and solve an inequality that describes the possible number of additional dollars Aaron can spend and still remain in the $11.00 shipping fee category. Let d represent the additional dollars. Explain your solution in terms of the problem situation.

To **solve an inequality** means to determine the value of the variable that makes the inequality true. The objective when solving an inequality is similar to the objective when solving an equation. You want to isolate the variable on one side of the inequality symbol by using the operations of addition, subtraction, multiplication, and division.

2. Describe the steps you would take to solve the equation $3x - 2 = 7$. Then, solve the equation.

3. A list of possible solutions for the inequality is shown. Circle the solutions that make the inequality true. Then, list three additional solutions to the inequality.

   a. $3x - 2 \geq 7$

   $-2, -1, 0, 1, 2, 3, 4, 5, 6, 7$

   b. $3x \geq 9$

   $-2, -1, 0, 1, 2, 3, 4, 5, 6, 7$

c. $x \geq 3$

$-2, -1, 0, 1, 2, 3, 4, 5, 6, 7$

4. What do you notice about the solutions you circled in Question 3, parts (a) through (c)?

5. What do you notice about the three additional solutions you wrote for each inequality?

6. Compare the sequence of the three inequalities to the steps you used to solve the equation in Question 2. What do you notice? Explain your reasoning.

> Use a number line to graph this inequality. Remember there is a difference between a closed circle and an open circle.

7. Graph the solution for $3x - 2 \geq 7$.

<-----+---+---+---+---+---+---+---+---+---+---+---+---+---+---+---+----->
          -5 -4 -3 -2 -1 0 1 2 3 4 5 6 7 8 9 10

You can check your solution to an inequality by choosing a value that is in your solution set and substituting it into the original inequality. If that substituted value makes the inequality true, then you have verified a correct solution.

8. Choose a value from the solution set of the inequality $3x - 2 \geq 7$, and verify that it is a solution.

7

9. Solve each inequality or equation, and show your work. Then, graph your solution on a number line.

a. $2x + 5 < -17$

b. $97 \leq 8x + 1$

c. $6x - 11 = 7$

Problem 2   Who's Correct?

Jenna and Brendan think that solving an inequality is the same as solving an equation except for one special case. What happens if you have to multiply or divide both sides of an inequality by a negative value? They are trying to solve $-4x < 20$. Consider their solutions and explanations.

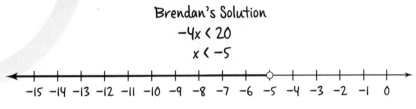

Brendan's Solution

$$-4x < 20$$
$$x < -5$$

I divided both sides by -4 to solve the inequality.

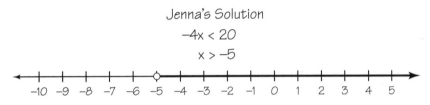

Jenna's Solution

$$-4x < 20$$
$$x > -5$$

I know that when I multiply or divide any given number by a negative number, I have to pay attention to the sign of my answer. So when I divide both sides of the inequality by -4, the inequality sign should reverse.

1. Check each solution and determine who is correct. List three values from each person's solution, and verify that those solutions make the original inequality $-4x < 20$ true. What do you notice? Explain your reasoning.

   Check for Brendan's solution.   Check for Jenna's solution.

It is necessary to reverse the inequality symbol when you multiply or divide both sides of an inequality by a negative value.

7

---

2. Circle the correct solution and explanation, and cross out the incorrect solution and explanation from Brendan's and Jenna's work in Question 1.

3. Solve each inequality, and then graph the solution.

   a. $8x > 16$

   b. $\dfrac{x}{3} \leq -4$

   c. $-5x < 35$

   d. $\dfrac{x}{-2} \geq 5$

   e. $10 < 2x - 3$

   f. $18 \geq -x + 7$

> The expression $-x$ is the same as $-1x$.

Be prepared to share your solutions and methods.

Key Terms

▶ equation (7.1)

▶ Properties of Equality (7.2)

▶ solve an inequality (7.5)

7.1   Representing Daily Life Situations Using Picture Algebra

Drawing a "picture" can be used to model a situation. In the picture, draw a rectangle or box to represent the unknown quantity. Combine the variable box with either boxes labeled with numbers or more boxes with the same variable to represent different amounts in relation to the variable. A picture can also be used to calculate a solution to the variable and each combination of boxes. Pictures can also be used to represent a mathematical sentence using operations and an equals sign. An equation is a mathematical sentence you create by placing an equals sign, $=$, between two expressions.

Example

Eli, Dixon, and Derek sold fruit bars to raise money for a school trip. Eli sold three times as many fruit bars as Dixon, and Derek sold 14 more fruit bars than Dixon. The picture drawn, and the calculation shows how to determine how many fruit bars each boy sold. Let c represent fruit bars.

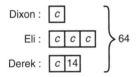

Drawing pictures and doodling are strategies that can help your brain focus and understand complicated problems.

$$c + (3c) + (c + 14) = 64$$
$$5c + 14 = 64$$
$$5c = 50$$
$$c = 10$$

Dixon sold 10 fruit bars, Eli sold $3 \times 10 = 30$ fruit bars, and Derek sold $10 + 14 = 24$ fruit bars.

7.2 Understanding Equality and Using a Balance Model

A representation can be shown on a balance. When subtraction of a quantity is done one one side, subtraction of the same quantity must occur on the other side to maintain a balance.

The same process must also be done to both sides when other operations like addition, multiplication, and division are done on one side of the balance.

Example

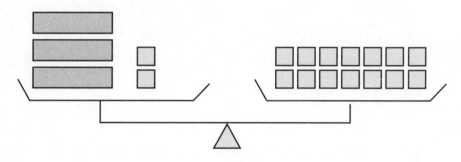

Subtract two squares from each side, which leaves three rectangles on one side and 12 squares on the other side. Then divide each side by 3, which leaves one rectangle on one side and four squares on the other side: 1 rectangle = 4 squares.

$$3x + 2 = 14$$
$$x = 4$$

7.2 Solving Two-Step Equations

To solve a two-step equation, the variable must be isolated on one side of the equation. Perform the inverse operations in the reverse order of operations found in the original equation. To determine if your solution is correct, substitute the value of the variable back into the original equation. If the equation remains balanced, then the calculation performed is the solution to the equation.

Example

The solution for the equation $\frac{b}{5} + 19 = 25$ for b is shown.

Subtract first, and then multiply.   Check the solution.

$$\frac{b}{5} + 19 = 25$$

$$\frac{b}{5} + 19 - 19 = 25 - 19 \qquad\qquad \frac{30}{5} + 19 = 25$$

$$\frac{b}{5} = 6 \qquad\qquad\qquad 6 + 19 = 25$$

$$5\left(\frac{b}{5}\right) = 5(6) \qquad\qquad\qquad 25 = 25$$

$$b = 30$$

7.3 Solving Two-Step Equations

Some equations require only two steps to isolate the variable and solve the equation. To isolate the variable, use the inverse operation of each operation contained within the equation. Verify the solution algebraically by substituting the value of the variable into the original equation to see if it makes the equation true.

Example

The solution of the two-step equation $4t + 17 = 1$ is shown. Subtract first, then divide.

$$4t + 17 = 1$$
$$4t + 17 - 17 = 1 - 17$$
$$\frac{4t}{4} = \frac{-16}{4}$$
$$t = -4$$

Verify the solution by substituting -4 for t in the original equation.

$$4(-4) + 17 \stackrel{?}{=} 1$$
$$1 = 1$$

7.3 Using Two-Step Equations to Solve a Problem

An equation can be written to represent a problem situation. When this occurs, variables must be defined, calculations are performed, and finally there is a verification of the solution.

Example

Kendra made three dozen breakfast rolls. She sold half of them at the bake sale and split the remaining rolls between her two brothers. The use of a two-step equation is shown to determine how many rolls each brother received.

Kendra made three dozen rolls, or 36 rolls. She sold half, or 18 rolls.

Let r represent the number of rolls each brother received. So, $36 = 18 + 2r$. The solution for the equation is shown.

$$36 = 18 + 2r$$
$$36 - 18 = 18 + 2r - 18$$
$$\frac{18}{2} = \frac{2r}{2}$$
$$9 = r$$

Verify the solution:

$$36 \stackrel{?}{=} 18 + 2(9)$$
$$36 = 36$$

Each brother received nine breakfast rolls.

7.4 Solving Two-Step Equations Involving the Distributive Property

Use the Distributive Property to simplify the equation before it can be solved. Then, apply the inverse operations to isolate the variable, and solve the equation.

Example

The steps for solving the equation $130 - 6(n - 2) = 220$ are shown.

$$130 - 6(n - 2) = 220$$
$$130 - 6n + 12 = 220$$
$$142 - 142 - 6n = 220 - 142$$
$$\frac{-6n}{-6} = \frac{78}{-6}$$
$$n = -13$$

7.4 Using Two-Step Equations and the Distributive Property to Solve a Problem with Decimals or Percents

Write an equation to represent a problem situation. Define your variables, solve, and verify your solution.

Example

Hong rented a bike to ride at the beach. The cost was $15 for the first hour and $5 per hour after that. If he paid $27.50, you can determine how many hours Hong rented the bike using a two-step equation and the Distributive Property.

Let h represent the number of hours for which the bike is rented. Then the equation is $27.50 = 15 + 5(h - 1)$. The solution to the equation is shown.

$$27.50 = 15 + 5(h - 1)$$
$$27.50 = 15 + 5h - 5$$
$$27.50 = 10 + 5h$$
$$27.50 - 10 = 10 - 10 + 5h$$
$$\frac{17.50}{5} = \frac{5h}{5}$$
$$3.5 = h$$

Verify the solution.

$$27.50 \stackrel{?}{=} 15 + 5(3.5 - 1)$$
$$27.50 \stackrel{?}{=} 15 + 17.5 - 5$$
$$27.50 = 27.50$$

Hong rented the bike for 3.5 hours.

7.5 Graphing One-Variable Inequalities

A number line can be used to represent inequalities. The graph of an inequality in one variable is the set of all points on a number line that make the inequality true. Any simple inequality can be represented on a number line by a ray whose starting point is an open or closed circle. A ray begins at a starting point and goes on forever in one direction. A closed circle means that the starting point is part of the solution. An open circle means that the starting point is not part of the solution.

Example

The graph of the inequality $x > 8$ is shown.

```
    ←—+—+—+—+—+—+—+—+—○—+—+—+—+—→
      0  1  2  3  4  5  6  7  8  9  10 11 12
```

7.5 Solving Simple Inequalities

To solve an inequality means to determine the values of the variable that make the inequality true. The objective when solving an inequality is similar to the objective when solving an equation. The variable must be isolated on one side of the inequality symbol by using the operations of addition, subtraction, multiplication, and division. It is necessary to reverse the inequality symbol when you multiply or divide each side of an inequality by a negative value.

Example

The steps for solving the inequality $21 - 7x > 28$ are shown.

$$21 - 7x > 28$$
$$21 - 21 - 7x > 28 - 21$$
$$-7x > 7$$
$$\frac{-7x}{-7} < \frac{7}{-7}$$
$$x < -1$$

8 SOLVING PROBLEMS WITH EQUATIONS AND INEQUALITIES

Can you spot the rock climbers in this picture? Those climbers are scaling El Capitan, in Yosemite National Park, California. In 2008, two rock climbers climbed El Capitan in record time–under 3 hours.

8

8.1
SOME PLACES ARE EXPENSIVE; SOME PLACES ARE MORE AFFORDABLE
Multiple Representations of Problem Situations

Learning Goals

In this lesson, you will:

▶ Use different methods to represent a problem situation.

▶ Identify advantages and disadvantages of using a particular representation.

▶ Solve two-step equations.

Have you ever heard the phrase "cost of living"? Cost of living is the expenses adults and families have to maintain living. Some cost of living expenses are food, housing, utilities like electricity or heating, and clothing. Do you think that the cost of living is the same throughout your entire state? Do you think that the cost of living is the same in different cities in the United States?

Problem 1   Cost of Living Increase? Prices Are Going Up?

Ms. Jackson translates books for a living. She decides to change her fees to keep up with the cost of living. She will charge an initial fee of $325 to manage each project and $25 per page of translated text. Ms. Jackson does not consider partial pages in her fees.

1. Name the quantities that change in this problem situation.

2. Name the quantities that remain constant.

3. Which quantity depends on the other?

4. Complete the table that shows the various projects that Ms. Jackson has managed recently.

Number of Pages	Project Fees (dollars)	Total Cost of the Project (dollars)
1		
2		
		400
		425
10		
		1150
		2100
92		

5. What is the least number of pages that Ms. Jackson could translate? What is the greatest number of pages that Ms. Jackson has translated recently?

6. What are the least and greatest amounts of money that Ms. Jackson has earned?

7. Consider the ranges of values you wrote in Questions 5 and 6 and choose upper bounds (they should be whole numbers) for the *x*- and *y*-axes that are slightly greater than your greatest values. Then, write the lower and upper bound values in the table shown for each quantity.

Variable Quantity	Lower Bound	Upper Bound	Interval
Pages Translated			
Earnings			

8. Calculate the difference between the upper and lower bounds for each quantity. Then, choose an interval that divides evenly into this number. Doing so will ensure even spacing between the grid lines on your graph. Write these intervals in the table.

9. Label the graph using the bounds and intervals. Then, create a graph of the data from the table in Question 4.

Earnings (dollars)

Pages Translated

Is there a pattern to the points I plotted?

10. Should the points you graphed be connected by a line? Are the data continuous or discrete? Explain your reasoning.

11. Describe the relationship between the two quantities represented in the graph.

12. Use the graph to answer each question. Explain your reasoning.

    a. Approximately how much money would Ms. Jackson earn if she translated 57 pages?

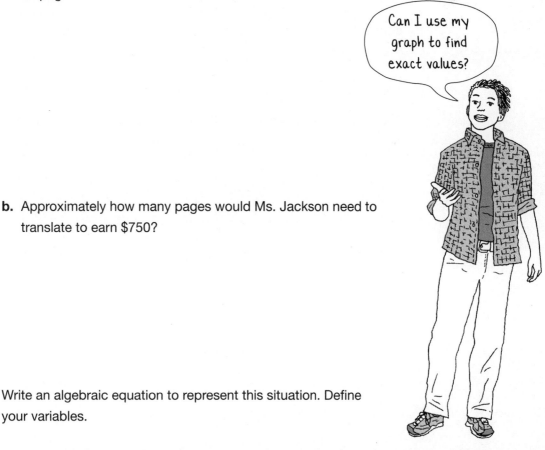

Can I use my graph to find exact values?

    b. Approximately how many pages would Ms. Jackson need to translate to earn $750?

13. Write an algebraic equation to represent this situation. Define your variables.

Problem 2 Who's Correct?

1. Ms. Jackson translated a 23-page technical manual for Technicians Reference Guide Inc. She received a check for $900. Was her check correct? If not, state the correct amount she should have received. Explain your reasoning in terms of the equation and the graph you created in Problem 1, Question 9.

2. Ms. Jackson translated a 42-page year-end report for Sanchez and Johnson Law Office. She received a check for $1050. Was her check correct? If not, state the correct amount she should have received. Explain your reasoning in terms of the equation and the graph you created.

3. Ms. Jackson translated a 35-page product specification document for Storage Pros. She received a check for $2075. Was her check correct? If not, state the correct amount she should have received. Explain your reasoning in terms of the equation and the graph you created.

Problem 3   Marketing

1. Ms. Jackson is planning a reception for potential clients. There is a flat fee of $275 to reserve a room at Mariano's Restaurant for the evening and a charge of $20 per person for food and a drink. If Ms. Jackson has $1250 to spend, what is the maximum number of potential clients she can invite? Write an equation, and show your work. Make sure to define your variable(s).

2. Ms. Jackson contracts with a marketing firm in hopes of building her business. The marketing firm will put together sets of marketing materials. Each set of materials will include packets to be mailed to 12 businesses. The marketing firm charges $125 to produce one set of materials. If Ms. Jackson has $500 to spend on this type of marketing, how many potential businesses can she contact? Make sure to define your variable(s).

Talk the Talk

Solve each equation. Verify your solution.

1. $16 = 3x - 4$

2. $1.2x + 5.3 = 5.9$

Be prepared to share your solutions and methods.

8.2 PLASTIC CONTAINERS
Using Two-Step Equations

8

Learning Goals

In this lesson, you will:

▶ Write and use two-step equations.

▶ Compare two problem situations.

Have you ever gotten a package in the mail or from a delivery company? If you have, chances are that your package contained some type of packaging material. One type of packaging material is packaging peanuts, or foam peanuts. The foam peanuts are poured into a box that contains an item or items being shipped. Even though foam peanuts are lightweight, they offer protection to the item being shipped.

Foam peanuts were invented in 1965 by the Dow Company as a way to cut shipping costs but, at the same time, protect valuables being shipped. Can you think of other materials or devices that can be used to ship items?

Problem 1 Different Shapes and Sizes

Your job at Storage Pros is to create new boxes to ship the company's plastic containers. Storage Pros makes all different shapes and sizes of plastic containers. To ship the containers, the lids are removed, allowing the containers to be stacked. Storage Pros wants to design its shipping boxes so that they will hold two dozen stacks of the plastic containers without lids in stacks of two dozen, regardless of the size or shape of the container.

The table shows the data gathered from measuring the heights of different-sized stacks of the various plastic containers.

> How are the stack heights changing?

Number of Containers	Stack Height (centimeters)	
	Round	Square
1	9	15
2	9.8	15.4
3	10.6	15.8
4	11.4	16.2
5	12.2	16.6
6		
7		

1. What are the variable quantities in this problem situation?

2. What quantity depends on the other?

3. Create a graph for each container shape's stack height in terms of the number of containers used. Determine the bounds and intervals and complete the table shown. Be sure to label your graph clearly. Use the symbols in the legend shown when graphing.

Variable Quantity	Lower Bound	Upper Bound	Interval
Number of Containers			
Stack Height			

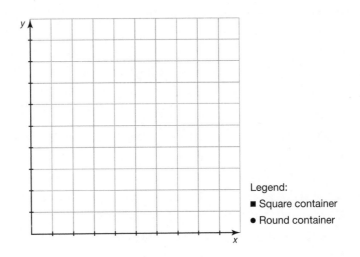

Legend:
■ Square container
● Round container

4. Did you connect the points on your graph? Why or why not?

5. What is the difference in height between a stack of two round containers and a stack of one round container? Explain your reasoning.

6. What is the difference in height between a stack of three round containers and a stack of two round containers?

I see a pattern!

7. What is the difference in height between a stack of four round containers and a stack of three round containers?

8. What is the difference in height between a stack of five round containers and a stack of four round containers?

9. How does the stack height change when one round container is added to a stack of round containers?

10. How does the stack height change when one square container is added to a stack of square containers? Explain your reasoning.

11. Determine the stack height for 6 and then 7 round and square containers. Then, complete the table and graph, Explain your strategy.

12. Determine the height of each stack of round containers. Show your work.

    a. What is the height of 10 round containers?

    b. What is the height of 15 round containers?

    c. What is the height of 20 round containers?

    d. Explain how you calculated each answer.

13. What does the expression $r - 1$ represent if you use r to represent the number of containers in a stack of round containers? Explain your reasoning.

14. Let h represent the stack height. Write an equation that represents the stack height of round containers in terms of the number of containers c in the stack.

15. Let *c* represent the number of containers in a stack of square containers, and let *h* represent the stack height. Write an equation that gives the stack height in terms of the number of containers in the stack.

16. How are the two equations you wrote similar? Why are these equations similar? Explain your reasoning.

17. How are the two equations you wrote different? Why are these equations different? Explain your reasoning.

18. Calculate the stack height of two dozen round containers using your equation. Show your work.

19. Calculate the stack height of two dozen square containers. Explain your reasoning.

20. Storage Pros had extra boxes that were 45 centimeters tall.

  a. How many square containers can be in each stack inside the box?

  b. How many round containers can be in each stack inside the box?

Talk the Talk

8

1. What is the advantage of the first table in Problem 1? What does it show?

2. What is the advantage of the graph in Problem 1? What does it show?

3. What is the advantage of using the equation? What does it show?

Be prepared to share your solutions and methods.

8.3

JUST ANOTHER SATURDAY

Solving More Complicated Equations

Learning Goals

In this lesson, you will:

▶ Solve equations containing fractions.

▶ Solve equations with variables on both sides.

▶ Verify solutions within a problem context.

Key Terms

▶ multiplicative inverse

▶ multiplying by the reciprocal

Cutting coupons has been a routine for U.S. citizens since the late 1800s. And who can blame Americans for trying to save money? Many sources agree that in the late 1800s, Atlanta business owner and pharmacist Asa Candler was one of the first to offer handwritten coupons to customers. By 1904, coupons had spread to the cereal market, and by 1930, coupons were a staple of American life. Besides in newspapers, where else have you seen coupons? Have you used coupons before?

Problem 1 Using a Recipe

Cousins Nic and Emily had plans on Saturday to visit the arcade at the mall. Before they could head out for the day, their Aunt Heather asked them for help baking cakes for the family reunion picnic on Sunday.

1. The recipe for the cake calls for $\frac{2}{3}$ of a cup of cocoa powder.
   The recipe for icing requires $\frac{3}{4}$ of a cup of sugar.

   a. Aunt Heather told the cousins that she has exactly four cups of cocoa powder. How many cakes can they make with the amount of cocoa powder they have? Write and solve an equation.

   b. How much sugar will they need to ice all the cakes? Write and solve an equation.

The one-step equation you solved in Question 1 contained a fractional coefficient. To solve an equation that contains a fractional coefficient, you can use *multiplicative inverses*. **Multiplicative inverses** are two numbers that when multiplied together equal 1. When you multiply a term with a fractional coefficient by the multiplicative inverse of the fraction, you can isolate the variable on one side of the equation. This is also known as **multiplying by the reciprocal.** When you multiply any number by its reciprocal, the result is 1.

> A coefficient is a number multiplied by a variable in an algebraic expression. Reciprocals are two numbers that when multiplied together result in a product of 1.

2. Consider the equation $26 = \frac{2}{3}x$. What number would you multiply $\frac{2}{3}$ by to get 1?

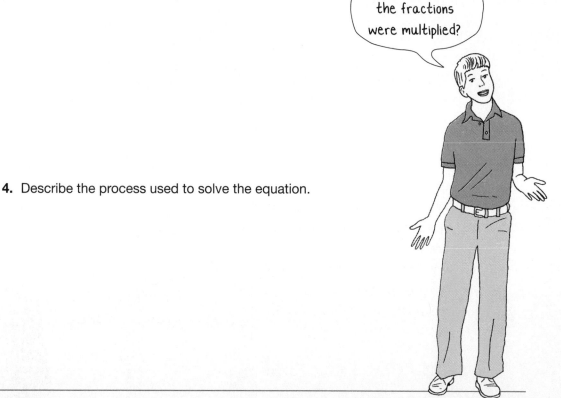

So, multiplying by the reciprocal IS like dividing the fraction by itself!

Analyze the solution to the equation $26 = \frac{2}{3}x$.

$$26 = \frac{2}{3}x$$

$$\frac{3}{2}(26) = \frac{3}{2}\left(\frac{2}{3}x\right)$$

$$\frac{3}{\overset{}{\underset{1}{2}}} \cdot \frac{\overset{13}{\cancel{26}}}{1} = 1x$$

$$3 \cdot 13 = 1x$$

$$39 = x$$

3. Verify that 39 is the solution.

Did you see how the fractions were multiplied?

4. Describe the process used to solve the equation.

5. Write a sentence to describe how to apply operations and inverse operations to solve each equation. Then, solve each equation and verify your solution.

a. $42 = \frac{3}{5}x + 12$

b. $-\frac{7}{3}x - 11 = -25$

c. $\frac{2}{9}x + \frac{7}{3} = -\frac{5}{3}$

d. $\frac{3}{4}(x - 1) + 2x = 15$

Problem 2 Can You Do Me A Favor?

After helping bake cakes for the family reunion picnic, Nic and Emily went to the mall. Just as they were leaving, Aunt Heather asked them to stop by the Super Cinema and check the prices of this year's Frequent Movie Viewer Discount Membership. Aunt Heather is considering buying a discount membership if she can save money throughout the year when she goes to the movies.

The box office associate at the Super Cinema told the cousins that a Frequent Movie Viewer membership costs $40. The membership is good for one year and allows the member to purchase movie tickets for $5.75 at any time with no restrictions. The regular price of a movie ticket is $9.25.

Would you recommend the discount card to Aunt Heather if she went to the movies once every two months? What if Aunt Heather went to the movies once a month? Would you recommend Aunt Heather purchase the discount card if she went to the movies every 3 weeks? What if Aunt Heather went to the movies twice a month?

It appears that you will need to determine the number of times Aunt Heather goes to the movies before you can suggest if she should purchase the discount membership.

1. Write an equation to represent the cost of purchasing a ticket without a membership. Let x represent the number of movie tickets and y represent the total cost of the movie tickets.

2. Use the equation you wrote in Question 1 to determine the cost of purchasing the specified number of tickets shown in a year.

   a. 6 tickets

b. 12 tickets

If I know the cost for 6 tickets, can I just double that for 12 tickets?

c. 18 tickets

d. 24 tickets

3. Write an equation to represent the cost of purchasing a ticket with a discount membership. Let *x* represent the number of movie tickets and *y* represent the total cost of the movie tickets.

4. Use your equation to determine the cost of purchasing the specified number of tickets shown in a year.

   a. 6 tickets

   b. 12 tickets

Why can't I just double the cost of 6 tickets and have the cost of 12 tickets?

   c. 18 tickets

   d. 24 tickets

5. Write an equation to represent when the cost without a membership and the cost with a membership would be the same.

To solve the equation you wrote in Question 5, you can move all the terms with variables to one side of the equals sign and keep all the constant terms on the other side.

A term is a number, a variable, or a product of numbers and variables in an equation. A constant term is a term that does not change its value.

6. If you do this, which term should you move? Describe the mathematical operation that should be used to begin solving this equation. Explain your reasoning.

7. Solve the equation you wrote in Question 5. Show your work.

8. Describe your solution in terms of the problem situation.

9. What recommendation would you provide Aunt Heather about purchasing a discount card?

Problem 3 A Party Surprise

1. While Nic and Emily were off to the mall, Aunt Heather was finalizing the details to rent a moon bounce for the family reunion picnic. She received cost estimates from two different companies that rent inflatable moon bounces.

   Walkin' On the Moon charges $55 per hour and a $100 delivery charge to rent a moon bounce. Moo-na Luna charges $65 per hour and a $75 delivery charge.

   a. Complete the table by writing an expression to represent the cost of renting a moon bounce from Walkin' on the Moon and Moo-na Luna. Then, evaluate the expressions for the given number of hours the moon bounce would be rented.

Moon Bounce Rental (hours)	Walkin' On the Moon (dollars)	Moo-na Luna (dollars)
h		
1		
1.5		
2		
2.5		
3		

   b. When is the cost of renting a moon bounce from Walkin' on the Moon the same as when renting from Moo-na Luna?

   c. Write an equation that represents the cost for the two companies being equal.

To solve this equation, you can move all the terms with variables to one side of the equals sign, and keep all the constant terms on the other side.

2. Describe the steps that you will use to solve this equation. Explain your reasoning.

3. Solve the equation. Show your work.

4. Describe your solution in terms of the problem situation.

5. Aunt Heather decides to rent the moon bounce for 3 hours. Which company should she call? Explain your reasoning.

Problem 4　Back at the Mall

Nic and Emily arrive at the arcade and head to their favorite games. Nic plays Dinosaur Tag, which costs $0.75 per game, and Emily plays Comet Avoidance, which costs $0.50 per game.

Nic has $15 to spend.

1. Write an equation to determine how much money Nic will have after playing Dinosaur Tag. Let x represent the number of games and let y represent the amount of money remaining.

2. Use your equation to determine how much money Nic has remaining after:

   a. 4 games.

   b. 6 games.

Emily has $13 to spend.

3. Write an equation to determine how much money Emily will have after playing Comet Avoidance. Let x represent the number of games, and let y represent the amount of money remaining.

4. Use your equation to determine how much money Emily has remaining after:

   a. 4 games.

   b. 6 games.

5. After how many games played will Nic and Emily have the same amount of money? Write an equation and solve. Explain your solution in terms of the problem situation.

 6. How much money will they each have left?

Problem 5   Just the Math

8

Solve each equation. Then check your answer.

1. $5x = 3x + 18$

2. $14x - 13 = 9x + 2$

3. $6x - 24 = 30$

4. $5x + 10 = 3x - 4$

5. $5x + 8 = 2(3x + 1)$

6. $4(3x - 1) = 2(x + 3)$

Be prepared to share your solutions and methods.

8.4 CLIMBING EL CAPITAN
Making Sense of Negative Solutions

Learning Goals

In this lesson, you will:

▶ Use multiple representations to analyze problem situations.

▶ Interpret negative solutions to problem situations.

▶ Identify independent and dependent variables.

▶ Evaluate algebraic expressions.

▶ Solve algebraic equations.

El Capitan is a 3000-foot vertical rock formation in Yosemite National Park in California. The granite cliff is one of the most popular challenges for experienced rock climbers. On July 3, 2008, Hans Florine and Yuji Hirayama scaled El Capitan in a record time of 2 hours 43 minutes and 33 seconds.

What type of equipment do you think these climbers used to climb El Capitan? Do you think that they used a map similar to a coordinate plane?

Problem 1   Rock Climbing

Two new climbers want to attempt to break the record by climbing El Capitan in 2 hours and 30 minutes.

1. If these climbers are to reach their goal, on average, how fast in feet per minute will they have to climb?

2. On average, about how fast in feet per minute did the record holders climb on average?

You want to watch the climbers attempt to break the record for climbing El Capitan. On the morning of the climb, you arrive late at 11:30 AM. When you arrive, the climbers are exactly halfway to the top.

3. How many feet high are the climbers?

4. Assuming they are climbing at the average rate needed, how many feet up the cliff will the climbers be:

    a. in two more minutes?

I have to pay attention to the units of measure!

b. in a quarter of an hour?

c. in one hour?

5. What are the two quantities that are changing in this problem situation?

6. Which quantity depends on the other?

7. Identify and define the independent and dependent variables with their units of measure for this situation.

8. Write the units of measure and the variables in the table. Then, complete the first four rows for this situation.

Quantities	Time	Height
Units of Measure		
Variables		
	0	
	2	
	15	
	60	

9. Write an equation or rule for calculating the value of the dependent variable when the value of the independent variable is given.

10. Use your equation to determine how long after 11:30 AM it will take the climbers to reach the top at 3000 feet. Make sure to show your work.

11. What time would the climbers reach the top?

12. Use your equation to determine when the climbers are 1400 feet up the cliff. Make sure to show your work.

13. What does this answer mean in terms of the problem situation?

14. Use your equation to determine how high up the cliff the climbers were:

    a. two minutes before 11:30.

    b. a half hour before 11:30.

15. Use your equation to determine how many minutes before 11:30 the climbers started to climb.

16. What time of day was that?

17. Write the values from Questions 10–15 in the table used in Question 8.

18. Plot the points from the table on the coordinate plane shown. Label the axes with the units of measure, and draw the graph of your equation.

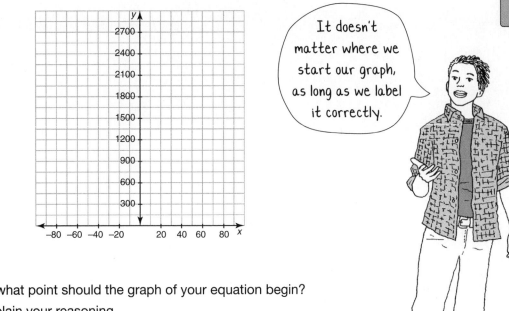

It doesn't matter where we start our graph, as long as we label it correctly.

19. At what point should the graph of your equation begin? Explain your reasoning.

20. At what point should the graph of your equation end? Explain your reasoning.

21. Locate the point at $x = -60$.

   a. What is the height of the climbers at this point?

   b. Interpret the meaning of this ordered pair in terms of the problem situation.

22. This analysis of the climbers' progress assumes that the climbers would climb at a steady rate of 20 feet per minute. In reality, would the climbers be able to do this during the whole climb?

23. Because of the first assumption that the climbers would climb at a steady rate of 20 feet per minute, the graph representing their height above the ground is a straight line. In reality, would this be a straight line?

24. The negative values of time on the graph represent "time ago" or "time before 11:30." Does this make sense?

 Be prepared to share your solutions and methods.

8.5 FLYING IN THE OCEAN
Rate of Change

8

Learning Goals

In this lesson, you will:

▶ Calculate the unit rate of change.

▶ Interpret the unit rate of change in a problem situation.

Key Term

▶ unit rate of change

To explore one of the last unknown regions on our planet, companies are starting to produce single-person, submersible deep-sea submarines like the Deep Flight I.

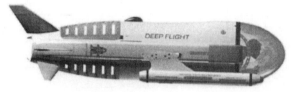

This submersible can dive to a depth of 3300 feet below sea level at a rate of 480 feet per minute.

Problem 1   Deep Flight 1

8

1. Suppose Deep Flight I is going to do a dive starting at sea level. Identify the independent and dependent quantities and their units of measure, and define variables for these quantities. Then, write an equation to represent Deep Flight I's depth.

> Depths in feet below sea level can be represented by negative numbers.

2. Use your equation to complete the table shown for this problem situation. Do not forget to define the quantities, units of measures, and variables for this situation.

	Independent Quantity	Dependent Quantity
Quantities		
Units of Measure		
Variables		
	0	
	1	
	2	
	3	
	4	
	5	
	6	

3. Why does the table end at 6 minutes for this problem situation?

4. Examine your table. What do you notice about each depth value in relation to the one before and the one after?

The **unit rate of change** is the amount that the dependent value changes for every one unit that the independent value changes.

5. In this problem, what is the unit rate of change?

6. How deep would the submersible be after:

   a. 2.5 minutes?

   b. 90 seconds?

   c. 45 seconds?

7. How many minutes would it take Deep Flight I to be:

    a. 1400 feet below sea level?

    b. 2100 feet below sea level?

c. at its maximum depth?

8. Construct a graph of this problem situation. Label the units on each axis. Then, plot all the points from the table and from Questions 6 and 7. Finally, draw the graph to represent the problem situation.

9. Use the graph to decide what times Deep Flight I will be:

a. above 1400 feet below sea level.

b. below 2100 feet below sea level.

How does this graph model the starting depth and maximum depth?

10. Write an inequality and solve it to determine the time Deep Flight I is:

    a. above 1400 feet below sea level.

    b. below 2100 feet below sea level.

11. How do your answers using the graph compare to those when you wrote and solved inequalities?

Problem 2   Deep Flight 2

Deep Flight I can dive to a depth of 3300 feet below sea level and can ascend to the surface at a rate of 650 feet per minute.

    1. Suppose Deep Flight I is going to ascend to sea level starting at its maximum depth of 3300 feet below sea level. Identify the independent and dependent quantities, define variables for these quantities, and write an equation to represent Deep Flight I's depth.

2. Use your equation to complete the table shown for this problem situation.

	Independent Quantity	Dependent Quantity
Quantities		
Units of Measure		
Variables		
	0	
	1	
	2	
	3	
	4	
	5	

3. Why does the table end at 5 minutes for this problem situation?

4. Examine your table. What do you notice about each depth value in relation to the one before and the one after?

5. In this problem, what is the unit rate of change?

6. How deep would the submersible be after ascending for:

    a. 2.5 minutes?

    b. 90 seconds?

    c. 45 seconds?

7. How many minutes would it take Deep Flight I to ascend to:

    a. 1000 feet below sea level?

    b. 2100 feet below sea level?

    c. sea level?

How do I represent "sea level" as a number?

8. Use this information to construct a graph of this problem situation. First, label the units of measure on each axis. Then, plot all the points from the table and from Questions 6 and 7. Finally, draw the graph to represent the problem situation.

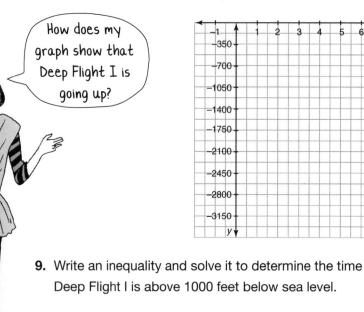

How does my graph show that Deep Flight I is going up?

9. Write an inequality and solve it to determine the time Deep Flight I is above 1000 feet below sea level.

You can use your graph to estimate first.

10. Write an inequality and solve it to determine the time Deep Flight I is below 2000 feet below sea level.

Be prepared to share your solutions and methods.

8.6

EMPTYING A TANK
Using Multiple Representations to Solve Problems

Learning Goal

In this lesson, you will:

▶ Use multiple representations to analyze problem situations.

Celsius and Fahrenheit seem to be always different. When it's freezing out, the Celsius temperature will be 0°, but the Fahrenheit temperature will be 32°. On a warm day, when it's about 75°F outside, the Celsius temperature will be about 24°.

There is one temperature where both Fahrenheit and Celsius are the same number. And you could use the formula $F = \frac{9}{5}C + 32$ to figure out what that number is. Can you do it?

Problem 1 Start with a Verbal Description

A tank that currently contains 2500 gallons of oil is being emptied at a rate of 25 gallons per minute. The capacity of this tank is 3000 gallons.

1. How many gallons are currently in the tank?

2. How fast is the tank being emptied?

3. What are the two quantities that are changing?

4. Define variables for these quantities. Then, identify which is the independent variable and which is the dependent variable.

5. What is the unit rate of change in this situation? Explain your reasoning.

6. Write an equation that relates the two quantities.

7. How many gallons will be in the tank after:

   a. a quarter of an hour?

   b. five and a half minutes?

   c. an hour and a half?

8. When will the tank be:

   a. half full?

b. empty?

9. How long ago did the tank contain 2600 gallons?

10. How long ago was the tank full?

11. Complete the table for this problem situation using your results from Questions 7–10.

	Independent Quantity	Dependent Quantity
Quantities		
Units of Measure		
Variables		

12. Label the units of measure on each axis and plot all the points from the table. Then, graph the equation for this situation. Make sure to label the units on the axes.

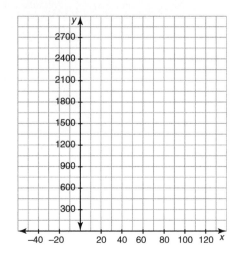

How does my graph show that the tank is being emptied?

Problem 2   Start with an Equation

The equation that converts a temperature in degrees Celsius to a temperature in degrees Fahrenheit is $F = \frac{9}{5}C + 32$, where F is the temperature in degrees Fahrenheit, and C is the temperature in degrees Celsius.

You can also write this formula as F = 1.8C + 32.

1. What is the temperature in degrees Fahrenheit if the temperature is:

    a. 36 degrees Celsius?

    b. −20 degrees Celsius?

2. What is the temperature in degrees Celsius if the temperature is:

a. 32 degrees Fahrenheit?

b. 212 degrees Fahrenheit?

3. What is the unit rate of change? Explain your reasoning.

4. At what temperature are both the Fahrenheit and Celsius temperatures equal? Show your work.

5. Complete the table with the information you calculated in Question 1 through Question 4.

	Independent Quantity	Dependent Quantity
Quantities		
Units of Measure		
Variables		

6. Label the units of measure on each axis and plot all the points from the table. Then, graph the equation for this situation.

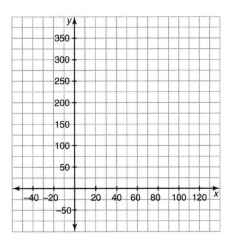

Problem 3 Start with a Table

Herman and Melville found this table.

Time in Minutes	Total Cost in Dollars
0	20
1	23
2	26
3	29
5	35
10	
20	
50	

The bottom three entries in the second column were smudged, and the boys couldn't read them.

Let's see if you can calculate the unknown values.

1. What is the unit rate of change shown in the table? Explain your reasoning.

2. Define variables for the quantities in the table, and write an equation that relates the two quantities.

3. Use your equation to complete the table. Show you work.

4. Use the completed table to construct a graph.

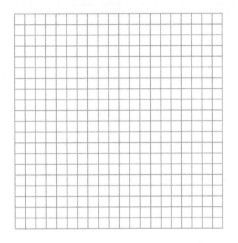

Problem 4   Start with a Graph

This graph shows the relationship between two quantities.

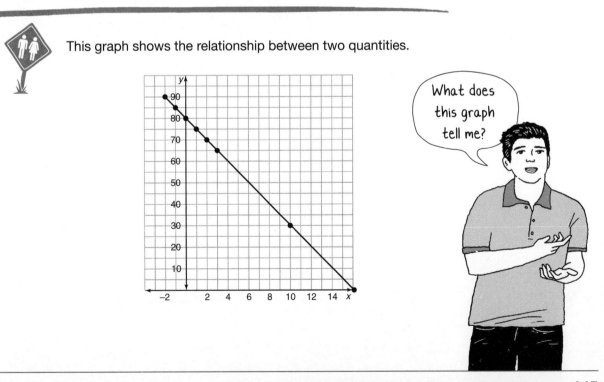

What does this graph tell me?

1. Complete the table using the information in the graph.

0	80

2. What is the unit rate of change? Explain your reasoning.

3. Write an equation for this relationship.

4. Write a problem situation that can be represented by this graph, table, and equation.

Be prepared to share your solutions and methods.

Chapter 8 Summary

Key Terms

▶ multiplicative inverse (8.3)

▶ multiplying by the reciprocal (8.3)

▶ unit rate of change (8.5)

8.1 Using a Table to Represent a Two-Step Problem Situation

To create a table to represent a problem situation, first decide which quantities change, which remain constant, and which quantity depends on the other. Label the independent quantity in the left column (or top row), the constant quality in the middle column (or middle row), and the dependent quantity in the right column (or bottom row). Label the units of measure for each quantity. Then, choose several values for the independent quantity, and determine the corresponding dependent quantity.

Example

A floral shop charges $2 per stem of flowers in an arrangement. It also charges a $4.50 delivery fee.

Number of Flowers (stem)	Delivery Fee (in dollars)	Total Cost of Arrangement (in dollars)
10	4.50	24.50
12	4.50	28.50
15	4.50	34.50
17	4.50	38.50
20	4.50	44.50

> Getting some sleep helps your brain learn complicated tasks. Work hard during the day and your brain will work hard for you at night!

8.1 Using a Graph to Represent a Two-Step Problem Situation

To create a graph to represent a problem situation, first decide which quantities change, which remain constant, and which quantity depends on the other. The dependent quantity is written along the *y*-axis and the independent quantity is written along the *x*-axis. Then, determine the upper and lower bounds, or greatest and least values, of the *x*- and *y*-axes. Calculate the difference between the upper and lower bounds for each quantity, and choose an interval that divides evenly into this number to ensure even spacing between the grid lines on your graph. Plot ordered pairs on the graph, and connect them in a line if they represent continuous data.

Example

Variable Quantity	Lower Bound	Upper Bound	Interval
Number of Flowers	10	20	1
Total Cost of Arrangement	5	50	5

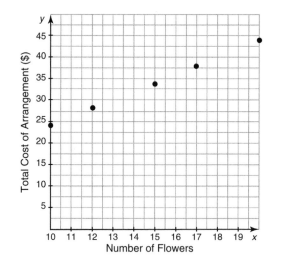

8.1 Using a Two-Step Equation to Represent a Problem Situation

Write a problem situation that is written in sentence form and requires two operations to solve as a two-step equation. Define unknown amounts in the situation as variables.

Example

Let C represent the total cost of an arrangement, and f represent the number of flowers in the arrangement.

The equation is $C = 2f + 4.50$.

8.1 Using an Equation and Graph to Determine if a Solution Is Correct

Substitute a value for the independent variable into the equation to see if the solution given is correct. You can also look at the graph to see if the solution given is represented as a point along the line in the graph of the equation.

Example

Victor takes an order for two dozen roses to be delivered tomorrow. He tells the customer that the arrangement will cost $54.50.

Victor's calculation is incorrect. The customer will owe $52.50. You can verify that Victor's calculation is incorrect by writing an equation.

$2(24) + 4.50 = 52.50$

The ordered pair (24, 54.50) is not a point along the line in the graph.

8.1 Solving Two-Step Equations

To solve a two-step equation, the variable must be isolated by performing two inverse operations. Perform the inverse operations in the reverse order of operations found in the original equation. To determine if your solution is correct, substitute the value of the variable back into the original equation. If the equation remains balanced, then you have calculated the solution of the equation.

Example

$$9x - 14 = 94$$
$$9x - 14 + 14 = 94 + 14$$
$$9x = 108$$
$$\frac{9x}{9} = \frac{108}{9}$$
$$x = 12$$

Check the solution.
$$9(12) - 14 = 94$$
$$108 - 14 = 94$$
$$94 = 94$$

8.2 Writing and Solving Two-Step Equations

Look at a table of values for a situation. Decide which set of values is the independent quantity, and which is the dependent quantity. Calculate the difference between consecutive independent quantities in the dependent quantity. Define the variables, and write the equation. Solve to answer questions about the situation.

Example

The table shows the cost to rent a car.

U Rent It Rental Costs per Day	
Number of Days	**Total Cost**
3	$240
4	$269
5	$298
6	$327
7	$356

8.2 Write an equation that represents the total cost, t, of renting a car from U Rent It in terms of the number of days rented, d.

$269 - 240 = 29$
$298 - 269 = 29$
$327 - 298 = 29$
$356 - 327 = 29$
$t = 240 + 29(d - 3)$

8.2   **Comparing Two Problem Situations**

To compare two problem situations, substitute the same value into two similar equations and compare their outcomes.

Example

Ronald needs to hire a caterer for the school picnic. He is comparing catering companies to find the most affordable option. The total cost, t, for a picnic lunch from Callie's Catering in terms of the number of students, s, is represented by the equation $t = 120 + 5(s - 20)$.

The total cost, t, for a picnic lunch from Paco's Picnics in terms of the number of students, s, is represented by the equation $t = 100 + 7.50(s - 15)$. Calculate the total cost for each company if Ronald estimates 200 students. Ronald can determine which company is more affordable for providing catering for 200 students.

Total Cost from Callie's Catering
$$t = 120 + 5(s - 20)$$
$$= 120 + 5(200 - 20)$$
$$= 120 + 900$$
$$= 1020$$

Total Cost from Paco's Picnics
$$t = 100 + 7.50(s - 15)$$
$$= 100 + 7.50(200 - 15)$$
$$= 100 + 1387.50$$
$$= 1487.50$$

For 200 students, Callie's Catering is more affordable.

8.3 Solving Equations with Fractions

To solve an equation that contains a fractional coefficient, you can use multiplicative inverses to isolate the variable on one side. This is also known as multiplying by the reciprocal.

Example

Solve the equation $\frac{4}{5}x = 16$.

$$\frac{4}{5}x = 16$$

$$\frac{5}{4}\left(\frac{4}{5}x\right) = \frac{5}{4}(16)$$

$$x = 20$$

Verify the solution.

$$\frac{4}{5}(20) \stackrel{?}{=} 16$$

$$16 = 16$$

8.3 Solving Equations with Variables on Both Sides

To solve an equation with variables on both sides, you must move all the terms with variables to one side of the equation and keep all the constant terms on the other side.

Example

Solve the equation $2x + 7 = 8(4 - x)$.

$2x + 7 = 8(4 - x)$

$2x + 7 = 32 - 8x$

$2x + 8x + 7 = 32 - 8x + 8x$

$10x + 7 - 7 = 32 - 7$

$\frac{10x}{10} = \frac{25}{10}$

$x = 2.5$

Verify the solution.

$2(2.5) + 7 \stackrel{?}{=} 8(4 - 2.5)$

$5 + 7 \stackrel{?}{=} 8(1.5)$

$12 = 12$

8.3 Verifying Solutions in a Problem Context

To determine when the outcomes of two similar situations will be the same, set the two equations equal to each other and solve. Verify the exact value of the outcome by substituting the solution for the variable in each equation.

Example

Kylie is buying balloons for the school dance. Better Balloons charges $0.10 per balloon plus a $6.00 inflating fee per order. Bouncy Balloons charges $0.18 per balloon plus a $0.04 inflating fee per balloon. Let t represent the total cost and b represent the number of balloons ordered. What number of balloons can Kylie order so that the cost of the order from both balloon stores will be the same? What is the total cost for that number of balloons?

$$0.1b + 6 = 0.18b + 0.04b$$
$$6 = 0.18b + 0.04b - 0.1b$$
$$6 = 0.12b$$
$$\frac{6}{0.12} = \frac{0.12b}{0.12}$$
$$50 = b$$

$$t = 0.1b + 6$$
$$= 0.1(50) + 6$$
$$= 11$$

$$t = 0.18b + 0.04b$$
$$= 0.18(50) + 0.04(50)$$
$$= 11$$

If Kylie buys 50 balloons, the cost will be the same from either store. Fifty balloons will cost $11.00.

8.4 Identifying Independent and Dependent Variables to Write and Solve Algebraic Equations

Algebraic equations can be used to represent and analyze problem situations. Identify and define the variables as the quantities that change in a problem situation. The dependent variable is the quantity that depends on the other. When given the dependent variable, an algebraic equation can be solved to determine the independent variable.

Example

Ling is competing in a 26-mile marathon. She hopes to run at an average rate of 5 miles per hour. It is now 3 hours after the beginning of the race, and Ling is 15 miles into the race. You can write and solve an equation to determine when Ling will reach the 20 mile mark.

Independent variable t = time in hours

Dependent variable d = total distance in miles

$$d = 15 + 5t$$
$$20 = 15 + 5t$$
$$5 = 5t$$
$$1 = t$$

Ling will reach the 20 mile mark of the race 1 hour from now, or 4 hours after the beginning of the race.

Interpreting Negative Solutions

Often a negative solution will arise when evaluating an algebraic equation with a valid dependent value. In the case of time, the solution can represent "time ago" or "time before." In the case of height or elevation, the solution can represent a value below the current level.

Example

Ling is competing in a 26-mile marathon. She hopes to run at an average rate of 5 miles per hour. It is now 3 hours after the beginning of the race, and Ling is 15 miles into the race. You can write and solve an equation to determine when Ling reached the halfway point of the race.

Independent variable t = time in hours

Dependent variable d = total distance in miles

$$d = 15 + 5t$$
$$13 = 15 + 5t$$
$$-2 = 5t$$
$$-0.4 = t$$

Ling reached the halfway point of the race 0.4 hour, or 24 minutes, ago.

8.5 Identifying Rate of Change

Algebraic equations can be used to represent problem situations. The unit rate of change is the amount the dependent value changes for every one unit the independent value changes.

Example

A helicopter is rising at 9.5 meters per second. You can write and solve an equation to determine how long it will take the helicopter to reach a height of 855 meters.

Independent variable t = time in seconds
Dependent variable h = height in meters
Unit rate of change = 9.5 meters per second

$$h = 9.5t$$
$$855 = 9.5t$$
$$90 = t$$

90 seconds = 1.5 minutes
The helicopter will take 1.5 minutes to reach 855 meters.

8.6 Using Multiple Representations

A problem situation can be represented in multiple ways. A verbal description, an algebraic equation, a table, or a graph can represent a problem situation.

Example

Manuel is using a garden hose to fill his backyard pool at 8 gallons per minute. After 5 minutes, the pool has 40 gallons of water. The capacity of the pool is 400 gallons. You can write and solve an equation to determine how many gallons of water will be in the pool after an additional 10 minutes.

Independent variable t = time in minutes
Dependent variable w = amount of water in gallons
Unit rate of change = 8 gallons per minute

$$w = 40 + 8t$$
$$w = 40 + 8(10)$$
$$w = 40 + 80$$
$$w = 120$$

8.6

There will be 120 gallons of water in the pool after an additional 10 minutes.

You can use a table to represent this problem situation.

	Independent Quantity	Dependent Quantity
Quantities	Time	Water
Units of Measure	Minutes	Gallons
Variables	t	w
	0	40
	5	80
	10	120
	15	160
	30	280
	45	400

You can also plot the points and graph the equation for this problem situation.

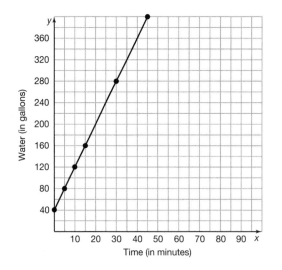

GLOSSARY

A

acute angle

An acute angle is an angle whose measure is greater than 0° but less than 90°.

Examples

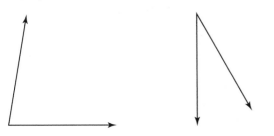

---

additive inverses

Two numbers with the sum of zero are called additive inverses. An Identity Property that states for every rational number a, $a + (-a) = 0$ designates the opposite of a number as the additive inverse.

Example

$$6 + (-6) = 0 \quad -0.45 + 0.45 = 0 \quad \frac{3}{13} + \frac{-3}{13} = 0$$

---

adjacent angles

Adjacent angles are two angles that share a common vertex and a common side.

Examples

Angles *BAC* and *CAD* are <u>adjacent angles</u>. The angles share the vertex *A* and the side *AC*.

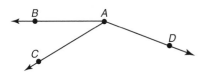

---

algebraic expression

An algebraic expression, sometimes shortened to be called an expression, is a mathematical phrase involving at least one variable and sometimes numbers and operation symbols.

Examples

$$a \quad 2a + b \quad xy \quad \frac{4}{p}$$
$$z^2 \quad \sqrt{(4y + 4)^2} \quad 2.5 \times 10^y$$

---

angle

An angle is formed by two rays that share a common endpoint.

Example

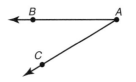

Angle *BAC* is formed by the rays $\overrightarrow{AB}$ and $\overrightarrow{AC}$ with a common endpoint at *A*.

---

angle bisector

If a ray is drawn through the vertex of an angle and divides that angle into two angles of equal measure, or two congruent angles, then the ray is called an angle bisector.

Example

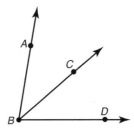

Ray *BC* is an <u>angle bisector</u>. It bisects angle *ABD* to create two congruent angles: angles *ABC* and *CBD*.

Glossary

arc

An arc is a part of a circle. It is the curve between two points on a circle.

Example

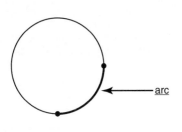

aspect ratio

An aspect ratio of an image is the ratio of its width to its height. Aspect ratios are written as two numbers separated by a colon (width : height).

Example

Aspect ratios are used to determine the screen sizes for movie screens and televisions.

—————— B ——————

bar notation

Bar notation is used for repeating decimals. A bar is drawn over digits that repeat.

Example

$\frac{2}{3} = 0.66666666\ldots = 0.\overline{6}$

base of a pyramid

The base of a pyramid is a single polygonal face. Similar to prisms, pyramids are classified by their bases.

Example

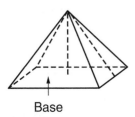

Base

bisect

To bisect means to divide into two equal parts.

—————— C ——————

census

A census is the collection of data from every member of a population.

Example

The U.S. <u>Census</u> is taken every 10 years. The U.S. government counts every member of the population every 10 years.

center of a circle

The center of a circle is the point from which all points on the circle are equidistant. Circles are named by their center point.

circle

A circle is a collection of points on the same plane equidistant from the same point.

coefficient

A coefficient is the number that is multiplied by a variable in an algebraic expression.

Examples

coefficient   The <u>coefficient</u> is 1 even though it is not shown.

combining like terms

When you simplify expressions by adding or subtracting like terms, you are combining like terms.

Example

$4x + 3p + x + 2 = 5x + 3p + 2$
$24a^2 + 2a - 9a^2 = 15a^2 + 2a$

commission

A commission is an amount of money a salesperson earns after selling a product.

Example

5% commission on \$350

$.05 \times 350 = \$17.50$ ←commission

Glossary

common factor

A common factor is a number or an algebraic expression that is a factor of two or more numbers of algebraic expressions.

Example

5(12) + 5(9) = 5(12 + 9)
5 is a common factor of both 5(12) and 5(9).

compass

A compass is a tool that is used to create arcs and circles.

complementary angles

Two angles are complementary angles if the sum of their angle measures is equal to 90°.

Example

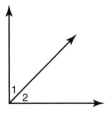

∠1 and ∠2 are complementary angles.

complementary events

Complementary events are events that consist of the desired outcome, and the remaining events that consist of all the undesired outcomes.

compound event

A compound event combines two or more events, using the word "and" or the word "or."

congruent

Congruent means to have the same size, shape, and measure.

congruent angles

Congruent angles are two or more angles that have equal measures.

congruent geometric figures

Congruent geometric figures are figures that have exactly the same size and shape. This means that each part of one figure is congruent to each corresponding part of the other figure.

congruent line segments

Line segments that have the same length are called congruent line segments.

constant of proportionality

In a proportional relationship, the ratio between two values is always the same, or constant. This is called the constant of proportionality. You can typically use the variable k to represent the constant of proportionality.

construct

When you construct a geometric figure, you create it using only a compass and a straightedge.

convert

To convert a measurement means to change it to an equivalent measurement in different units.

Example

To convert 36 inches to feet, you can multiply:

$$36 \text{ in.} \left(\frac{1 \text{ ft}}{12 \text{ in.}} \right) = \frac{36 \text{ ft}}{12}$$
$$= 3 \text{ ft}$$

coplanar lines

Coplanar lines are two or more lines that are located in the same plane.

Glossary

corresponding angles

Corresponding angles are angles that have the same relative positions in geometric figures.

Examples

Corresponding angles of the two quadrilaterals are listed below.

Angle *M* and angle *C* are corresponding angles.

Angle *A* and angle *O* are corresponding angles.

Angle *T* and angle *I* are corresponding angles.

Angle *H* and angle *N* are corresponding angles.

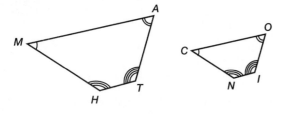

corresponding sides

Corresponding sides are sides that have the same relative positions in geometric figures.

Example

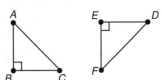

Sides *AB* and *DE* are corresponding sides.

cross-section

A cross-section of a solid is the two-dimensional figure formed by the intersection of a plane and a solid when a plane passes through the solid.

Example

The cross section of the cylinder is a circle.

data

When information is collected, the facts or numbers gathered are called data.

Examples

Heights of different animals at the zoo, area covered by different U.S. cities in square miles.

degrees

One unit of measure of angles is degrees (°).

depreciation

Depreciation is the decline in value of an item over time.

Example

The value of a car usually depreciates, or decreases in value, over time.

diameter

The diameter of a circle is the distance across the circle through the center. The diameter is equal to twice the radius of the circle.

Example

In circle *O*, segment *AB* is a diameter. The diameter *AB* is equal to twice the radius *OA*. The radius *OA* is 6 centimeters, so the diameter *AB* is 12 centimeters.

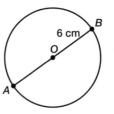

direct proportion

When two variables, *y* and *x*, are related in such a way that $y = kx$ with *k* being the constant of proportionality, the variables form a direct proportion. You can say that *y* is directly proportional to *x*.

Glossary

direct variation

A function represents a direct variation if the ratio between the output values and input values is a constant. The quantities are said to vary directly.

Example

If Melissa earns $8.25 per hour, then the amount she earns is in direct variation with the number of hours she works. The amount $8.25 is the constant of proportionality.

Distributive Property of Division over Addition

The Distributive Property of Division over Addition states that if a, b, and c are real numbers and $c \neq 0$, then $\frac{a+b}{c} = \frac{a}{c} + \frac{b}{c}$.

Examples

$$\frac{1+2}{4} = \frac{1}{4} + \frac{2}{4}$$

$$\frac{3}{4} \qquad \frac{3}{4}$$

$$\frac{3}{16} + \frac{9}{16} = \frac{3+9}{16}$$

$$\frac{12}{16} = \frac{3}{4} \qquad \frac{12}{16} = \frac{3}{4}$$

Distributive Property of Division over Subtraction

The Distributive Property of Division over Subtraction states that if a, b, and c are real numbers and $c \neq 0$, then $\frac{a-b}{c} = \frac{a}{c} - \frac{b}{c}$.

Examples

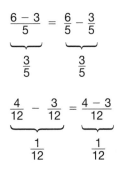

$$\frac{6-3}{5} = \frac{6}{5} - \frac{3}{5}$$

$$\frac{3}{5} \qquad \frac{3}{5}$$

$$\frac{4}{12} - \frac{3}{12} = \frac{4-3}{12}$$

$$\frac{1}{12} \qquad \frac{1}{12}$$

Distributive Property of Multiplication over Addition

The Distributive Property of Multiplication over Addition states that for any real numbers a, b, and c, $a \cdot (b + c) = a \cdot b + a \cdot c$

Examples

$$2(13 + 5) = 2(13) + 2(5)$$
$$2(18) = 26 + 10$$
$$36 = 36$$

$$\frac{1}{4} \cdot (8 + 4) = (\frac{1}{4} \cdot 8) + (\frac{1}{4} \cdot 4)$$

$$\frac{1}{4} \cdot 12 = \frac{8}{4} + \frac{4}{4}$$

$$\frac{12}{4} = \frac{12}{4}$$

Distributive Property of Multiplication over Subtraction

The Distributive Property of Multiplication over Subtraction states that if a, b, and c are any real numbers, then $a \cdot (b - c) = a \cdot b - a \cdot c$.

Examples

$$2(13 - 5) = 2(13) - 2(5)$$
$$2(8) = 26 - 10$$
$$16 = 16$$

$$\frac{1}{4} \cdot (8 - 4) = (\frac{1}{4} \cdot 8) - (\frac{1}{4} \cdot 4)$$

$$\frac{1}{4} \cdot 4 = \frac{8}{4} - \frac{4}{4}$$

$$\frac{4}{4} = \frac{4}{4}$$

draw

When you draw a geometric figure, you create it using tools such as a ruler, a straightedge, a compass, or a protractor.

endpoints

The endpoints of a line segment are the points where the line segment begins and ends.

Example

endpoint   endpoint

equally likely

When the probabilities of all the outcomes of an experiment are equal, then the probabilities are called equally likely.

equation

An equation is a mathematical sentence that is created by placing an equals sign, $=$, between two expressions.

Examples

$y = 2x + 4$

$6 = 3 + 3$

$2(8) = 26 - 10$

$\frac{1}{4} \cdot 4 = \frac{8}{4} - \frac{4}{4}$

equivalent ratios

Equivalent ratios are ratios that represent the same part-to-part or the same part-to-whole relationship.

evaluate an algebraic expression

To evaluate an algebraic expression, replace each variable in the expression with a number or numerical expression and then perform all possible mathematical operations.

Example

Evaluate the expression $\dfrac{4x + (2^3 - y)}{p}$ for $x = 2.5$, $y = 8$, and $p = 2$.

• First replace the variables with numbers:

$$\frac{4\mathbf{(2.5)} + (2^3 - \mathbf{8})}{\mathbf{2}}$$

• Then calculate the value of the expression:

$$\frac{10 + 0}{2} = \frac{10}{2} = 5$$

event

An event is one or a group of possible outcomes for a given situation.

experiment

An experiment is a situation involving chance that leads to results, or outcomes.

experimental probability

Experimental probability is the ratio of the number of times an event occurs to the total number of trials performed.

Exterior Angle Inequality Theorem

The Exterior Angle Inequality Theorem states that the measure of an exterior angle of a triangle is greater than the measure of either of the remote interior angles of the triangle.

Exterior Angle Theorem

The Exterior Angle Theorem states that the measure of the exterior angle of a triangle is equal to the sum of the measures of the two remote interior angles of the triangle.

factoring

To factor an expression means to rewrite the expression as a product of factors.

Example

$5(12) + 5(9) = 5(12 + 9)$

geometric construction

When a figure is created using only a compass and a straightedge, it is called a geometric construction.

geometric figures

Geometric figures are figures composed of lines, line segments, points, lines, rays, angles, and arcs.

Glossary

greatest common factor (GCF)

The greatest common factor (GCF) is the largest factor that two or more number or terms have in common.

Example

$14x + 35$
Since 7 is the greatest common factor of 14 and 35 this expression can be written as
$7(2x + 5)$

 **H**

height of a pyramid

The height of a pyramid is the perpendicular distance from the vertex of the pyramid to the base of the pyramid.

Example

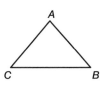
Height

 **I**

included angle

An included angle is the angle whose sides are made up of the specific sides of the triangle.

Example

In triangle ABC, angle A is the included angle formed by consecutive sides $\overline{AB}$ and $\overline{AC}$.

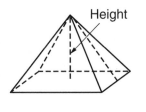

included side

An included side is a side between the two specific angles of the triangle.

Example

In triangle ABC, $\overline{AB}$ is the included side formed by consecutive angles A and B.

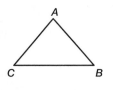

inscribed circle

An inscribed circle is a circle that fits exactly within the boundaries of another shape. It is the largest possible circle that will fit inside a plane figure.

Example

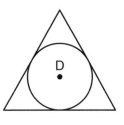

interest

When you save money in a bank savings account, the bank pays you money each year and adds it to your account. This additional money is interest.

intersection

An intersection is the point at which two or more lines or arcs intersect, or cross.

Example

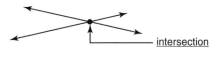
intersection

inverse operations

Inverse operations are operations that undo each other.

Examples

Addition and subtraction are inverse operations: $351 + 25 - 25 = 351$.

Multiplication and division are inverse operations: $351 \times 25 \div 25 = 351$.

 **L**

lateral edges of a pyramid

The lateral edges of a pyramid are the edges formed by the intersection of two lateral faces.

Example

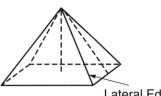
Lateral Edge

lateral faces of a pyramid

The lateral faces of a pyramid are the triangular faces of the pyramid. All lateral faces of a pyramid intersect at a common point.

Example

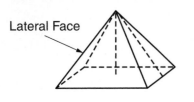

Lateral Face

like terms

Terms whose variable portions are the same are called like terms.

Examples

like terms

$$4x + 3p + x + 2 = 5x + 3p + 2$$

like terms

$$24a^2 + 2a - 9a^2 = 15a^2 + 2^a$$

no like terms

$$m + m^2 - x + x^3$$

line

A line is described as a straight, continuous arrangement of an infinite number of points.

line segment

A line segment is a portion of a line that includes two points and all the points between those two points.

Example

A   B

$\overline{AB}$ is a line segment.

linear pair

A linear pair of angles are two adjacent angles that have noncommon sides that form a line.

Example

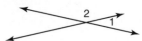

2

1

Angles 1 and 2 are a <u>linear pair</u>.

M

mean absolute deviation

The mean absolute deviation is the average of the absolute values of the deviations of each data value from the mean.

means and extremes method

The means and extremes method involves solving a proportion by setting the product of the means equal to the product of the extremes and then solving the resulting equation to find the unknown quantity.

Example

$$\frac{1}{2} = \frac{x}{9}$$
$$9 \times 1 = 2x$$
$$\frac{9}{2} = x$$
$$4.5 = x$$

midpoint of a segment

The midpoint of a segment is a point that divides the segment into two congruent segments, or two segments of equal length.

Example

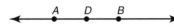

A   D   B

Point *D* is the midpoint of line segment *AB*.

multiplicative inverse

Multiplicative inverses are two numbers that when multiplied together equal 1.

Examples

The <u>multiplicative inverse</u> of $\frac{3}{7}$ is $\frac{7}{3}$:

$$\frac{3}{7} \times \frac{7}{3} = \frac{21}{21} = 1.$$

The <u>multiplicative inverse</u> of 5 is $\frac{1}{5}$:

$$\frac{5}{1} \times \frac{1}{5} = \frac{5}{5} = 1.$$

multiplying by the reciprocal

When you multiply a term with a fractional coefficient by the multiplicative inverse of the fraction, you can isolate the variable on one side of the equation. This is known as multiplying by the reciprocal. When you multiply any number by its reciprocal, the result is 1.

Example

$10 = \frac{1}{2}x$ multiplying by the reciprocal

$$\frac{2}{1}(10) = \frac{2}{1}(\frac{1}{2}x)$$

$$20 = 1x$$

— N —

non-repeating decimal

A non-repeating decimal neither terminates nor repeats.

Examples

$\sqrt{2} = 1.414213562373095\ldots$
$\sqrt{29} = 5.385164807134504\ldots$

---

non-terminating decimal

A non-terminating decimal is a decimal that continues without end.

Examples

$\sqrt{2} = 1.414\ldots$ $\sqrt{29} = 5.385\ldots$

$\frac{2}{3} = 0.6666666\ldots$

---

non-uniform probability model

When all probabilities in a probability model are not equivalent to each other, it is called a non-uniform probability model.

— O —

obtuse angle

An obtuse angle is an angle whose measure is greater than 90° but less than 180°.

Example

origin

The origin is the point on a graph with ordered pair (0, 0).

Example

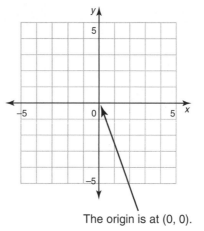

The origin is at (0, 0).

---

outcome

An outcome is the result of a single trial of an experiment.

— P —

parameter

When data are gathered from a population, the characteristic used to describe the population is called a parameter.

Example

If you wanted to find out the average height of the students at your school, and you measured every student at the school, the characteristic "average height" would be a parameter.

---

percent decrease

A percent decrease occurs when the new amount is less than the original amount. It is a ratio of the amount of decrease to the original amount.

Example

The price of a $12 shirt has decreased to $8.

$$\frac{\$12 - \$8}{\$12} = \frac{\$4}{\$12} = 0.\overline{3} = 33.\overline{3}\%$$

The percent decrease is 33.$\overline{3}$%.

percent equation

A percent equation is written in the form percent × whole = part, where the percent is often written as a decimal.

Example

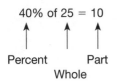

percent increase

A percent increase occurs when the new amount is greater than the original amount. It is a ratio of the amount of increase to the original amount.

Example

The price of a $12 shirt has increased to $13.20.

$$\frac{\$13.20 - \$12}{\$12} = \frac{\$1.20}{\$12} = 0.1 = 10\%$$

The <u>percent increase</u> is 10%

perpendicular

Two lines, line segments, or rays are perpendicular if they intersect to form 90° angles. The perpendicular symbol is ⊥.

Example

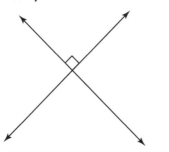

perpendicular bisector

A perpendicular bisector is a line, line segment, or ray that intersects the midpoint of a line segment at a 90° angle.

Example

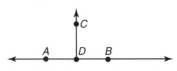

Ray *DC* is a <u>perpendicular bisector</u> of line segment *AB*.

pi (π)

The number pi is the ratio of the circumference of a circle to its diameter. That is,

$$pi = \frac{circumference\ of\ a\ circle}{diameter\ of\ a\ circle}.$$

plane

A plane is described as a flat surface. A plane has infinite length and width but no depth.

point

A point is described as a location in space.

population

The population is the entire set of items from which data can be selected. When you decide what you want to study, the population is the set of all elements in which you are interested. The elements of that population can be people or objects.

Example

If you wanted to find out the average height of the students at your school, the number of students at the school would be the <u>population</u>.

probability

Probability is a measure of the likelihood that an event will occur.

principal

The original amount of money originally invested is the principal.

probability model

A probability model is a list of each possible outcome along with its probability.

Properties of Equality

The Properties of Equality allow you to balance and solve equations involving any number. These properties include the Addition Property of Equality, the Subtraction Property of Equality, the Multiplication Property of Equality, and the Division Property of Equality.

Examples

Addition Property of Equality:
    If $a = b$, then $a + c = b + c$.

Subtraction Property of Equality:
    If $a = b$, then $a - c = b - c$.

Multiplication Property of Equality:
    If $a = b$, then $a \times c = b \times c$.

Division Property of Equality:
    If $a = b$, and $c \neq 0$, then $\frac{a}{c} = \frac{b}{c}$.

proportion

A proportion is an equation that states that two ratios are equal.

Example

$$\frac{1}{2} = \frac{4.5}{9}$$

protractor

A protractor is a tool that can be used to approximate the measure of an angle.

pyramid

A pyramid is a polyhedron formed by connecting one polygonal face to several triangular faces.

Example

A pyramid is named according to the shape of its base. The pyramid below is a triangular pyramid.

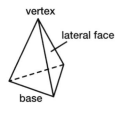

vertex

lateral face

base

R

radius

The radius is the distance from the center of a circle to a point on the circle.

Example

In the circle, O is the center and the length of segment OA is the radius.

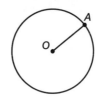

random number generator

A random number generator is any computer program or calculator that can generate numbers such that each number has an equal chance of occurring each time.

Example

You can use a graphing calculator and follow steps to generate random numbers.

random number tables

Random number tables are tables that display random numbers. These tables can contain hundreds of digits.

Example

Line 7	54621	62117	55516	40467
	11268	80811	14821	74154
	83479	55516		

random sample

A random sample is a sample that is selected from the population in such a way that every member of the population has the same chance of being selected.

Example

If you wanted to find out the average height of the students at your school, you could choose just a certain number of students randomly and measure their heights. This group of students would be a <u>random sample</u>.

range

The range of the data refers to the minimum and maximum values in a data set.

rate

A rate is a ratio that compares two quantities that are measured in different units.

Example

The speed of 60 miles in two hours is a <u>rate</u>:
$$\frac{60 \text{ mi}}{2 \text{ h}} = \frac{30 \text{ mi}}{1 \text{ h}}.$$

ratio

A ratio is a comparison of two quantities that uses division.

Example

The <u>ratio</u> of stars to circles is $\frac{3}{2}$, or 3:2, or 3 to 2.

The <u>ratio</u> of circles to stars is $\frac{2}{3}$, or 2:3, or 2 to 3.

ray

A ray is a portion of a line that begins at a point and extends infinitely in one direction. Rays are named using two points. The first point represents the starting point, and the second point can be any other point on the ray.

Examples

A   D   B

There are five rays labeled: ray *DA*, ray *BA*, ray *BD*, ray *DB*, and ray *AB*.

regular pyramid

A regular pyramid is a pyramid in which the base is a regular polygon.

remote interior angle of a triangle

The remote interior angles of a triangle are the two angles that are not adjacent to the specified exterior angle.

Example

The remote interior angles with respect to exterior angle 4 are angles 1 and 2.

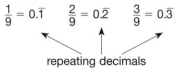

repeating decimal

A repeating decimal is a decimal in which a digit or a group of digits repeats without end.

Examples

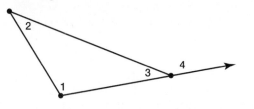

$$\frac{1}{9} = 0.\overline{1} \qquad \frac{2}{9} = 0.\overline{2} \qquad \frac{3}{9} = 0.\overline{3}$$

repeating decimals

right angle

A right angle is an angle whose measure is equal to 90°. A square drawn at the vertex of the angle is used to indicate a right angle in geometric figures.

Example

─────── S ───────

sample

When data are collected from a part of the population, the data are called a sample.

Example

If you wanted to find out the average height of the students in your school, you could choose just a certain number of students and measure their heights. The heights of the students in this group would be your <u>sample</u>.

sample size

When selecting a random sample, the number of members of the population selected to be in the sample is called the sample size.

Example

If you wanted to find out the average height of the students in your school, you could choose just a certain number of students randomly and measure their heights. The number of students in this group would be your <u>sample size</u>.

sample space

A list of all possible outcomes of an experiment is called a sample space.

scale drawings

Scale drawings are representations of real objects or places that are in proportion to the objects or places they represent.

Example

Maps and blueprints are examples of <u>scale drawings</u>.

scale factor

The ratio of side lengths in the scaled figure to those of the original figure is called the scale factor.

Example

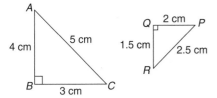

The <u>scale factor</u> from triangle ABC to triangle PQR is $\frac{1}{2}$.

scaling down

Scaling down means you divide the numerator and denominator by the same factor.

Example

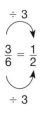

scaling up

Scaling up means you multiply the numerator and denominator by the same factor.

Example

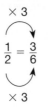

segment bisector

A segment bisector is a line, line segment, or ray that divides a line segment into two line segments of equal measure, or two congruent line segments.

Example

Ray CD is a <u>segment bisector</u>. It bisects line segment AB.

sides of an angle

The sides of an angle are the two rays that form the angle.

simple event

A simple event is an event consisting of one outcome.

simple interest

Simple interest is a fixed percentage of the principal. Simple interest is paid over a specific period of time—twice a year or once a year, for example.

simulation

A simulation is an experiment that models a real-life situation.

sketch

When you sketch a geometric figure, you create it without the use of tools.

Glossary

skew lines

Skew lines, or non-coplanar lines, are lines that are not located in the same plane.

Example

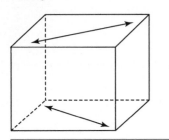

slant height of a pyramid

The slant height of a regular pyramid is the altitude of the lateral faces.

Example

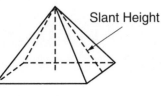

Slant Height

solve a proportion

To solve a proportion means to determine all the values of the variables that make the proportion true.

solve an equation

When you set expressions equivalent to each other and identify which value or values could replace the variable to make the equation true, you are solving an equation.

spread

The spread of data describes how "spread out" the data is. This can also be called the variability of the data.

spreadsheet

A spreadsheet is a computer document that allows you to organize information in rows and columns. Computer spreadsheets typically have a number of tools such as mathematical formulas and functions that make it easy to analyze information.

statistic

When data are gathered from a sample, the characteristic used to describe the sample is called a statistic.

Example

If you wanted to find out the average height of the students in your school, and you chose just a certain number of students randomly and measured their heights, the characteristic "average height" would be called a statistic.

straight angle

A straight angle is an angle whose measure is equal to 180°.

Example

∠ADB is a straight angle.

straightedge

A straightedge is a ruler with no numbers.

supplementary angles

Two angles are supplementary angles if the sum of their angle measures is equal to 180°.

Example

∠1 and ∠2 are supplementary angles.

surface area

The surface area of a solid three-dimensional object is the total area of the outside surfaces of the solid. Surface area is described using square units of measure.

Glossary

survey

A survey is one method of collecting information about a certain group of people. It involves asking a question or set of questions of those people.

Example

A restaurant may ask its customers to complete a survey with the following questions:

- On a scale of 1–10, with 1 meaning "poor" and 10 meaning "excellent," how would you rate the food you ate?

  ☐ 1 ☐ 2 ☐ 3 ☐ 4 ☐ 5 ☐ 6 ☐ 7 ☐ 8 ☐ 9 ☐ 10

- On a scale of 1–10, with 1 meaning "poor" and 10 meaning "excellent," how would you rate the friendliness of your server?

  ☐ 1 ☐ 2 ☐ 3 ☐ 4 ☐ 5 ☐ 6 ☐ 7 ☐ 8 ☐ 9 ☐ 10

T
---

terminating decimal

A terminating decimal has a finite number of digits, meaning that the decimal will end, or terminate.

Example

$$\begin{array}{r} 0.9 \\ 3\overline{)2.7} \end{array} \longleftarrow \text{terminating decimal}$$

theoretical probability

Theoretical probability is the mathematical calculation that an event will happen in theory.

tree diagram

A tree diagram is a tree-shaped diagram that illustrates sequentially the possible outcomes of a given situation.

Example

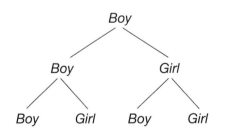

trial

Each time you repeat an experiment, it is called a trial.

Triangle Inequality Theorem

The Triangle Inequality Theorem states that the sum of the lengths of any two sides of a triangle is greater than the length of the third side.

Triangle Sum Theorem

The Triangle Sum Theorem states that the sum of the measures of the interior angles of a triangle is 180°.

two-step equation

A two-step equation requires that two inverse operations be performed in order to isolate the variable.

U
---

uniform probability model

A uniform probability model occurs when all the probabilities in a probability model are equally likely to occur.

unit rate

A unit rate is a comparison of two measurements in which the denominator has a value of one unit.

Example

The speed 60 miles in 2 hours can be written as a unit rate:

$$\frac{60\ \text{mi}}{2\ \text{h}} = \frac{30\ \text{mi}}{1\ \text{h}}.$$

The unit rate is $\frac{30\ \text{mi}}{1\ \text{h}}$, or 30 miles per hour.

unit rate of change

The unit rate of change is the amount the dependent value changes for every unit the independent value changes.

V
---

variability

The variability of data describes how spread out or clustered the data are in a data set.

Example

Range is one measure of the <u>variability</u> in a data set.

variable

In algebra, a variable is a letter or symbol that is used to represent a quantity.

Examples

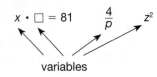

variables

vertex

The vertex of an angle is the common endpoint its two rays share.

Example

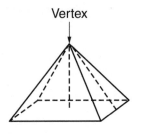

The <u>vertex</u> of angle *BAC* is point *A*.

vertex of a pyramid

The vertex of a pyramid is the point formed by the intersection of all lateral faces.

Example

Vertex

vertical angles

Vertical angles are two nonadjacent congruent angles that are formed by two intersecting lines.

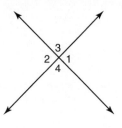

∠1 and ∠2 are <u>vertical angles</u>.
∠3 and ∠4 are <u>vertical angles</u>.

volume

The volume of a solid three-dimensional object is the amount of space contained inside the object. Volume is described using cubic units of measure.

— Z —

zero pair

The integers −1 and +1 are a zero pair because their sum is 0.

INDEX

Index